BEYOND PURE REASON

Leonard Hastings Schoff Memorial Lectures

**UNIVERSITY SEMINARS**
Leonard Hastings Schoff Memorial Lectures

The University Seminars at Columbia University sponsor an annual series of lectures, with the support of the Leonard Hastings Schoff and Suzanne Levick Schoff Memorial Fund. A member of the Columbia faculty is invited to deliver before a general audience three lectures on a topic of his or her choosing. Columbia University Press publishes the lectures.

David Cannadine, *The Rise and Fall of Class in Britain*  1993
Charles Larmore, *The Romantic Legacy*  1994
Saskia Sassen, *Sovereignty Transformed: States and the New
    Transnational Actors*  1995
Robert Pollack, *The Faith of Biology and the Biology of Faith: Order,
    Meaning, and Free Will in Modern Medical Science*  2000
Ira Katznelson, *Desolation and Enlightenment: Political Knowledge
    After the Holocaust, Totalitarianism, and Total War*  2003
Lisa Anderson, *Pursuing Truth, Exercising Power: Social Science and
    Public Policy in the Twenty-first Century*  2003
Partha Chatterjee, *The Politics of the Governed: Reflections on
    Popular Politics in Most of the World*  2004
David Rosand, *The Invention of Painting in America*  2004
George Rupp, *Globalization Challenged: Conviction, Conflict,
    Community*  2007
Lesley A. Sharp, *Bodies, Commodities, nd Technologies*  2007
Robert Hanning, *Serious Play: Desire and Authority in the Poetry of
    Ovid, Chaucer, and Ariosto*  2010

# BEYOND PURE REASON

Ferdinand de Saussure's
Philosophy of Language and
Its Early Romantic Antecedents

**BORIS GASPAROV**

Columbia University Press   New York

Columbia University Press
*Publishers Since 1893*
New York   Chichester, West Sussex
cup.columbia.edu

Copyright © 2013 Columbia University Press
All rights reserved

Library of Congress Cataloging-in-Publication Data
Gasparov, B.
Beyond pure reason: Ferdinand de Saussure's philosophy of language and its early romantic antecedents / Boris Gasparov.
p. cm. —(Leonard Hastings Schoff memorial lectures)
Includes bibliographical references and index.
ISBN 978-0-231-15780-3 (cloth: alk. paper) —ISBN 978-0-231-50445-4 (e-book)
1. Saussure, Ferdinand de, 1857–1913. 2. Linguistics—Philosophy. 3. Linguistics—History. 4. Structural linguistics—History. 5. Semiotics. I. Title.

P85.S18G38  2012
410.92—dc23                                  2012003959

Columbia University Press books are printed on permanent and durable acid-free paper.
This book is printed on paper with recycled content.
Printed in the United States of America

c 10 9 8 7 6 5 4 3 2 1

Cover image courtesy of L'Herne, Paris.

References to Internet Web sites (URLs) were accurate at the time of writing. Neither the author nor Columbia University Press is responsible for URLs that may have expired or changed since the manuscript was prepared.

The grammarian must become philosopher, and the philosopher grammarian.

—Friedrich Schlegel, "Athenaeum Fragmente," no. 92

# Contents

*Acknowledgments* ix
*Abbreviations* xi

Introduction: Saussure, "Saussurism," and "Saussurology"   1

**PART 1**   Voluble Silence: Saussure and His Legacy
1. The Person   15
     The Roots   16
     Years of Learning   20
     Paris and Geneva   28
2. The Writings   37
     The Published and the Perishable   37
     Fragmentariness   46
     Reading the *Course in General Linguistics*   52

**PART 2**   Postulates About Language and Their Demise
3. Antinomies of the Sign   63
     Linguistics in Search of Its Subject   63
     The Double Nature of the Sign   66
     Arbitrariness and Negativity: Language as Pure Form   70

Immutability and Mutability of Signs: An Indissoluble
    Antinomy   80
  Freedom and Aporia   84
4. Fragmentation and Progressivity: Saussure's Semiotics in the Mirror of
Early Romantic Epistemology   87
  In Search of Saussure's Intellectual Roots   87
  A Missing Link? From "Progressive Education" to "General
    Linguistics"   92
  The Speaker of *la langue* and the Early Romantic Subject: Saussure and
    Novalis   101
5. Diachrony and History   111
  Toward Immutability: Constructing the Past   111
  Toward Mutability: Duration   120
  A World in Transition: Saussure and Friedrich Schlegel   128
  A Tentative Compromise: Linguistics as a "Natural" and a
    "Historical" Science   130

**PART 3**   Language in Discourse
6. The Anagram   139
7. Linguistics of Speech: An Unrealizable Promise?   150
  From Language to Speech: Bridging the Metaphysical Gap   150
  "Linguistics of Speech" and "Romantic Poetry"   156
  The Mystery   161

Conclusion: Freedom and Mystery—the Peripathetic Nature
of Language   170
  Made in Leipzig   170
  From "Science" to Philosophy   174
  "To Have a System and to Have None Is Equally Deadening for
    the Spirit"   177
  Anxiety and Stoicism   179

  *Notes*   183
  *Works Cited*   207
  *Index*   221

# Acknowledgments

This book grew out of the Leonard Schoff Memorial Lectures at Columbia University, which I delivered in the fall of 2006. I am immensely grateful to Columbia University Seminars and their director, Professor Robert Belknap, for having given me this tremendous opportunity to bring into focus ideas concerning Saussure's heritage that I had been musing about for quite a while. To a large extent, this project emerged from many exciting discussions of various facets of early Romanticism in the framework of the University Seminar on Romanticism at Columbia, which Lydia Goehr and I co-chaired for a number of years.

The extensive library and documentary research involved in this project would not have been possible without the support I received from Columbia University, which granted me an academic leave in 2006–7, and Wissenschaftskolleg at Berlin, where I was a fellow in 2009–10. I wish to express my profound gratitude to these institutions for not only giving me an opportunity to complete my work but providing a stimulating and inspirational intellectual environment. Finally, I am grateful to several academic and public libraries—Columbia University's Butler Library, the Library of Congress, the Staatsbibliothek in Berlin, the Bibliothèque Nationale in Paris, and the Library of the University of Helsinki (Helsingin Yliopiston kirjasto)—whose outstanding collections and excellent facilities proved to be instrumental for my studies.

Beyond the Schoff Memorial Lectures, I have had a number of stimulating opportunities to present parts of my study to various audiences—most memorably, at the Universities of Stockholm, Oxford, Lausanne, Moscow (the State University for the Humanities), and Tomsk. The support and encouragement I received from my colleagues on those occasions has been vital in carrying this project through. No less important in this regard, the nascent program in general linguistics at Columbia, whose students' vivid interest in the theoretical problems of linguistics and philosophy of language and determination to keep the spirit of theoretical linguistic exploration at Columbia alive, has been a constant source of energy and intellectual stimulus in my writing.

Amy Aires was very helpful in shaping an early version of the book. As for the final stage, I simply do not know how to express my gratitude to Nancy Workman for all the precision and intellectual empathy she has shown in her editing.

# Abbreviations

| | |
|---|---|
| AB | "Das allgemeine Bruillon." Novalis 1983:242–479. |
| AF | "Athenaeum Fragmente." Schlegel et al. 1798. |
| BS | "Blutenstaub." Novalis 1981:412–474. |
| CFS | *Cahiers Ferdinand de Saussure*, vols. 1–60 (Genève: Société genèvoise de linguistique, 1941–2007). |
| CLG | *Course de linguistique générale*. Saussure 1967a [1916]. |
| ELG | *Écrits de linguistique générale*. Saussure 2002. |
| FDA | "Fragmente oder Denkaufgaben." Novalis 1981:564–566. |
| FNS | "Freiberger naturwissenschaftliche Studien 1798/99." Novalis 1983:34–205. |
| FS | "Fichte-Studien." Novalis 1981:104–298. |
| GL | "Glauben und Liebe, oder Der König und die Königin." Novalis 1981:485–498. |
| LF | Novalis, "Logologische Fragmente." Novalis 1981:522–534. |
| PhL | *Philosophische Lehrjahre*. Schlegel 1963. |
| TF | "Teplitzer Fragmente." Novalis 1981:596–622. |
| VF | "Vermishte Fragmente." Novalis 1981:539–363. |

In all quotations from *CLG* and *ELG* the translation is mine. The double pagination in brackets refers to the French original and to the corresponding passage in the English edition (Saussure 1986 and Sassure 2006, respectively).

# Introduction

## *Saussure, "Saussurism," and "Saussurology"*

Saussure's *Course in General Linguistics* appeared in 1916, three years after his death; it was in fact a compilation of his students' notes from three lecture courses Saussure taught in Geneva between 1906 and 1911.[1] Despite disruptions to international communications, the appeal of the book was momentous.[2] During the period between the two world wars, all over the world, scholars specializing in linguistics, literary theory, and studies of the sign and meaning found themselves in an intense dialogue with the book—interpreting, refining, and challenging its ideas, building various descriptive models of language and literature according to its premises, opening up entirely new areas of study along its methodological guidelines. To its readers, the book offered a set of postulates about language, presumably laid out by Saussure in his courses, which built the foundation for a radically new approach to language and, furthermore, to the whole semiotic environment of human society and culture. Among those postulates were the contradistinction between the transempirical phenomenon of the inner language knowledge of speakers, which Saussure called *la langue*, and its manifestation in observable acts of speaking (*la parole*), with a clear emphasis on the former; the vision of that inner structure as an immanent mechanism whose parameters are defined solely as a "system" of mutual relations; and finally, the foregrounding of the principle of "synchrony," according to which the inner structure is presented as if frozen at a given moment, exempt from all the accidents of "external" influences. Although some of those principles could be found in works by Saussure's contemporaries—such as Jan Baudouin de Courtenay, Gottlob Frege (1892), Ludwig Wittgenstein (of the *Tractatus*), and C. K. Ogden and I. A. Richards (1923)—the *Course* articulated them in the most systematic and unequivocal way. Consequently, the book bearing Saussure's name looms in the background of numerous "structural" models in linguistics, literary theory, cultural anthropology, psychology, philosophy of meaning, and the study of social behavior.

It would not be an exaggeration to say that all the major concepts and scholarly bodies concerned with theoretical linguistics that emerged in Europe between the two world wars—the Prague linguistic circle, the Moscow linguistic circle, the Copenhagen linguistic circle (the birthplace of glossematics), the "Swiss school" (Charles Bally, Albert Sechehaye, Sèrge Karcevsky), the leading theoretical linguists in France (Émile Benveniste, André Matrinet)—treated the *Course* as the starting point from which their respective approaches were derived.[3] The *Course*'s distinction between *langue* and *parole* laid the foundation for the Prague school's phonology—an entirely new discipline, defined by Nicholas Trubetzkoy as the study of the sound structure of language, in contradistinction to the description of the physical properties of speech sounds relegated to phonetics;[4] Louis Hjelmslev's glossematics (1953) carried the structural premises of the *Course* to their logical conclusion, building a dizzyingly abstract picture of language as a system of purely relational values. Beyond continental Europe, American "descriptive linguistics" of the Bloomfieldian mold, although manifesting a higher degree of independence, maintained a dialogue with Saussure.[5] As to works on meaning in language and art, among the most significant resonances the *Course* evoked in the first twenty years of its reception were Ogden and Richards's seminal *The Meaning of Meaning* (1923), followed by the emergence of New Criticism and a later stage of the Formal school in Russia (late 1920s).[6] The launching in 1941 of *Cahiers Ferdinand de Saussure*, an international series entirely dedicated to Saussurean linguistics and its contexts, reflected the universal interest in Saussure and his work.[7]

For the first two decades after the Second World War, the impact of Saussure's ideas (or rather, of what the postwar generation was willing and able to draw from the book published under his name) continued to grow exponentially in both scope and depth. In her recent book on Saussure, Claudine Normand recalls how her generation—eager to move forward from the horrors of the recent past and perceiving their vigorous struggle against intellectual routine as an integral part of challenges to the compromised social and moral order—enthusiastically embraced the "radical modernism" of the *Course*, alongside other major influences of the time: Freud, Marx, and Nietzsche (Normand 2000:10). Indeed, it was during that period that the *Course* was widely recognized beyond the domain of theoretical linguistics as a pivotal work on philosophy of language and meaning, alongside such major events of the turn of the century as works by Charles Peirce, Frege, Wittgenstein, and Ernst Cassirer. Consequently, the (presumably Saussurean) idea of "structure" spread far beyond the study of language. In the domain of literary criticism and aesthetics, it gave rise to structural poetics (Roman Jakobson), narratology (Claude Brémond), and the relativist theory of aesthetic value (Jan Mukařovský). The principle of structure also proved to be seminal for the theory of psychological development (Jean Piaget), anthropology (Claude Lévi-Strauss), and eventually for the kind of studies of the infinite variety of forms of cultural behavior that thrived at the time under the umbrella name of semiotics—in particular, in Paris (Barthes 1957; Todorov 1967) and Eastern Europe (the Tartu-Moscow school: Lotman 1977 [1970]). When Piaget summarized the premises and principal achievements of "structuralism" (1968), he treated the concept as a major intellectual paradigm whose applicability seemed to have no limits.

Meanwhile, it was precisely in the late sixties that the fortunes of the *Course* began to decline. Derrida came out with a powerful if not always fair critique of Saussure's theory of the sign in his *Of Grammatology* (1967). Another piece of insightful critique of Saussure, V. N. Voloshinov's *Marxism and the Philosophy of Language* (1973 [1928]), inspired by Bakhtin's ideas of meaning and discourse, although written forty years earlier, became widely known at that time. Yet another shattering blow to the idea of the preponderance of *la langue* came from Jacques Lacan's *Seminars* with their very deliberate emphasis on *la parole*. The impact of Lacan's and Bakhtin's ideas on literary and cultural studies was to a large extent responsible for the evolution of poetics and semiotics, in the late 1960s and the 1970s, from a rigid structuralism to models of artistic works and culture that emphasized the openness of meaning and the interactive (dialogical) character of its construction. A similar transformation could be seen in anthropology, in particular, in Lévi-Strauss's later works (notably *La pensée sauvage*, 1962), as well as those by Clifford Geertz (1973). As to theoretical linguistics proper, Chomsky (1965:14), while adopting the Saussurean language-versus-speech dichotomy (which he redefined as linguistic competence versus performance), took on Saussure for his preoccupation with the "inventory of signs" at the expense of syntax, making the latter the core of generative grammar.

By the end of the 1970s, the "structural" model was viewed by many as a paradigm of the past—a brainchild of turn-of-the-century modernism whose vision of the totalized structural organization of culture and behavior had not withstood the social and cultural turmoil of the 1960s. The new intellectual generation found inspiration in a sweeping critique of the postulates laid down in the *Course*. The terms *poststructuralism* and *postmodernism,* which grew fashionable to the point of virtual meaninglessness, reflected the spirit of opposition out of which the new trend was born and with which it identified itself; the very nebulousness of the content of these terms testified to the ubiquitousness of the new intellectual trend. For a scholar in the 1960s, a single glance at any cultural phenomenon—be it language, a work of art or literature, cultural mythology, social institutions, or everyday behavior—instantly revealed recurrent patterns pointing to a coherent structure, presumably preprogrammed in the minds of all "speakers" of a certain cultural *langue*. With equal predictability, a glance at the same object cast by a scholar in the 1980s revealed inconsistencies, contradictory voices, and disrupted discourses whose discontinuity and inconclusiveness suggested a phenomenon in the making, an "open work" immersed in a flow of ceaseless interpretational challenges.[8] Ideas that had looked to the generation of the 1950s and 1960s like a methodological ground from which they could challenge the traditional order of things now appeared to be a deadening routine, an intellectual affirmation of all the faults of the existing order. In the new intellectual climate, the enormous and universal recognition that the *Course* had enjoyed in the previous half-century made it a prime target of deconstructing critique. In this sense, Saussure and his *Course* continued to occupy a prominent place in the "postmodern" epoch, this time as one of the most conspicuous emblems of the old (that is, modernist) intellectual regime, with its authoritarian rationalism and its paternalistic idealization of universal order.[9]

For a long time, it was assumed that whatever Saussure himself may have written, whether in preparation for his lecture courses or otherwise, was either lost or remained so sketchy as to be of virtually no practical use. The ostensible paucity of written documents seemed to agree with the well-known fact of Saussure's severe problems concerning writing and publishing, which condemned him to almost total silence (barring his lecturing to very small audiences at the University of Geneva) during the last two decades of his life. It was this understanding that led Charles Bally and

Albert Sechehaye, who compiled the *Course* and published it under Saussure's name, to rely almost entirely on his students' notes, as well as their own awareness of their former teacher's ideas, with only minimal use of portions of Saussure's writing that surfaced at the time. For more than forty years following the book's appearance, nobody questioned either its publishers' sources or their editorial judgment. Such a remarkable lack of textological curiosity was perhaps due to the fact that the intellectual presence of the book was so powerful as to make it an inexorable force, rendering moot any questions about its provenance. The invisibility of the "ultimate" author, whose word reached the world only through his disciples' varied renditions, only added to the book's charisma a certain touch of mystery.

It was about the time when the fortunes of the "structural" paradigm of thought, which had found in the *Course* the most vocal expression and the foremost authority, began to decline that Saussure's genuine writing started to emerge. The publication of Robert Godel's *Les sources manuscrites de Cours de linguistique générale de F. de Saussure* in 1957 brought a revolutionary change to the perception of the corpus of Saussure's heritage—if not yet, at that time, of its tenor. As it turned out, during the last twenty years of his life, while suffering from severe writer's block as far as published works were concerned, Saussure was engaged in intense, at times feverish writing that addressed a broad spectrum of problems. Though never coalescing into something that could amount to even a draft of a publishable work, Saussure's private notes accumulated through the years into a corpus of fragments of enormous summary volume and formidable if inconclusive consequence. Godel's study allowed the first glimpse of this hidden treasure.

Another discovery, perhaps even more sensational, came to light with the appearance of Jean Starobinski's *Les mots sous les mots: Les anagrammes de Ferdinand de Saussure* in 1971. It exposed for the first time another major area of Saussure's private writing, of which the scholarly community at large had hitherto remained totally unaware. During the years 1906 to 1909— at the time when he began teaching his course in general linguistics— Saussure was intensely pursuing his perceived discovery of cryptographic clues, conveyed through patterns of sound repetition, in various poetic texts. Saussure's preoccupation, late in life, with "anagrams"—about which he himself remained rather secretive—fortuitously fell on the fertile ground of a starry-eyed fascination with the transrational at the time when this line of his work was revealed. For at least a part of the post-1960s intellectual and artistic world, Saussure, the rationalist of slightly dour bent, had suddenly turned into a prophet of oneiric truths.[10] The issue of the anagram helped to maintain the perpetual fascination of Saussure's "mystery"; at the same time, it cast a certain ambiguity upon his overall intellectual profile.[11]

As if all this were not enough, archival research done in the 1990s brought to light several other facets of Saussure's private studies and note writing, whose importance is only now beginning to emerge. In the first half of the first decade of the 1900s, Saussure embarked on extensive studies of medieval legends, in particular, of the Nibelung epos, its historical and mythological sources, and later transformations.[12] Finally, a close examination of the "Harvard papers" (another part of Saussure's archive that was bought by Harvard University in the 1960s) yielded yet another strand in Saussure's notes, dedicated to Hindu philosophy, theology, and linguistic thought, which he pursued in 1906 (Saussure 1993a; Saussure 1994b).

The stream of discoveries, publications, and critical responses to new findings during the last half-century has been tremendous; it has intensified particularly in the past fifteen or twenty years. This "archeological" research into Saussure's heritage, together with the interpretation that ensued, grew into a particular new branch of Saussurean studies—"Saussurology," to use the mildly bantering name given to it by one of its prominent proponents, René Amacker.[13] In many respects, the new attitude toward Saussure set itself in explicit opposition to views that were dominant during the first half of the twentieth century. It has become habitual among "Saussurologists" to address the now-refuted earlier Saussurean paradigm as *Saussurism*—a term loaded with a deprecatory *ism*. One could sense the almost religious zeal with which the new breed of Saussure scholars strove to refute the writing on which Saussurism was founded as apocryphal and to restore the "true" letter and spirit of Saussure's teaching.

The principal strategy of Saussurological critical analysis of the *Course*, beginning with Godel, consisted in rejecting as inauthentic virtually all the statements in it upon which the structural approach was built: the strict separation of language as an immanent structure from the empirical data of speech, the treatment of language as a synchronic "state," indifferent to any "diachronic" development, and the view of language as a conventional inevitability about which individual speakers have no choice but that of accepting it the way it is. It was precisely these points that most greatly irritated the generation that emerged after the major paradigm shift in the late 1960s.

The major claim of Saussurology has been that all those ideas, now exposed as fallacious, have nothing whatsoever to do with Saussure; the responsibility should be redirected to his editors instead. The stronger the desire to exculpate Saussure from all the sins of structuralism grew, the more vehemently denunciations of the published book as the betrayal or even "falsification" of Saussure resounded.[14] The *Course*, that gospel of the preceding epoch, is now habitually referred to as Saussure's *vulgate*—yet another addition to Saussurean Christology,[15] artfully balancing the authentic Latin meaning of the word (*vulgatus:* "made public," i.e., "published") and its modernized interpretation as "vulgarized."

Indeed, as one navigates through Saussure's desperately fragmented writing, one finds ample evidence of his recognition of the importance of *la parole* and, moreover, his awareness of the predominance of speech, with its ceaseless improvisations and transformations, as the only real-life condition under which *la langue* exists. Saussure's despair at the apparent impossibility of capturing this unceasing movement in a "state" is palpable. Saussure's thought itself appears to be perpetually evolving and vacillating, a far cry from the neat system of theoretical postulates that the *Course* was (rightly or wrongly) universally perceived to be.

However, I find efforts to exempt Saussure, on the strength of his notes, from the faults and illusions of an era, for which the book under his name (be it what it may) stood as a major intellectual catalyst, and to make him our contemporary—that is, a participant in our own faults and illusions—as problematic as the earlier unquestioning acceptance of and rhapsodizing upon the assertions of the *Course*. Inevitably, Saussure's notes, with their fragmentary and sketchy character, feature a variety of statements, some difficult to reconcile with each other. Even more important, when one reads the *Course* with the awareness of Saussure's notes, one can discern, under the veneer of the lucid and orderly narrative in which it is clad (apparently, a trademark of Saussure's oral presentations), hidden contradictions, barely perceptible shifts of earlier premises, and instances of a subject being abruptly abandoned when it turns out that its explication is leading nowhere—all features that become manifest in Saussure's private writing. Rhetorically, the *Course* and the notes stand worlds apart; nevertheless, their intellectual kinship is indisputable.

We are greatly indebted to the scholars who spent years searching for, reading, editing, and publishing much of the enormous accumulation of Saussure's lonely writing. Thanks to their determined and skillful effort, what might have looked (and for a long time, did look) like an incoherent and almost illegible pile of fragmentary scribblings has emerged as a palpable if labile textual corpus whose importance for the history of ideas cannot be overestimated. What makes the premises of Saussurological studies questionable is that restoring the meaning of Saussure's ideas to its historical context and restoring the authentic purity of his message often appears in them as one and the same task. As a result, at times the struggle with what "genuine" Saussurean thought was *not* seems to override the task of interpreting what it was.

It was an irony of Saussurology that its attitude toward Saussure's heritage was based on the very premises from which it strove to exculpate the "true" Saussure. The treatment of the *Course* as an integral (albeit falsified) "text" whose content preprogrammed all the faults of its readers was nothing but a fine example of Saussurism. This position does not take into account that what the generations of the 1920s and 1950s saw in the *Course*, rightly or wrongly, was as much a product of their own intellectual needs and preferences as of what was present in the "text" of the book itself. A differently contextualized reading of the *Course*—greatly facilitated by the presence of its manuscript background—can expose in the fabric of the book itself important clues adherents of various strains of structuralism neither saw nor wanted to see.[16]

To recapitulate: revealing the nearly full corpus of Saussure's writing has been a tremendous scholarly achievement, but this philological work cannot and should not be combined with the task of the historical reevaluation of Saussure's heritage. Neither burying Saussure in the mass grave of structuralism nor proclaiming his resurrection as our soul mate serves the purpose of his historical contextualization.

Much has been said about the "sadness" that seemed to engulf Saussure in the last years of his life. What Saussure's biographers invariably pass over—perhaps because of a certain hagiographic halo that surrounds his conventional image—is his characteristic outbursts of frustration and contemptuous anger, which on numerous occasions disrupted the train of his argument. The sound and fury of rhetorical exclamation marks, such as *véritable, unique, indubitable, absolument certain,* coupled with vehemently denunciatory epithets, such as *enfantine, stupide, obtuse, bizarre, ridicule, absolument faux,* proliferate in Saussure's private writing. They only contribute to the chaos into which Saussure's notes disintegrate sooner or later, with a depressing inevitability. One can sense Saussure's despair in the way that, again and again, after a spirited start, his writing eventually falls apart into a pile of unfinished sentences, abrupt changes of topic, distracting asides, and laborious yet obscure examples—until the piece is finally abandoned, proving to be yet another failed attempt in a passionate but ever-inconclusive intellectual pursuit. The rest is silence—Saussure's prolonged and notorious silence as a publishing scholar.

The remarkable contradiction between impassive rationalism and a very personal fury, charismatic assertiveness and anxious vacillations, striving for a comprehensive systematization of knowledge and feverish fragmentariness of reasoning and writing, was more than just a personal character trait of Saussure. It reflected the peculiar nature of his epistemological pursuit.

As has often been pointed out in recent studies, Saussure's approach to language was that of a philosopher rather than a "linguist," in whatever conventional sense of the term you will.[17] In contrast to Jakobson—one of the foremost figures of the epoch of Saussurism—who proudly declared, "Linguista sum: linguistici nihil a me alienum puto" (I am a linguist: there is nothing in linguistics that I feel to be alien to me). Saussure's approach to every subject of his study—be it language, poetry, or ancient legend—was epistemological rather than descriptive. In the *Course*, as well as in Saussure's notes on general linguistics, one finds few systematic descriptions of concrete features either of language in general or of particular languages. Language enters Saussure's explication of the problems of general linguistics only by way of isolated examples—which, moreover, are not always well chosen and occasionally do more harm than good to his theoretical argument.

Saussure's concern with the epistemological foundations of the study of language places his work in the arena of major developments in the theory of cognition in the 1890s and 1900s. A common basis for such trends as the neo-Kantian theory of cognition, phenomenology, and works on the foundations of mathematics and the natural sciences was their critique of the limitations of the "positivism" of the second part of the nineteenth century. Beginning in the 1890s—precisely the time when this trend arose—Saussure shows similar concerns and an ensuing awareness of methodological problems. The principal target of his fury was the "obtuse" positivism of the 1870s to 1880s, whose proponents—his early mentors at Leipzig first and foremost—kept themselves busy with "elementary operations" with language material, while "never giving themselves the trouble to explain the nature of the object of their studies" (*CLG*, 16/3).

Having begun as an enthusiastic and uniquely gifted language explorer, Saussure eventually came to realize the insufficiency of the notion of linguistics as a discipline occupied with "language." As he emphatically declared, studies of language would never amount to anything more than a "childish" (one of his favorite words) groping in the dark unless one first determined what is to be studied and to what purpose. Saussure's notion of *la langue* separated language as the postulated object of linguistics from language as an observable phenomenon that could be approached from a plurality of perspectives. Saussure's "speaker"—or, more precisely, his construction thereof—was conceived as close kin to the cognizing subject of phenomenology. To ask why the Saussurean ideal speaker, as he is presented in the *Course*, never gets around to the business of speaking (that is, to *la parole*) would be as pointless as to reproach Husserl's exposition of phenomenology for the overuse of an elementary example of "2+2=4."

And yet this dispassionate inferential reasoning—presenting language as a "chain of theorems," as he once put it—reflects only one side of Saussure. While carefully building a new discipline whose premises would respond to the cognitive guidelines universally accepted at the time, Saussure continued to be tormented by the thought that the object he had constructed with such tenacious intellectual labor would turn out to be unviable and ungraspable. Language as a form, that is, a network of pure relations, exists only as a state; yet the essence of language is that it never ceases to change. The very principle of the arbitrariness of semiotic value, upon which the notion of the form was founded, meant that there could be no logical limit to the volatility of that form—no "substantial" factor that could check or direct its incessant movement. Saussure, the rationalist versed in modernist epistemology, saw the necessity of reductive critique in order to reach language as a cognizable object; nevertheless, he could not cast aside his realization that *la langue*, thus constructed, could not be sustained in use for even a fraction of a second. Aware as he was of this dilemma, Saussure vacillated between cognitive coherence and a penetrating vision, allowing them to undermine—to *spoil*, to use his own word—each other as a result.

Saussure's inability to reach an ultimate solution, while setting him apart from the messianic assertiveness of many of his modernist contemporaries, can be seen as being similar to the spirit of our own time, with its penchant for delving into contradictions and exposing—and celebrating— inconsistencies. The idea of Saussure's kinship with postmodernism has circulated widely in recent Saussure studies. Yet there is a crucial dividing line that separates Saussure from "postmodern" skepticism. Saussure's unique combination of the passion with which he pursued the elusive essence of the matter and the "grand sobriety" (enjoined in the concluding chapter of the *Course*) of recognizing the impossibility of ever reaching it is no more consonant with the atmosphere of postmodernist skeptical complaisance than it was with modernist messianic triumphalism.

I believe that the vector of Saussure's contradictory and in a way self-defeating position points not to the century after but to the century before him. It shows Saussure's kinship with the epistemological, historical, and linguistic thought of early Romanticism.

Saussure's relation to early Romantic thought remains virtually unexplored. Indeed, evoking Romanticism in connection with Saussure's ideas about language can easily become misleading. Saussure's negative attitude toward Romantic linguistics is well known. He referred with mild skepticism even to the work of his revered mentor, Adolph Pictet. When approaching the problem of "Saussure and Romanticism," however, we need to keep in mind what was said earlier about the character of Saussure's "general linguistics": namely, that it was a philosophy of language more than a linguistic model proper. To a late-nineteenth-century linguist, the purely "linguistic" judgment of the Romantics could not sound anything but childish. However, when one considers the Jena school philosophical critique, an integral part of which was philosophy of language and meaning, its relation to Saussure's epistemological effort appears in a different light. Separating Romantic philosophy of language from "Romantic linguistics" is therefore a prerequisite for approaching the problem of Saussure's relationship to Romanticism.

It is Saussure's adherence to epistemological problems of his time that makes perceptible his connection with early Romantic philosophy of cognition. Saussure's position vis-à-vis neo-Kantian and phenomenological epistemology had much in common with the Jena Romantics' reaction to Kant's critique of pure reason. An observer who follows Saussure's struggle with the irreconcilable contradictions of his cognizing pursuit is struck by its similarity to the predicament of the early Romantics. I know no other phenomenon in the history of ideas in which the sober realization of the cognitive constraints laid out by Kantian critique, on the one hand, and the relentless pursuit of the absolute, in the face of the manifest impossibility of reaching it, on the other, stood in such a palpable and unresolved tension, as the one that found its representation in the thousands of semi-improvised fragments written by Novalis and Friedrich Schlegel in the period between 1795 and 1801.

Addressing Saussure's thinking about language in the contemporary context of the modernist epistemological revolution and exploring the threads in its lineage that point to the metaphysics of early Romanticism constitute the two related principal goals of this book. I believe that projecting Saussure's views against the background of Jena Romanticism can be illuminating for both. Doing so highlights features in these intellectual phenomena that made him stand out among this contemporaries and immediate successors; by the same token, it shows their relevance for our time.

Voluble Silence | **PART I**

*Saussure and His Legacy*

# The Person | ONE

Despite the appearance of impassive objectivity that characterizes the rhetorical surface of both celebrated books of Ferdinand de Saussure (1857–1913)—his early *Note on the Original System of Indo-European Vowels* (1879) and the posthumous *Course in General Linguistics* (1916)—his life and personality always attracted keen interest among those who were stirred, one way or another, by his ideas. Emile Benveniste expressed this sentiment admirably in an article dedicated to the fiftieth anniversary of Saussure's death: "A certain mystery surrounds his human life [*sa vie humaine*], which withdrew so early into silence";[1] we are invited, as it were, to muse about the mystery of another, transcendent life of Saussure beyond the silence of the "human" one. Even before the mass of Saussure's private notes came to light, one could always sense behind the impersonal calm of his published works something that hinted at their author's kinship with the kind of charismatic intellectual figures, so typical of the late nineteenth and early twentieth centuries, whose Werk would remain incomplete without the text of their Leben—a paradoxical perception, given Saussure's extreme reticence, even shyness, a trait that deepened through the years, leading eventually to his almost complete withdrawal from any public expression save that directed at a tiny group of disciples in a classroom.

Thanks to the tremendous research efforts of those who have made accessible and commented on all the relevant correspondence, reviews, obituaries, official documents, and memoirs, all crowned by Saussure's own sketchy "Souvenirs" of 1903 about his early years,[2] we now know more about Saussure's life and career than perhaps about any other personality in the history of linguistics and philosophy of language, with the possible exception of Roman Jakobson. And yet this factual knowledge neither alters the impression of an almost enigmatic silence surrounding Saussure nor diminishes the intensity with which his human presence can be felt in his work. It therefore seems unavoidable that yet another attempt at reading Saussure should begin with an assessment of his life and personality.

## THE ROOTS

One aspect of the biographic data about Saussure that has always been available in abundance concerns his family. The Saussures traced their lineage back to the fifteenth century. The family originated in Lotharingy, whence it migrated to Geneva in a time of religious turmoil in the sixteenth century.[3] The migratory pattern of Saussure's remote ancestors replicated events of the sixth century (in which Saussure showed keen interest late in his life): the political and religious turmoil in Burgundy that forced one section of its population to move to the Helvetic area. In the 1900s Saussure sought traces of the Germanic language of their origin in various toponyms in the Vaudois area (the locality of the Saussures' summer residence). The way a German and a French element were melded together in this story was characteristic of Saussure's own intellectual biography.

Many generations of the Saussures belonged to an exclusive circle of the most prominent Genevan families. Saussure grew up in a patrician atmosphere in which material opulence, even luxury, was combined with an intensity of spiritual life, a high ethical sensibility, and a strong sense of familial tradition. When Saussure submitted his doctoral dissertation in Leipzig in 1880, one of his reviewers, the renowned philologist Georg Curtius, added to his praise of the author's scholarship a few words of somewhat naive admiration for a young scholar so profoundly dedicated to his studies despite the "shining material circumstances" of his life.[4] This little episode is characteristic of the cultural rift between Saussure the patrician and the Bürgertum of German academia. That sociocultural alienation resulted in a certain antipathy on both sides, which occasionally erupted in professional and personal confrontations. The overt frictions, exacerbated by German-French political antagonisms of the time, are usually highlighted in the (predominantly francophone) Saussure biographical literature, with the effect of obfuscating Saussure's profound indebtedness to the German philosophical and scientific tradition.

From the second half of the eighteenth century on, the Saussures were known as a family of outstanding scientists. Both Saussure's grandfather Nicolas-Théodore and his father Henri were eminent scholars; so was his younger brother René, a distinguished mathematician. At the beginning of that tradition stood the towering figure of Horace Bénédict de Saussure (1740–1799), of whom it was suggested that he was second only to Rousseau among the famous Genevans of the century.[5] Like his great-grandson a century later, Saussure the elder was precocious in his academic career, becoming a professor of philosophy and natural sciences at the age of twenty-two. Horace Bénédict's most important scientific discovery (which involved a celebrated ascent of Mont Blanc) concerned the contingency of surface temperature on the density of the atmosphere; as he demonstrated in ingenious experiments, it is not the amount of sun heat itself, which is the same at zero altitude and the top of Mont Blanc, that accounts for the difference in temperature between the two points, but the different atmospheric conditions under which they receive the energy.

Yet later in his life Saussure took pains to distance his theoretical approach to language from the outright scientific paradigm professed by most of his contemporaries, most notably his teachers at Leipzig; again and again he reiterated in his notes that language is fundamentally different from any object of the natural sciences because of the unlimited freedom (arbitrariness) of its inner structuring, which causes its systemic values to be permanently in flux. The inapplicability of a scientific approach to language seemed to leave Saussure at once dismayed and gleeful. He missed no occasion to condemn attempts to build an artificial international language, expressing his conviction that all efforts to shape language rationally were futile: the moment such a creation, however brilliant, was put to use, it would dissolve into an unpredictable and uncontrollable spontaneous development. The "familial" subtext of these assertions becomes clear if we remember that Saussure's brother René was a prominent champion of Esperanto (at one point, he served as the president of the International Esperanto Association); in 1911 René published a book on the subject under a characteristic title, *Principes logiques de la construction des mots en esperanto,* in which he extolled the "modernity" of artificial languages, in contradistinction to the idiosyncratic backwardness of natural ones.

The tension between rationalist universalism and an exceptionalist vision of language constituted the fundamental contradiction around which Saussure's theoretical thought revolved. The complexity and originality of the Saussure phenomenon comes from the fact that no matter how much he might wish to succeed in casting language as a succession of "theorems,"[6] he never lost sight of its other side—the one that condemned any rationally built systemic model to dissolution upon encountering the volatile "mystery" of language usage.

This "other side" of Saussure also had its roots in the familial tradition. While Saussure's biographers habitually dwell on the male lineage of Saussure's family and its formidable scientific credentials, another outstanding representative of the family's intellectual tradition has so far attracted little attention. I mean Saussure's great-aunt (Horace Bénédict's daughter), Albertine Adrienne Necker de Saussure, a prominent figure of early Romanticism. Necker de Saussure's most notable achievement, her book *L'éducation progressive* (three volumes, 1829–1837), offered a bold revision of Enlightenment ideas about education, from Kant to Rousseau, in the spirit of early Romanticism. Her "progressive" (i.e., evolutionary) vision of education was deeply rooted in early Romantic ideas about language and cognition, particularly those held by Novalis, Friedrich Schlegel, and Friedrich Schleiermacher. We will return to the question of Saussure's intellectual relationship to his great-aunt—and through her, and together with her, to the world of Jena Romanticism—in more detail later.

Albertine Necker de Saussure died before Saussure was born. (Her library, apparently containing works by the Schlegels, Novalis, Schleiermacher, Jean Paul, Germaine de Staël, François-René de Chateaubriand, and Benjamin Constant, remained at the Saussures' summer residence in Vufflens: Stancati 2004:186). The key figure in the continuity of this lineage of the family tradition was Adolphe Pictet, a younger friend and distant relative of Necker de Saussure,[7] who played a crucial formative role in Saussure's adolescent years: it was Pictet who introduced the thirteen-year-old Saussure to the theoretical foundations of Indo-European linguistics.

Pictet was a dedicated champion of German Romanticism and idealist philosophy. Like French, English, and Russian Romantics since the beginning of the century, he made a journey to Germany, where he became acquainted with A. W. Schlegel (with whom he maintained an important correspondence over the course of many years), Goethe, Hegel, Schleiermacher, and Schelling. Pictet's early "absorption," in his words, in contemporary philosophy and aesthetics is reflected in his book *The Beautiful in Nature, Art, and Poetry* (1856). While closely following Schelling's system of transcendental idealism, the book was also clearly influenced by *L'éducation progressive*, in particular, by its vision of the ability to admire the beautiful as the principal force for spiritual freedom that resists the rationalist drive toward conformity (originally a Schillerean idea adopted by the Jena Romantics). In the spirit of earlier wars between "romantics" and "classics" (a little outmoded by the 1850s), Pictet envisioned Romanticism, with its embrace of pluralism and freedom of invention, as standing in sharp opposition to Classicism, the embodiment of systemic compactness and uniformity.

True to his profession of Romantic versatility, Pictet established himself as a person of many interests and vocations. But first and foremost, he was an accomplished Indo-Europeanist. Pictet's Indo-European studies naturally led to his intimate acquaintance with Sanskrit and Vedic poetry. In accordance with his Romantic philosophical predisposition, he perceived in the Rig Veda a proto-"Romantic" phenomenon, which he counterpoised to the proto-"Classical" Homeric epos—an opposition that would surface many years later in Saussure's notes.

Pictet represented the first, Romantic generation of historical linguists, for whom the history of language went hand in hand with the history of the material and spiritual being of the people who spoke it. His magnum opus was the two-volume *Origines indo-européennes: Essai de paléontologie linguistique* (1859–63); the second edition of the book appeared in 1877, two years after the author's death and only a year prior to Saussure's *Mémoire*. It was a monumental attempt, in the tradition of Friedrich Schlegel and Jakob Grimm, to reconstruct the whole world of the proto-Indo-Europeans. Largely speculative, as such a reconstruction (as well as all those that followed it) inevitably was, it nevertheless summoned a massive and diverse body of data concerning the language, mythology, religion, and material culture of scores of Indo-European nations, from the Indian peninsula to the western extremities of Europe. In his autobiographical essay (1960 [1903]:16), while giving a sober assessment of this work of his first mentor, Saussure speaks of the enthusiasm it inspired in him in his adolescent years: "The idea that one could, with the help of two or three Sanskrit syllables—for that was the idea of the book itself and of the whole linguistics of that epoch—retrieve the life of vanished people, inflamed me with an enthusiasm, unmatched in its naivety; and I have no memories more exquisite and truer to the joy of linguistic studies than those brought to me even today by a whiff of recollection of that childhood reading." Later, in his review of the second edition of Pictet's book,[8] Saussure cast his recently deceased mentor's quest for vanished civilizations in the likeness of "Oedipus in front of the Sphinx." Saussure's review spoke of Pictet's willingness to make leaps from known facts to the unknown, shuttling between "science" and "imagination." Needless to say, in his mature years Saussure far outgrew his first mentor in his understanding of the intellectual stakes involved in the dilemma of the rationally constructed versus the ungraspable, which he came to see as inherent in linguistic studies.

## YEARS OF LEARNING

When Saussure first met Pictet—during summers in Vufflens, where they were neighbors—he was full of enthusiasm for the "magic" of etymology. According to Saussure's own account, he caught the etymological fever from his maternal uncle, whose two hobbies—pursued "without a method, but with a wealth of ideas"—were building yachts after a mathematical system of his own devising and making etymologies; as Saussure noted wryly, both tended to sink equally fast (Saussure 1960 [1903]:16–17). (This healthy irony notwithstanding, Saussure never lost his own passion for venturesome etymologies.)

During the following two years, Pictet became Saussure's principal intellectual mentor. At the age of fifteen, Saussure presented for his teacher's judgment his "Essay on reducing words of Greek, Latin, and German to a small number of roots."[9] Using the three languages he knew well by that time, he first, with one stroke of the pen, "reduced" all vowels to a single proto-vowel. (Curiously enough, this was precisely what Saussure would do again—on the strength of an extremely sophisticated argument—six years later in his reconstruction of proto-Indo-European vowels.) The "Essay" then proceeded, with the same ease, to reduce the number of consonants, by grouping them according to their articulatory features: p, b, f, v = P; t, d, s, z = T, etc. The vocal and consonantal abstractions obtained by this method were then linked in twelve triple combinations (KAK, KAT, KAP, TAT, TAP, etc.), which Saussure proclaimed to be the twelve proto-roots. Each abstract formula of a proto-root could give rise to a multiplicity of concrete stems: for example, under Saussure's formula, the proto-root PAK could accommodate a throng of words in various languages, from fog to bush. Each root was supposed to have a certain proto-meaning, which had to be extremely broad—broad enough to contain in a nutshell the whole spectrum of meanings featured in all its presumable later representations in a plurality of languages. For instance, Saussure suggested that the combination RAK had originally stood for a proto-idea of "violent power," on the evidence of such words as Lat. *rex* "king," Gr. ῥήγνυμι, "tear, crush," Germ. *Rache* "vengeance" or *rügen* "to thrash," and so on. It is curious the extent to which this naive exercise recalls Velimir Khlebnikov's attempt to create a universal poetic language some forty years later, an intellectual event that (alongside Saussure's *Course*) had a major impact on Jakobson's theory of phonological universalia.[10] As for Saussure himself, one gets a glimpse of his later feelings about the matter in a sudden and seemingly unmotivated outburst in one of his notes concerning the futility of studying "roots" (Saussure 1993a:195).

Perhaps the most interesting moment in this adolescent effort comes at its conclusion: "If I could be sure that the rest were true, naturally I would study all these difficult points in more detail. With this, I could have advanced further, especially if I knew Oriental languages, in grouping all the words along a dozen roots. But I see that I have lost myself in dreams, and need to recall the fable about the milk pot" (Saussure 1960 [1903]:101).

The La Fontaine fable in question tells the story of a milkmaid who was so excited by reveries about her future profits from selling her milk that she stumbled and broke her milk pot. The close cohabitation of defiant assertiveness and self-deprecating scepticism evident in this excerpt would become a trademark of Saussure's thinking and writing.

Although Pictet's criticism of his disciple's opus was mild, Saussure's experience with this *enfantillage,* as he would later call it (a word he did not hesitate to use in his private assessment of many past and contemporary linguistic theories as well), caused him to "forget" about linguistics for a while.[11] "Conforming to a sort of family tradition" (as he put it),[12] Saussure entered the program in science at the University of Geneva in 1875. He had been ready for the university by the age of fifteen, but his parents, having decided that he was too young at the time, made him languish for two years in a pre-university college program whose academic content was for him totally superfluous. During Saussure's first semester there, a curious episode occurred that was to play an important role in his life and academic career. While half-heartedly following the reading of Herodotus in class—a boring exercise for a pupil who already knew both the language and the author through and through—Saussure spotted an unusual form of the perfect that contained a vowel in lieu of the nasal consonant of the standard form.

A sudden explanation came to his mind: the unusual vowel-consonant alternation could be explained if one supposed that at an earlier stage in language the nasal sonants [n] and [m], like vowels, could form a syllable; when they lost this ability later, they turned either into a full-scale vowel or into a consonant, depending on position: hence the alternation. However, upon consulting Bopp's Sanskrit grammar, the fifteen-year-old Saussure found that in this work of the foremost authority the occasional examples of syllabic sonants in Sanskrit were declared to be of "no consequence." Still cringing from "timidity" after the debacle with his essay, Saussure kept his observation to himself.[13] The issue of "syllabic sonants" eventually turned out to stand at the core of the argument in Saussure's sensational book on the system of Indo-European vowels, which appeared just a few years later. At the same time, as we will see, this episode cast a shadow over Saussure's relationship (or his perception thereof) with his German academic mentors.

During the single year Saussure spent at the University of Geneva, he took courses in chemistry and physics, but also in philosophy and art history (De Mauro 1967a:291). One subject he avoided at Geneva was "general linguistics," taught by professor Joseph Wertheimer—a noted specialist on the Kabbalah (he was the grand rabbi of Geneva) but apparently a mediocre linguist. The "Souvenirs" offers a terse evaluation of Wertheimer's work as a "copy" (*démarquage*) of Michel Bréal. It was Wertheimer's retirement many years later (in 1906) that led to Saussure assuming teaching responsibilities for the course.

The reasons behind Saussure's decision to enter the program in linguistics at Leipzig after just a year of studies in Geneva are not clear. Those biographers who tend to emphasize his alienation from the German academic world highlight a rather trivial aspect of the matter: namely, that his choice was motivated by the presence in Leipzig of a sizable colony of students from Geneva, whose company Saussure enjoyed; if this were the reason, however, why should he have left Geneva in the first place? Saussure himself—at least at moments when he wished to be impartial—acknowledged his indebtedness to his Leipzig education. In the early pages of the "Souvenirs" (before his writing erupted in an outburst of anger and went into a standstill) he speaks of the University of Leipzig as "the principal center, during the years of 1876 and 1877, of a scholarly movement that had fortunate consequences for Indo-European linguistics," adding: "There is no one who, upon evaluating this book [the *Mémoire*], would not quite easily and naturally conclude that for better or worse, it was a fruit that grew from the soil of Leipzig of 1876–77."[14]

It is true that Saussure felt uncomfortable in the atmosphere of no-nonsense directness, at times verging on brashness, that reigned among Leipzig adepts of the "science of language,"[15] and he was extremely hurt by the tepid and occasionally hostile reception in Germany of his first major book,[16] which stood in stark contrast to the enthusiasm shown by the French and Russians.[17] Later, at times he could not contain his sarcasm toward works by "Germans" (including those to whom he showed respect in his calmer moments); in characteristic instances of uncontrollable anger, he even spoke of their "monstrous obtuseness" and "idiocy," although he always kept such outbursts to himself (as in the case of the aborted "Souvenirs"). The "Germans" on their part were upset by what they perceived as Saussure's "French" oversqueamishness and secretiveness.[18] All along, however, both Brugmann and Saussure took pains to emphasize that their personal relationship remained "on good terms" (*auf guten Fuss gestanden:* Brugmann)[19] or "amiable" (Saussure), although Brugmann did not fail to add that after Saussure left Leipzig he stopped any communication with Osthoff and himself—"written, that is."

The episode with the publication of Saussure's first (in fact only) book is characteristic in its mixture of the attraction and repulsion its author must have felt toward his Leipzig academic environment. In a way, the whole affair was a follow-up to Saussure's early encounter with the phenomenon of nasal-vowel alternation in his adolescent years. Just at the moment Saussure entered the program at Leipzig, Brugmann, defying Bopp, came out with the idea of the existence of "syllabic sonants" in proto-Indo-European. According to Saussure's testimony (1960 [1903]:21), he "could not believe his ears" upon learning about the "great agitation" that surrounded Brugmann's thesis, about which he could only remark "timidly" to himself that the matter looked "neither extraordinary nor new" to him. Feeling that Brugmann's lectures interfered with his own budding ideas, Saussure abruptly abandoned his course, which was the centerpiece of the program, and eventually interrupted his studies at Leipzig to spend a year in Berlin, under the pretext of continuing Sanskrit classes, whence he submitted his sensational book for publication in Leipzig. One can understand that Saussure might feel a need to distance himself from the bustling intellectual atmosphere at Leipzig in order to be able to follow through with his thoughts; in a sense, it was an early sign of a behavioral pattern that would become dominant late in his life. But his reticence understandably upset his Leipzig mentors and was probably one of the reasons for the sour welcome Saussure's book received from them. Saussure, on his part, felt bitter about having to acknowledge

Brugmann and Osthoff for the idea of syllabic sonants, contrary to his inner conviction of his own priority.[20] Throughout all his mature life, Saussure harbored bitter feelings about the injustice he perceived to have been done to him, to the point of erupting on a few occasions in vehement allegations of "plagiarism"—which, objectively speaking, were quite irrational. It was with the express wish of setting the record of this "priority" straight once and for all that he embarked in 1903 on writing about his student years in the "Souvenirs," in which he described the precise timing and circumstances of what he felt was his discovery.

The antagonism between Saussure and the world of German scholarship was apparently exacerbated by French-German animosities that began in the 1870s and eventually erupted in the First World War a year after Saussure's death. Saussure's sojourn in Germany took place in the wake of the German seizure of Lotharingy, his ancestral Urheimat. Confrontations about Saussure's heritage persisted between the two sides after his death. While his Swiss disciples were busy compiling the *Course in General Linguistics* for publication, Saussure's German colleagues—particularly Wilhelm Streitberg, with whom he remained cordial all his life—decided to publish a volume of his small articles on various problems of Indo-European linguistics and phonology, which were scattered through various linguistic magazines. Eventually, however, to his utmost discomfiture, Streitberg was informed by his Swiss counterparts that it had been decided to publish the volume in Geneva after all.[21] As it turned out, there was no money for the project in Switzerland; it had to wait until 1922, when it was finally published in Germany.

One should be careful not to give all this *Menschliches, allzu Menschliches* (both personal and national) more than its due. In Leipzig Saussure found resolute separation of linguistics, as a discipline based on scientific methods, from the methodological nebulousness of philological studies—a distinction an elder generation of Indo-European linguists (Pictet among them) was not able to draw. To cite one of Brugmann's later remarks, Saussure had come to Leipzig still under the "Curtius spell," an attitude out of which his *Mémoire* could never have emerged. The militant brashness of the "young Turks" from Leipzig, in Brugmann's word (or *Junggrammatiker*, the name under which they eventually went down in the history of linguistics), may have repelled and hurt Saussure. Their "obtuse" home-grown scientism, lacking in philosophical culture (German as much as French) and hence remaining oblivious to the fundamental problems of epistemology that had begun to be raised at the time, drew contemptuous remarks from the mature Saussure. But the spirit of making the study of language an orderly and coherent discipline, free from the motley of diverse approaches and goals, could not fail to appeal to the "scientific" side of Saussure. It is this spirit that dominates the *Mémoire;* Brugmann had some reason to feel hurt by Saussure's (and his Francophone champions') unwillingness to give credit to Leipzig for his achievement.[22] Even in Saussure's notes from the 1890s and in the *Course,* one can sense distant but palpable echoes of Leipzig, in particular, in his reiteration of the principle of the "blindness" of phonetic changes, which, although more narrowly understood, represented one of the cornerstones of the Leipzig school. Saussure might vehemently denounce the "sheep-like stupidity [*moutonnièreté*] of the Germans" for lumping together phonetic change and the psychological mechanism of analogy. Yet the very idea of those two factors standing vis-à-vis each other as the two major forces of language formation was, to paraphrase Brugmann, "made in Leipzig."

Even more important, the trivia of personal frictions obfuscate the extent to which Saussure's identity was rooted in the both Francophone and the German traditions. In the politically correct world of today, no one would hurl derogatory remarks about the "French," "Germans," and so on with the naive straightforwardness habitual in the world of a century (and two world wars) ago. Yet in assessing Saussure's heritage antagonistic undercurrents still persist, albeit in a more sophisticated form, and they are hindering the chance of giving Saussure's thought a full and balanced contextualization. They can be seen in efforts by some modern Saussurologists to diminish Saussure's connection to German philosophy—be it the Romantic metaphysics of the turn of the nineteenth century or the neo-Kantian philosophy and phenomenology of his own time.[23] To be sure, Saussure's dialogue with eighteenth-century French philosophy of language, whose conventionalist approach to language he particularly appreciated, was intense. But excluding his relationship with German philosophical tradition from the picture drastically narrows the scope of the philosophical dimensions of Saussure's thought—an effect that runs counter to exhortations in recent Saussure studies to liberate Saussure the philosopher from the purely "linguistic" straitjacket ostensibly imposed on him by the editors of the *Course.*

In connection with this issue, it is worth remembering Saussure's perception of the kingdom of Burgundy and its modern incarnation, Lotharingy, as his primordial homeland. In his notes on Germanic legends, he spoke of ancient Burgundy as a "pan-Germanic playground" of diverse peoples and languages—a historical cauldron whose echoes spread across time and space into the Romance world to reach the contemporary scene that surrounded him at Suisse Romaine and Vaud.

In any event, the recognition Saussure's *Mémoire* received upon its appearance was far-reaching if somewhat controversial. While praising the author's knowledge, Brugmann criticized his approach as "speculative," while Osthoff flatly rejected Saussure's construction. Still, even in Germany Saussure's work became instantly and universally known. As to the book's standing in the francophone world, it was nothing short of monumental. Even today's accounts coming from French readers hail the *Mémoire* as an event of historical proportions that broke the German "monopoly" in the field.

Despite the book's universal celebrity/notoriety, its practical impact on Indo-European studies remained marginal during Saussure's lifetime, a fact that caused him considerable bitterness and may have contributed to his later general sense of alienation. It was only later discoveries of hitherto unknown linguistic data, made soon after Saussure's death, that showed how far-reaching his deductive insights had been, propelling his early work into a pivotal position in twentieth-century comparative linguistics (Gmür 1986).

During Saussure's stay in Berlin, an episode occurred whose echoes can be perceived in the later progress of his ideas. In his notes of the 1890s Saussure repeatedly praised William Dwight Whitney for emphasizing the socially conventional nature of linguistic signs. Although Saussure clearly indicated the difference between his approach to conventionality and that of Whitney (as well as the French philosophes), references to him stand out as a rare bright spot in the bleak picture of contemporary theoretical linguistics painted in Saussure's notes. As a later-discovered letter of Saussure's to Whitney of April 7, 1879, attested, the two men even met each other—apparently very briefly—in early 1879 (Joseph 1988). Thus there is little doubt about Saussure's early familiarity with the conventionalist approach to language, which went against the grain of the treatment of language as a "natural" phenomenon according to the Leipzig school doctrine.

Meanwhile, the author of the *Mémoire*, who was twenty-one years old at the time of its appearance, returned to his school, where he eventually presented his dissertation on the genitive absolute in Sanskrit (Saussure 1881). Nothing in that work recalls the scope and glamour of the *Mémoire*. The annals of Saussurology cherish an anecdote about a Leipzig professor (Zarnke) who, upon meeting the modest junior scholar, asked him whether he was a relative of the author of the celebrated book. Saussure's dissertation was a pedestrian, even routine academic work: a diligent double classification—according to formal features and meaning—of a narrowly carved-out phenomenon, based on its representation in relevant texts: a proven recipe by which hundreds if not thousands of linguistic dissertations have been written and defended all around the world up to our day. Saussure was praised for the breadth of his knowledge and the scrupulousness with which he worked with his data and granted the mark of summa cum laude et dissertatione egregia.[24] Yet even his approving reviewers expressed a mild rebuke for the author's avoidance of what could have been the most interesting aspect of his study, namely, the construction's history.[25] Speaking in later Saussurean terms, his description of the genitive absolute turned out to be consistently "synchronic."

Even the most detailed accounts of Saussure's life and oeuvre mention the dissertation episode only in passing; I have never encountered any substantial discussion of this work. Nonetheless, its content appears in a different light if one pays attention to the work's second part, "Recueil d'exemples," in which all the data, after having been arranged in a dry and rather trivial classification, are presented in their original contexts. At first glance, this section serves merely as an appendix to the study proper; this is how it was apparently taken by the examiners, who never so much as mentioned it. Yet something interesting happens in the course of what seems to be a simple listing of the processed material. The classificatory chapters took the object of classification—the genitive absolute construction—for granted; it turns out, however, that when looked at in their respective contexts, the supposed examples of the phenomenon never coalesce into something coherent and unequivocally definable. What can be seen in the data is instead an agglomeration of phenomena partially resembling each other, whose contiguity "flows within limits that are rather uncertain" (Saussure 1881:33). What seem like representations of an abstract grammatical category provide a continuum whose various members show different degrees of affinity—sometimes quite "remote"—to the core notion (34). The ambiguity of the data, stemming from the syntactic looseness of the Indian epic style, with its penchant for ellipses, as well as from the damaged state of the texts, often makes it a matter of opinion whether one or another passage should be deemed an example of the construction in question. What may look like a "genitive absolute" (i.e., a genitive construction with no grammatical subject to which it could be related) could turn out to be an ordinary subordinate genitive construction, if one considers the possibility of an implied (elliptic) subject or chooses to treat the absence of the subject as the result of damage occurring in the process of the text's transmission.[26] The object of the study in effect dissolves under the scrutiny of particular cases. Saussure seems to be addressing his own old work when he states in one of his later notes that a grammatical category, "as for example genitive," is "completely ungraspable [*insaisissable*]"; its conventional name is a "word literally devoid of any sense," since the meaning of genitive is always "extended from one moment of use to another, one page to another"; to speak about genitive as a category is to imply that there is an idea "above signs, outside signs, independent of signs" (*ELG*, 55/35)—in other words, to treat it the way the main part of Saussure's dissertation did and not the way in which it was presented in the supplement.

For all the narrowness of the scope of the dissertation, the implicit tension between its first and second halves presages the contradiction between Saussure's later efforts to construct the subject of linguistics and his recognition of its ungraspable fluidity. In this sense, paradoxically, the work could be seen as a step forward from the *Mémoire* to the Saussure of the 1890s and 1900s.

## PARIS AND GENEVA

After receiving his degree, Saussure went to Paris, where he soon assumed the position of *maître de conférence* (roughly, associate professor) of Gothic and Old High German at the École pratique des hautes études at the Sorbonne. Among his students were some of the leading French linguists of the next generation, such as Antoine Meillet and Maurice Grammond. Saussure's teaching there has become legendary.[27] As to the specific content of Saussure's courses, little is known beyond his terse yearly reports indicating the subjects he taught and the number of students in each class (Benveniste 1965:22). Meillet later claimed that Saussure formed his ideas about general linguistics "very early,"[28] that is, during his Paris years. Godel (1957:33), on the other hand, pointed out that nothing is known of the development of Saussure's fundamental ideas prior to 1891, the date of the earliest notes. These claims should be entertained with some caution, the result of a benign yet palpable rivalry between Paris and Geneva—specifically, between Meillet and Bally and their respective circles—over Saussure's heritage. It is probable, though, that some of Saussure's core ideas, particularly those concerning the systemic aspect of language, transpired in his Paris lectures on Germanic and Indo-European comparative grammar, as they could be implicitly felt already in the *Mémoire*.[29]

Saussure's level of professional involvement in his Paris years can be seen in the pivotal role he played at the Linguistic Society of Paris, in particular as an editor of its series Mémoires de la Société de linguistique (Benveniste 1965). His activity in the society brought him in contact with many prominent linguists—notably Hugo Schuhardt, later a vocal critic of Leipzig positivism, and Baudouin de Courtenay, whose work (and even more that of his collaborator Mikołaj Kruszewski) on phonemes is universally acknowledged as the closest kin to Saussure's theoretical views—at least, to their "linguistic" aspect proper.

Saussure taught in Paris for ten years, excluding a leave for health reasons (whose cause, it seems, was fatigue) in 1889.[30] He used a part of his leave for a trip to Lithuania. The trip could not have been more productive; the law of the accentual shift that Saussure subsequently formulated constituted a major contribution to Balto-Slavic accentology. At the same time, this trip probably played a decisive role in developing his feelings of anxiety about the methodological foundation (or lack thereof) of comparative studies and, ultimately, of linguistics in general. In his private notes on the subject, Saussure called the positivist belief that language material itself constitutes the object of description "simply gibberish" (*simple charabia*) (Saussure 2003b:334).

Little is known about Saussure's life during those ten Paris years beyond the classrooms at the Sorbonne and the proceedings of the Linguistic Society. In 1891 he received the order of the Legion of Honor for his work as an educator (a fact very few people were aware of at the time, so tacit did he remain about it). Yet it was exactly at that point that he accepted an offer from the University of Geneva to create for him an "extraordinary" (i.e., not permanently inscribed in the university's academic programs) chair in Indo-European linguistics (it became "ordinary" a few years later). Saussure's move from the glamour and professional accomplishment of his Paris position to a smaller academic world has become a much-debated issue in Saussurean studies. Its "mystery" seemed to be heightened by the suggestion—first raised by Favre and later repeated by many others—that Bréal, who was instrumental in Saussure's original appointment, was certain to have nominated Saussure as his successor for the chair in linguistics at the College de France upon his own (ostensibly imminent) retirement. This issue led to speculation that Saussure's fierce Swiss patriotism may have prompted him to decline the College de France chair, as it would have required him to take French citizenship (De Mauro 1967a:31). It is only recently that Arrivé (2007:27) pointed out the plain fact that there was no question of Bréal's retirement at the time of Saussure's departure; he retired only in 1906 (whereupon he was succeeded by Meillet). Saussure's decision to assume a chair in the area of his principal scholarly specialization was logical in terms of academic career. Another reason for the transfer may have been his general fatigue.[31] Still, Saussure's move to Geneva was a clear retreat. It signified his increasing need to distance himself from the world outside intimately familiar confines.[32]

Saussure's teaching in Geneva remained as charismatic and productive as ever. Among his students were some who would become leading Swiss linguists, including the eventual editors of the *Course*; Sechehaye took Saussure's courses from 1891 to 1893, while Bally visited his classes occasionally till 1906. It was now Bally's turn to witness, as he would later testify, "the dazzling clarity of vision" one experienced at Saussure's lectures.[33] Less illustrious members of the audience remembered their teacher with awe ("a piece of chalk in hand since the moment of his arrival, always on his feet, never consulting any notes"), proliferating typical classroom anecdotes, for example, how he once gave a student zero on the exam for confusing a short and a long [a] in a Sanskrit text.[34] The energy of Saussure's Paris years can still be sensed in the early 1890s, in particular, in his efforts to organize in Geneva in 1894 a major Congress of Orientalists (a field that in the French academic tradition included Slavic and Baltic studies, which were of particular interest to Saussure in those years). This outward activity cost him considerable effort, as can be seen from his correspondence. Eventually, any public role became difficult. In 1908 Meillet and others among his former students in Paris and Geneva published a volume on the occasion of Saussure's fiftieth birthday,[35] which was presented to him at a festive ceremony in Geneva. Whether despite his profound modesty or because of it, Saussure cherished recognition of his work; he was genuinely happy and grateful for the event, but the ceremony itself rendered him virtually mute, overwhelmed by shyness. On a similar occasion, upon his election as a corresponding member of the Institute de France in December 1911, he wrote to Meillet of being "a little frustrated by congratulations for an honor little aspired to"; he even took a short trip out of the city "so as not to listen to any more talks about the Institute and all that pomp."[36]

By the late 1890s, Saussure had almost completely withdrawn into private life (he was married in 1894 to the daughter of another prominent Genevan family; they had two children) and a stable regimen of teaching, consolidated around a yearly course on Sanskrit and only occasionally punctuated with such subjects of choice as French versification (1899) and the epos of the Nibelungs (1904).³⁷ Having spent fifteen years outside his native country, Saussure now almost never went abroad. In all those years he visited Paris just once. (He and his wife also spent a few months in Rome in 1906 when he took a semester-long leave).

One of the signs of Saussure's progressing reticence was what he himself called his epistolophobia or graphophobia. His letters to colleagues almost invariably began with apologies for a delay (sometimes of years) in responding. Particularly dramatic was an episode that occurred in 1903. In a letter to the highly sympathetic Streitberg, Saussure, venting his longtime frustration with the perceived lack of real recognition of the *Mémoire*, complained with the utmost bitterness that Carl Verner (a Danish linguist whose famous "Verner's law" was hailed at Leipzig as a spectacular confirmation of the methodological premises of the school) had plagiarized some of its ideas. (A jab at Verner's law later appeared in the *Course*, where it was cited as an example of the "imprecisions" of contemporary historical studies: CLG 200/145). Once again, the unfortunate case of priority in the discovery of syllabic nasals came forth. Saussure asked permission to deposit with Streitberg his written account of the matter, with which he wanted to set the record straight regarding his own priority; the manner in which he thanks Streitberg in March 1904 for granting his request implies that the document in question is forthcoming. A month later, Saussure apologizes for the delay; another note followed on August 1, with a reference to his graphophobia; finally, a week later, Saussure tersely informs Streitberg that the current state of his family affairs makes it impossible for him to accomplish this project (Villani 1990:24–26). A sketch of the document, indeed written in 1903, is now known as "Souvenirs d'enfance et d'études." Like all of Saussure's writing of the time, its text, especially the later parts, is fragmentary, larded with aborted sentences. Particularly striking is the way the narrative gradually deteriorates from the quiet, mildly ironic tone with which Saussure depicts the events of his early years—among others, his grandiose adolescent endeavor at creating a universal linguistic system—to almost paranoid outbursts against perceived detractors, until it stops abruptly on the last phrase, "Montre moutonnièreté des Allemands"; one can see why Streitberg never received the document.

During the 1880s and early 1890s Saussure's scholarly production consisted of a number of articles of high quality but narrow scope: for the most part minuscule etymological notes and review articles. Precious as those "exhibition pieces" (*Kabinettsstücke*, in Wackernagel's word) of quality scholarship were, there was nothing in them to recall the drive toward a grand general picture that underscored the *Mémoire*. Yet by the time of Saussure's return to Geneva even this mode of scholarly expression began to fade. He experienced increasing difficulty in shaping even a narrowly focused work into a definitive form suitable for publication. During the 1900s, Saussure's published scholarly production was all but nonexistent. Writing an article or a review that he had promised proved on a number of occasions an insurmountable challenge.[38] In a note, he confesses to "a morbid horror of the pen," which makes his work "an experience of sheer torture, quite out of proportion to its relative unimportance."[39] Even a semipopular lecture on the etymology of some toponyms in the vicinity of Geneva, which Saussure delivered in 1904 at the Historical and Archeological Society of Geneva, is known to us only thanks to the minutes of the meeting, which have been preserved. The lecture itself was characteristic of the late Saussure. On the surface, it looked like a typical academic "dinner talk" before a company of enlightened nonspecialists; Saussure amused his colleagues by offering a sophisticated (and sometimes pretty fancy) etymological interpretation of some toponyms in the vicinity. What could be inferred from his examples, however, was a vision of the dizzyingly winding path by which the memory of remote historical events could be transmitted through all the vicissitudes of migration and interfering influences—a subject to which Saussure devoted much of his note writing at the time.

Looking at Saussure's outward activity in the late 1890s to early 1900s, one can easily get the impression of an aging professor who is set on doing respectable but routine academic work until his retirement. This picture, however, is refuted by the evidence of the thousands of pages Saussure was covering at the time, of which even his closest academic associates knew very little.

Insurmountable inner obstacles prevented this solitary writing from becoming public. As we have seen, the environment of Saussure's early formative years was extremely rich but perhaps also burdensome. The weight of family tradition can be sensed in the extreme feeling of intellectual responsibility that, after the bold generalizations of his early years, made Saussure increasingly cautious (in his word, *timid*) in asserting anything of which he could not be absolutely certain (a state he never seemed to reach).[40] We can see Saussure's growing dejection in the face of mounting ambiguities concerning the most fundamental premises of the subject of his studies.

Saussure himself was aware of the underlying cause of his malaise. Beginning in the early 1890s, he refers repeatedly in his letters to his extreme difficulty in addressing any question involving language, even a particular topic that seemed perfectly clear in itself, in the awareness that he still remained in the dark about the most fundamental premises concerning the nature of language and, consequently, about the way in which the topic he intended to write about could and should be addressed. He expressed these thoughts most eloquently in the now-famous letter to Meillet of January 4, 1894. Commenting on his recent studies of Lithuanian accentuation (a work that, by all appearances, was extremely successful), Saussure adds: "But I am quite disgusted with all of this, and with general difficulties in writing even ten lines that would make common sense in regard to facts of language. . . . I am seeing more and more both the immensity of labor that is needed to show a linguist what he is doing . . . and at the same time, the fairly great vanity in thinking that anything could, in the final account, be done in linguistics."[41]

This is the reason, he adds, why he has failed to deliver another article he had promised, even though its "material" aspect did not pose any difficulty. Responding to Meillet's enthusiasm about his new accentological studies and gentle nudging to move on with them, Saussure adds that the "ineptitude" of the current state of affairs in linguistics "spoiled" for him the "pleasures of historical studies" (*vient gâter mon plaisir historique*) of his earlier years. As he now sees it, he would in the end have to produce, "despite himself," a book in which, "with neither enthusiasm nor passion, I'll make it clear why there is no single piece of terminology employed in linguistics about which I would concede that it has any sense whatsoever. And it is only after that, I avow, that I would be able to resume my work at the point at which I left it."[42]

Champions of the "authentic Saussure" often cite this last passage as evidence of his determination to produce a "book" which, if accomplished, could have become his "real" Course in General Linguistics, in contradistinction to the "vulgate" manufactured by his disciples. Yet even at this early stage the omens seemed unfavorable. Saussure's fear of the unbearable intellectual burden he would have to take upon himself, his anticipation of the ultimate "vanity" of this effort, his hoping against hope to regain the lost "pleasures" of his subject studies after acquitting himself of the superhuman labor of theorizing—his language at times evoking the image of the defeated hero of an epic—did not portend a happy outcome. One can sense Saussure's gripping frustration, which renders him mute after a few energetic yet vague declarations.

This debilitating preoccupation with the foundations of the discipline became a palpable task when, upon Wertheimer's retirement in the fall of

1906, general linguistics was appended to Saussure's Indo-European chair. (I venture to guess that the primary reason for this wise decision was economic—that is, patching together two esoteric fields, each attracting few students—rather than a response to Saussure's intellectual interests). It now became Saussure's duty to teach the subject on a regular basis. He taught a two-semester lecture course in general linguistics three times, offering it every other academic year. The first course started belatedly in January of 1907, in the midst of the winter semester; the other two followed in 1908 to 1909 and 1910 to 1911. Course attendance steadily increased from six students in 1907 to eleven in 1908 to twelve in 1910;[43] several of his students took the course twice.

There is some evidence that, at least in the beginning, Saussure took his new duty, to use his expression, "sans enthousiasme ni passion."[44] Unlike other courses he taught, "linguistique générale" did not have a definitive subject. At the time, the term *linguistique générale* denoted more of an "administrative unity" that put together certain subjects related to the study of language (the basics of historical linguistics, phonetics, writing, typology of languages, etc.) than an exploration of linguistic theory (Bouquet 1998/99:188). As the now-published notes of Saussure's students show, he vacillated between these two foci; as a result, the content of the three courses he taught only partially overlapped (Bota 2002:142, 153). His uncertainty about their didactic content reflected a broader problem of "vacillations and uncertainty in Saussure's thought" (De Mauro 1967a:324).

Far from resolving the earlier doubts Saussure expressed in his notes at the start of the 1890s, the experience of teaching the courses apparently contributed to his feeling of dejection and defeat in the last years of his life. As De Mauro (1967a:325) notes, "a certain sadness dominates [Saussure's] late conversations with Riedlinger and L. Gautier" (another dedicated student and diligent note taker) in 1911. In a similar vein, Arrivé (2007:23) speaks about the "melancholy" and "bitterness" exuded by Saussure's "Souvenirs," while a remark by Matsuzawa (2003:320) shrouds this perception in a "Christological" aura: "The silence in which Saussure was wrapped in his last years seems to us to be a sign of a passion which the success of structuralism prevented from being shared." (One is tempted to interpret "passion" in this context as the Gospel's Passion). Having almost reached the end of his third course, Saussure confessed to Gautier that he was worried (*tracassé*) about his teaching. Should he present the subject in all its complexity, revealing to the students all its ambiguities and unsolvable dilemmas, which would ill serve their purpose of simply getting credit for the course, or simplify the matter, compromising the complexity of the issues to adapt them to the needs of the audience? (Gautier 2005:69). One should take the scruples of this conscientious educator with a grain of salt. It was not just for the sake of his students that Saussure could not force himself to embark upon a definitive strategy for the presentation of his ideas. Both in the published *Course* and in the notes, one can see the same recurring pattern: as Saussure moves forward with dazzling revelations about the most fundamental features of language, he eventually reaches a point at which he realizes that the way he defined his subject makes it purely negative and, as a consequence, impossible to seize upon, let alone describe in a systematic way; at this point, he rushes away from the abyss with ad hoc comments and spotty examples. They seem to remedy the situation at the rhetorical level, giving the discourse an appearance of coherence. Yet this forced clarity always proves to be short-lived: it dissipates once Saussure resumes his penetrating distinctions.

In the fall of 1912, Saussure was scheduled to teach his course for the fourth time. A sudden illness (apparently throat cancer) whose first symptoms had appeared as early as 1909 caused him to take leave from the university. The Saussures retreated to the castle of his wife's family at Vufflens. The task of teaching the course was given to Bally, an assignment that brought him into closer contact with students from previous courses and their notes. (After Saussure's death, Bally was appointed to his chair in general linguistics.)

During the last months of his life, Saussure embarked on the study of Chinese. Curiously, this was yet another issue with a "familial" subtext. One of Saussure's younger brothers, Léopold, was a politician and expert Sinologist. A champion of the French colonization of Southeast Asia, he used a linguistic argument to support his views. In his book *Psychologie de la colonisation français dans ses rapports avec les sociétés indigènes* (1899), he defended the thesis of the constitutional inferiority of "monosyllabic" languages, such as Chinese or Vietnamese, which ostensibly reflected the intellectual inferiority of their speakers. One can sense an implicit yet pointed answer to Léopold's linguistic racism in the way the *Course* ends with an irate denial of any connection between language and race and a passionate advocacy of the idea of the equal value of all structural types of languages. Still, Saussure did not abandon the idea that some structural differences between languages can be fundamental. On a few occasions, in his notes, he suggested the possibility that basic semiotic units (words) in "monosyllabic" languages may be less susceptible to unceasing changes of the kind characteristic of languages with highly developed inflection, such as Indo-European, Semitic, or Finno-Ugric (*ELG* 269/193 and 301–302/210). Did he hope to find in Chinese less relativity and, consequently, a firmer ground for linguistic analysis?

Saussure died on February 22, 1913; the best-known picture of him—formally dressed, immaculately trim, the shadow of an inwardly directed smile on his lips under a formidable "Nietzschean" moustache—was taken one day before his death.

## The Writings    TWO

### THE PUBLISHED AND THE PERISHABLE

Saussure's writing difficulties, underlain by perpetual doubt, did not affect his performance as a teacher. In his notes, moments of dazzling clarity of vision are not rare but are typically short-lived, dissolving rapidly into a fog of aborted theses, sudden diversions, and incomplete or even plainly ungrammatical phrases. In class, however, Saussure consistently maintained what Bally called "une clarté de vision étonnante." Saussure's trademark was his ability to shape even problems of the utmost complexity into an intellectual edifice whose logic of construction—or at least its rhetorical scaffolding—looked perfectly transparent. He always spoke spontaneously, using few notes or none at all.

When the lectures in linguistics began, quite a few among Saussure's disciples in Geneva—the older ones, like Bally and Sechehaye, as well as members of the generation of the 1900s (Albert Riedlinger, Sèrge Karcevsky, Léopold Gautier), realized their importance and were eager to see them published. The well-shaped character of Saussure's oral presentations left no doubt that he must have had a comprehensive draft of the course in his files; the only problem seemed to be how to overcome Saussure's notorious procrastinaton about preparing his works for publication.

The champions of the "genuine" Saussure cite, as evidence that only sudden death prevented him from writing the book he had in mind all along, his words in the famous letter to Meillet of January 1894, in which he said that he would eventually have to embark on writing a theoretical book, a burden he viewed with dread. But this letter—as well as the occasional mention in Saussure's notes that this or that fragmentary sketch would eventually constitute a "chapter" of the future book—was written back in the 1890s. By the time of his courses, when giving a systematic account of "general linguistics" had become a palpable and even pressing task, Saussure responded to numerous inquiries, encouragements, and offers of help with unambiguous reticence. In 1909, he wrote to a student, apparently in response to his inquiry about when one could expect a book on the subject of his lectures: "As to a book on this subject, one cannot dream of it: it should offer the definitive thought of its author"[1]—definitiveness being what Saussure felt himself to be totally lacking. Two years later, another student, Léopold Gautier, approached Saussure with similar inquiries. The conversation that ensued—in May 1911, a few weeks before the end of the last lecture cycle—poignantly revealed Saussure's state of mind in the wake of his courses:

—I [Gautier] told him that one would be very eager to learn at least a part of his system of philosophy of language.
"I don't believe so. All this is not worked out sufficiently."
—I asked him whether he had not occupied himself with these questions prior to Wertheimer's death. [It was actually Wertheimer's retirement that made Saussure responsible for teaching general linguistics].
"On the contrary, I have not added anything since then. These are matters that occupied me well before 1900." . . .
—I asked him if he had put his ideas on paper.
"Yes, I have some notes, but they are lost in those piles, so I wouldn't be able to retrieve them."
—I impressed it on him that he should publish something about these matters.
"It would be absurd to begin the lengthy research work [needed] for a publication, while I have here (he made a pointing gesture) lots and lots of works yet unpublished."[2]

Indeed, "piles" of Saussure's notes remained lost until 1996, when a renovation in the *orangerie* of the Saussures' residence led to the discovery of a large cache of documents (Bouquet 2003b).

Finally, Bally, himself already the author of a highly regarded book, offered the venerable *maître* any secretarial help he might need in order to turn his lectures into a book. The expressions with which Saussure cordially thanked his younger colleague for his selfless offer left no doubt that the project would never come to fruition.³

After Saussure's sudden death, the idea of publishing his legacy in some form emerged immediately in both Paris and Geneva. One of Saussure's students, P. Regard, who by then had moved to Paris, had taken extensive notes in the second and third courses, which gave Meillet the idea of publishing just these notes. On his part, Bally sought a way "to put on record memories that we all respect."⁴

Bally himself did not attend the courses; he initially became acquainted with them thanks to the "admirably maintained" notes of one of Saussure's students. That Bally had first-hand knowledge of Saussure's ideas as well is attested by his regret, upon reading the notes, that he himself did not keep a record of his numerous conversations with "our *maître*."⁵ After consulting the notes of various students, Bally came to the conclusion that, first, Saussure's successive courses differed widely in content, and therefore no single set of notes could represent his teaching as a whole; and second, that Regard's notes diverged from those of other students, apparently because they contained many of his own comments. It was perhaps in the aftermath of this conclusion by Bally that Saussure's widow, in a letter to Meillet (May 25), pointedly reminded him about the "scrupulous conscience" of her late husband in regard to his work and urged caution.⁶ As a result, Meillet decided to abort the project of publishing Regard's notes; it was now his turn to speak, in a letter to Bally (May 31), about his "great scruples" against posthumous publications and, even more so, against merging the diverse courses (Bally 1990:104). Later, when Bally sent to Meillet Saussure's copy of the *Mémoire* with the author's notes in the margins, asking his opinion about whether they could be incorporated into the book now being compiled, Meillet advised against it, arguing that any editorial decision of this kind would be "too delicate, almost impossible," since nobody could tell how much importance Saussure attached to this or that momentary thought whose traces he left in the margins; those notes were "obsolete" (*caduque*) anyway (letter of March 9, 1914; 109).

One can sense an implicit rivalry, however tactfully expressed, between the two places in which Saussure had taught and the two branches of the following his teaching had inspired: Paris, where his theoretical ideas were perceived largely as an outgrowth of his Indo-European studies and teaching, and Geneva, where his philosophical and synchronic approach to language, which came to the foreground in the 1900s, resonated strongly with his Swiss disciples' own preferences. One can sympathize with Meillet's heightened sense of academic and personal responsibility toward the heritage of his venerable teacher and colleague; it is undeniable that Bally and Sechehaye "forced" on Saussure the publication of something which he himself had a "strong reluctance" (Linda 1998/99: 226) to make public. Still, their edition was neither the first nor the last book of historical importance made public against an author's express wishes. And, as the recent publication of some separate sets of the students' notes has shown, in their primary form none of them could have evoked the response the *Cours de linguistique générale* did.

Apparently, Bally's original idea was that he and Sechehaye would do what he had not been able to convince Saussure to accomplish with his help, namely, take Saussure's draft and shape it into a book, with help from students' notes. In the preface to the first edition of the *Course*, Bally and Sechehaye speak of their astonishment when, after approaching Saussure's widow with a request to search for Saussure's notes, they found among them nothing even remotely resembling a coherent draft or synopsis of the course(s) he taught.[7]

This episode is curious in view of what is now known about the massive quantity of Saussure's writing. Saussure did make some notes (although not many) for each of the three courses. Yet they, as well as other documents in that "heap," remained hidden in plain sight, so to speak. Although written in clear and neat handwriting, the notes seemed virtually unusable. Saussure was putting down his thoughts on paper the moment they occurred to him, without giving heed to what preceded or would follow and with little consideration for coherent rhetorical presentation or even grammar. For years, beginning in the early 1890s, he continued this fragmentary writing, only to wave it aside in a remark to Gautier: "Oui, j'ai des notes mais perdues dans des monceaux, aussi ne saurais-je les retrouver." It took almost a century, and a tremendous amount of editorial work, before Saussure's notes began to be made public in close to their original form.

Not having found much by way of usable documents in Saussure's own writing,[8] the editors turned to his students. However, as the eventual (in the 1990s) separate publication of some of the students' notes from each of the three consecutive courses (Saussure 1996; Saussure 1997; Saussure 1993b have shown, Saussure perpetually vacillated about the course's design; at no point did any of the three courses reach a definitive form in regard to the issues they addressed, theoretical arguments, or the terminology in which key concepts were represented.

The first course—taught in a shortened format because of its late beginning—more or less followed the patchwork of topics traditionally associated with "general linguistics": after a brief introduction (characteristically dedicated to "Analysis of Errors of Linguistics" and "Principles of Phonology," two of Saussure's hobbyhorses), it proceeds to discuss at length the two types of language change—phonetic evolution and change by analogy—and methods of comparative grammar.

It was only on the second attempt that Saussure resolved to address the cardinal theoretical problems that constituted the core of his thoughts and writing in the 1890s: the necessity of constructing language as the object of linguistics, the negative value of linguistic signs, the mutability and immutability of signs, and the distinction between synchrony and diachrony. As a result, the first half of the second course turned out to be almost completely devoid of the descriptive issues traditionally associated with "general linguistics." This sharp change initially upset even such a devoted student as Albert Riedlinger, whose notes would eventually serve as one of the most reliable sources for the *Course*. Riedlinger, who was taking the course for the second time, wrote in his notes on January 19, 1909, a month into the semester: "The introduction that Mr. de Saussure has made so far to his course in general linguistics is nothing but small talk [*causérie*]. If the course is to continue, it had better change completely."[9] In the same January of 1909, in a conversation with Riedlinger, Saussure himself acknowledged his dissatisfaction with how his course had progressed so far: "Language is a closed system, and the theory must also be a system, as closed as language itself. Here lies the difficulty, since there is nothing to indicate any sequence in posing one or another question about language; everything has to be coordinated in a united system"; he then suggested that the current course should serve as a "preparation for a philosophical course in linguistics."[10] Riedlinger eventually came to appreciate what he initially perceived as "causérie," that is, Saussure's turning away from the inventory of the linguistic household in favor of a theoretical inquiry. Fifty years later, reversing his position entirely in the wake of Godel's critique of the published *Course*, he complained about the omission in the published version of the "magnificent Introduction" to the second course.[11]

The third and last course, which eventually served as the template for the published compilation, strove to achieve a balance between revolutionary theoretical ideas and the body of conventional knowledge. Yet Saussure's vacillations did not desert him at that point either. In the middle of the course, he suddenly announced that the rest of it would be dedicated to "comments" on subjects hitherto discussed. Indeed, the last third of the course followed almost precisely all the topics raised—at times elliptically—in the first part, offering various elaborations and definitions of previously introduced concepts and occasionally casting them in new terminology. It was on this paraphrastic round that some of Saussure's key terms such as *signifier* and *signified* appeared for the first time.

Bally, who emerged as the principal supervisor of the publication project (after Meillet graciously conceded primacy to Geneva), repeatedly emphasized the importance of rendering Saussure's teaching as precisely as possible. His idea was to (re)construct the *Course* as a coherent book by incorporating the notes of various students from the different courses as fully as possible without compromising the book's integrity.[12] Certain omissions were unavoidable, but the editors seemed resolved to make no additions of their own to the courses' content, as the episode with Regard's notes showed. On a few occasions when the editors felt something was wanting in the available material, they suggested the missing point in an editorial footnote—keeping it, however, separate from the main text. When the result of this reconstruction appeared in print in 1916, its title page was as follows: "Ferdinand de Saussure, *Course de linguistique générale*, publié par Charles Bally et Albert Sechehaye, avec collaboration de A. Riedlinger."

The scale of the response to the publication of the *Course* is well known. The book created a new paradigm in which various concepts emerging in different fields—from linguistics and the theory of signs to literary criticism, psychology, and anthropology—resonated with each other, reinforcing the paradigm's fundamental premises. It should be emphasized that this paradigm stemmed from the initial *reception* of the *Course*, i.e., from a selective and directed reading of the book, a process that turned a blind eye to what, at the time, seemed "irrelevant" or marginal in its content, to say nothing of the total ignorance at the time—and moreover, total lack of curiosity—about the unpublished writings of Saussure that stood behind the book's terse declarations. In a poignant way, the fate of the *Course* manifested in itself the Saussurean principle of arbitrariness: once the meaning of a sign is established as a given fact within the community of its users, it is futile to ask whither and by what vicissitudes of transformation it has arrived at a given point. From Voloshinov's (1973 [1928]) critique of the *Course*'s "objectivism" from the perspective of Bakhtin's theory of dialogism to Benveniste's and Jakobson's challenge of the principle of arbitrariness (Benveniste 1966a;

Jakobson and Waugh 1987:chapter 4) to Derrida's assault on the Saussurean "metaphysics of presence," the phenomenon of "Saussure's *Course*" was treated as a given fact whose meaning, constrained by convention, was presumed apparent.

Robert Godel's study of Saussure's manuscripts, while it exposed for the first time serious discrepancies between the published book and Saussure's own writings, did not shaken the fundamental premises of the established Saussurean paradigm. In his selection of Saussure's notes, Godel downplayed what might appear incoherent or even bewildering in the intellectual atmosphere of the 1950s; in particular, he mentioned the issue of the anagram—soon to become a sensation—only in passing. Nevertheless, Godel's book established an important precedent. Within a decade, critical editions of the *Course* appeared in which its text was confronted with various manuscript sources (Saussure's own as well as his students').

The available corpus of Saussure's writing about language and linguistics further expanded in the 1990s when a large cache of his papers was accidentally discovered in the hothouse of his family's mansion. This finding resulted in a new, comprehensive edition of Saussure's writings on general linguistics (Saussure 2002), in which the new material was added to that introduced by Godel and incorporated into Engler's critical edition of the *Course*.

Saussure neither dated his notes nor arranged them in any order. At first glance, it seems natural to attribute his writing on general linguistics to the time when he was teaching his courses on the subject. Yet Saussure spoke the truth when he told Gautier that the matter had occupied him "before 1900," and that he had not done anything substantial in that area "since then." Most if not all of Saussure's writing on general linguistics (save sparse preparatory lecture notes) was done in the first half of the 1890s. At one point, Saussure discusses the name "Félix," mentioning in passing that it is the name of the "new president" of the French Republic (*ELG*, 134/89); Félix Favre was the French president from 1895 to 1899.[13] It seems safe to accept the years 1891 to 1895 as the time when the foundations of linguistics stood at the epicenter of Saussure's interests; it was at that time that he spoke about his concerns about the issue in his correspondence with Meillet.

At the initial stages of their search, Saussure scholars understandably concentrated their attention on Saussure's writing about language, brushing aside other subjects as marginal. An altogether new phase in appraising Saussure's heritage began in 1971 with the appearance of Starobinski's account of Saussure's "anagram studies." Saussure's relatively short-lived

(1906 to 1909) but extremely intense, verging on obsessive, preoccupation with the subject resulted in scores of notebooks filled with analyses (few of which have been published so far beyond the excerpts presented in Starobinski's book) of anagrams in a wide variety of poetic texts.[14] If the revisions of the published *Course* resulted in the "softening" of its perceived cerebral constructionism, Starobinski's presentation unveiled an entirely different side of Saussure, strikingly remote from the conventional view of him as an inexorable system builder.

The quest for "the other Saussure" has led to new discoveries and new publications. It was well known, for instance, that throughout most of his academic career Saussure was interested in the Germanic epos; he taught courses on the subject both in Paris and Geneva. His notes on the subject, however, were made later, sometime between 1903 and 1911 (Fehr 1997:547). When a large cache of Saussure's papers dedicated to studies of legends and their transmission and transformation, from the Theseus myth to the Nibelung epos, finally came to light (Saussure 2003a), it turned out to be extremely important for illuminating Saussure's ideas about the nature of historical change. While the precise date when these notes were made is not available, Saussure's lecture of 1904 on the residue of Burgundian toponyms in the Vaudois area indicated that his ideas concerning the role of sixth-century Burgundy as the principal historical source of the Nibelung epos were only at the budding stage at the time.[15]

For a long time, research into Saussure's papers concentrated on the part of his archive bequeathed by his family to the Bibliothèque Nationale at Geneva. Meanwhile, another large part of Saussure's heritage, bought by the Widener Library of Harvard from Saussure's son in 1960, remained practically unexplored, beyond an initial survey done by Jakobson (who had initiated the purchase), until Herman Parret's publications in the 1990s (Saussure 1993a; Saussure 1994b). As it turned out, the "Harvard papers" contained Saussure's extensive notes on the Rig Veda and Brahman mythology and religion. Written apparently around 1906, when Saussure was supposed to be preparing for the first of his courses, the notes addressed linguistic matters indirectly at best.[16] Together with the anagrammatic studies of the same period, they presented alternative currents within Saussure's thought, whose remoteness—at least, on the surface—from questions of linguistic theory was such that a reader used to the public image of Saussure might feel "scandalized" (Parret 1995/96: 89).

Altogether, the corpus of Saussure's manuscript legacy at Geneva and Harvard comprises roughly nine thousand pages, plus about a hundred notebooks with anagrammatic studies.[17] Although many documents cannot be dated precisely, the entire span of Saussure's private writing covers about two decades—from 1891 (i.e., soon after Saussure's move to Geneva) to 1910 (the date of his preparatory notes for the third course in linguistics). The accumulation of notes was not a steady process; there were periods of particularly intense writing interspersed with intervals during which little seems to have been written. One such creative outburst came between 1891 and 1895, when Saussure was driven by his awareness that linguistic studies lacked a proper methodological foundation. Notes from this period are dedicated to insights into the fundamental nature of language and to the problem of "whence to begin?" that is, to the method (in the Cartesian sense) of constructing language as the object of linguistic inquiry. Another period of feverish activity came between 1906 and 1907.

During these two peak periods of activity, Saussure proved able to overcome his "epistolophobia" on a few occasions, so eager was he to share his thoughts with those whom he trusted most: Meillet in 1894 concerning the state of linguistic affairs, Bally and again Meillet in 1906 and 1907 in connection with his discovery of the anagram. We can note that both outbursts of creative energy came in the aftermath of a leave of absence Saussure had to take from his teaching duties due to exhaustion; Parret (1995/96:114–115) even suggests that these two periods coincided with two "crises" experienced by Saussure. The pattern of emerging from a spiritual "crisis" with a feverish outburst of revelatory creativity was itself characteristic of the turn of the century. Moreover, the very choice of issues with which Saussure felt preoccupied at those pivotal moments reflected intellectual and spiritual tides of the times. Saussure's soul-searching in quest of the ultimate goal of linguistics coincided with the philosophical crisis of positivism and the revival of Kantian epistemology and Hegelian phenomenology in the context of modern science, while his plunging, a decade later, into the enigma of the anagram and the world of Brahman theology reflected the overheated and misty spiritual atmosphere of early modernism.

Both periods of creative upsurge were followed by years of retreat. Saussure's "Souvenirs" of 1903 reveals a person who feels that his work has been unappreciated and his ideas looted by "plagiarizers." In the last years of his life, Saussure apparently felt himself to have been defeated on all fronts. After increasingly defiant (and by the same token, increasingly desperate) assertions that the presence of the anagram in diverse texts—whose scope was meanwhile expanding at a disastrous rate—had been proven beyond any doubt, Saussure suddenly broke off his analyses in the fall of 1909. As to his courses in general linguistics, his conversations with his students showed that he was neither satisfied with their content nor felt any hope of ever achieving, or any desire to strive for, the theoretical clarity whose vital importance for the field he had realized two decades earlier.

Virtually all the works Saussure published in his lifetime were dedicated to various problems of Indo-European linguistics. Yet even though he continued publishing some miscellaneous articles on the subject through the 1890s, he had essentially ceased to be an "Indo-European linguist" since the beginning of his inquiry into the nature of language. Looking now at the whole scope of Saussure's oeuvre, including what he himself was resigned to let perish, we can say that Saussure eventually ceased to be a "linguist" altogether.

Yet it was, perhaps, precisely the fact that Saussure had ceased to be a "linguist"—had in fact given up linguistics in his private writing—that bestowed on his course an almost transcendent force. His students and associates invariably felt the presence of a mysterious intensity behind Saussure's lectures and conversations that seemed luminously clear in the moment yet proved elusive in retrospect. This feeling left its traces in the persistent aura of "Christological" allusions that continued to surround accounts of Saussure's life, personality, and oeuvre. Yet it proved difficult to capture the spirit that had evoked this aura—as it proved impossible for Saussure himself to externalize what he sensed and tried to convey, if only to himself, in his notes.

## FRAGMENTARINESS

One reason Saussure proved unable to accomplish, and in the end unwilling even to attempt, the theoretical labor whose vital importance for the whole future of linguistics he had realized earlier, was the growing discontinuity of his writing. Late in his life, whatever came from his pen turned out to be hopelessly fragmentary. Saussure's book on Indo-European vowels, written when he was in his early twenties, was the only book-length work to which he managed to give a definitive shape. With its clarity and contained energy of explication, the book was as brilliantly lucid and logical in its discourse as in its content, a remarkable achievement given the enormous complexity of its subject. Although the book carried within itself some of the seeds of Saussure's later theoretical ideas, it exemplifies a happy epoch in his career when his inquiries had not yet been aggravated by the unbearably weighty theoretical concerns of later years. Oblivious to the abysses at its foundation, the book exuded the intellectual "pleasures" of sophisticated model building, about which Saussure spoke nostalgically years afterward. His dissertation, written three years later, already showed signs of dissolution, with its classification and the subsequent empirical presentation of the data standing in muted contradiction. Over the following twenty years, as far as his publishing activity was concerned, Saussure took upon himself only very limited, clearly definable tasks; yet eventually it became impossible for him to sustain even this strictly delimited format. It was at about the time of this crisis that Saussure embarked on his massive campaign of note writing.

The most striking immediate impression given by Saussure's notes is their improvised and scattered character. When expressing himself in private, Saussure casts off the conventional constrains of sequentiality, coherence—in short, any academic or stylistic "good manners." In Rastier's eloquent description (2003:25), the notes are "riddled with loopholes, feverish as it were, sometimes lacking proper orthography, and often remote from the academic style"—the last phrase being a diplomatic allusion to the angry, spiteful, and at times appallingly rude expressions that abound in Saussure's notes.

Saussure strives to register his thought at the very moment of its inception, as it surfaced at that moment, free of any polishing or organizing. This race between Saussure's pen and his thoughts recalls what he said about the inexorable development of language, whose every act of usage brings a change into its previously achieved systemic "state." Similarly, Saussure's thought seems to be thwarted by the very effort to express it; as a consequence, it remains as perpetually elusive as the synchronic state of language whose apparition Saussure pursued.

Saussure's notes abound in abbreviations, ellipses, and unfinished sentences. Above all, they defy continuity: a thought may be abruptly abandoned, to be followed by something radically deviating from or contradicting the previous argument. Passages of some continuity, amounting to a few printed pages, are rare, but even they are replete with repetitions and omitted logical links. The overall picture of Saussure's writing evolves as a maze of partially overlapping sketches; the same problem is approached in various passages from different angles, which inspire different concurrent sets of terminology. Overlapping notes partly support or rephrase, partly undermine each other.[18]

The relentless flow of Saussure's thought makes it hard to sustain the steady linear progress needed for expository prose. The writer's hand cannot keep up with his thought, which, faced with several alternative paths, rushes forth simultaneously in different directions. To keep up with the pace at which the text evolves in his mind, the writer resorts to shortcuts, bypassing single words or entire phrases, perhaps in the hope that those lacunae must be self-evident and could be filled out later. As such discontinuities accumulate, however, they take over the discourse, turning it into a kaleidoscope of overlapping, often telegraphically cryptic statements.

An additional problem arises from the oppositional manner in which Saussure's thought often evolves. Saussure tends to build his argument negatively, outlining a problem through a series of refutations of what he sees as its misrepresentation. What makes this approach problematic is his inability to stay calm in the course of such critique. The more he feels frustrated with the glaring inadequacies of his real or imagined opponents, the more he grows frustrated with his own struggle, as the precarious path between intellectual traps and snares along which he strives to navigate his thoughts becomes increasingly elusive.

Saussure's attempt to write a commissioned article about W. D. Whitney, following the latter's death in 1894, an effort that resulted in one of his most extensive manuscript pieces (about twenty printed pages), represents these features in a poignant way. Saussure always valued Whitney's theoretical ideas highly, particularly his emphasis on the nature of language as a social institution, which Saussure considered the closest to (although not identical with) his own. He embarked on the task with enthusiasm, seeing in it an opportunity to make his own most intimate thoughts public by relating them to Whitney's. The beginning in medias res, with a crisp formulation of the bipolarity of the linguistic sign, followed by praise for the "loftiness" of Whitney's theoretical views and fond memories of his formidable temperament as a polemicist, came out well. Under circumstances such as the present occasion, Saussure notes animatedly, "it is extremely easy to let one's pen run" ("Il est plus facile dans ces conditions de laisser courir sa plume"; *ELG*, 204/141). Even this part, however, is not without some omissions of single words and phrases, those worrisome trademarks of Saussure's private writing.

The first sign of trouble comes at the point when Saussure opposes to Whitney's conventionalist approach the idea of language as organism, a trend "born in Germany, developed in Germany, cherished in Germany by an innumerable category of individuals (*innombrable catégorie d'individues*)" (*ELG*, 205/142). When, inevitably, the name of August Schleicher—the bluntest proponent of the idea—surfaces, Saussure's writing loses all semblance of sequential narrative. Angry name-calling (*risible, son propre ridicule, la plus complete médiocrité, totalement inintelligible*) abounds, mixed with dark hints at those who steal other people's ideas (Whitney's?—surely Schleicher could not be plagiarizing *Saussure*). They are followed by emphatic yet sorrowfully inarticulate reassertions of the "double nature" of language, of whose "essence" one should ask oneself whether it is "preeminently historical—or preeminently of an abstract nature, escaping historical forces by virtue of being posited fundamentally and without coercion, which in a chess game is the initial convention reemerging with every move, while in language it is the totally ineluctable action of signs vis-à-vis the spirit, which establishes itself with every event, every move."[19] (This unfortunate comparison of language with the game of chess, of which Saussure was very fond, contributed much, I believe, to the misinterpretation of his ideas.) The discourse deteriorates precipitously into ellipses, frenetic fresh starts, and sudden excursions into elaborate examples of questionable relevance. Finally, Saussure abruptly addresses his commissioners with the request to relieve him "immediately" of the task of speaking about Whitney's works on linguistics, "while this occasion is much . . ."—the phrase remains unfinished.[20] This resignation, however, is forgotten the moment it is submitted; immediately afterward, Saussure compiles a "revised" list of points he wants to make, in a clear attempt to regain control. Yet, very soon, the realization of this new plan comes to a halt as well; just a page down, another revised list of discussion points appears, to be followed eventually by yet another, shortly after which the writing of the document is abruptly abandoned.

Saussure's inability to sustain a coherent line of writing extended itself even to the most elementary level of a single sentence. Facing alternative turns of speech by which a thought could be expressed, he procrastinated, incessantly trying and retrying various versions, unable to make any definitive move. When Saussure complained, in a draft of a letter, that "one is tempted to rewrite five or six times between the beginning and end of a sentence"[21]—a situation he attributed to the parlous state of the conceptual apparatus of linguistics—he spoke the literal truth, as far as his own writing was concerned. A good example of Saussure's tortured writing process is the hesitant beginning of his review (never finished) of Eduard Sievers's *Grundzüge der Phonetik*:

> En regard de Sievers avec // Ce Sievers consacre une page et démi à cette question des phonèmes que peuve ce suivre dans la syllabe // La question du présent travail, le genre de connexitée [replaced by *relation, rapport,* and again *connexité*] qui existe entre la syllabe et la nature de divers phénomènes, est traité en une page et démi par M. Sievers // M. Sievers a réussi à traiter en une

page et démi la question que nous ne faisons // En moins d'une page et démi M. Sievers s'acquitte de la tâche // Il n'y a pas une page démi dans Sievers sur la question ...²²

What made the fragmentariness of the late Saussure's writing irremediable was the fact that its cause was not a lack of rhetorical skill or authorial will. Saussure's writing problems were homomorphous with the essence of his ideas about the nature of language. It is striking to what extent the very fabric of Saussure's writing could be seen as a representation of his theoretical thought.

Saussure's hesitation in choosing among alternative representations of a thought reflected, on the level of rhetoric, one of the fundamental premises of his theory, that of the infinite plurality of arbitrarily shaped systems of signs. He tries in vain to escape the unbearable volatility of the semiotic situation by declaring that at any given moment speakers accept the particular state of the system as a given fact, without thinking of possible alternatives—as if a speaker were telling the language "Choose!" only to add: "It is going to be this sign and not another" (*CLG*, 104/71). When Saussure the writer finds himself in the shoes of that presumable "speaker," he proves unable to "choose." Saussure's indecision stems from his acute awareness of the plurality of alternative possibilities by which his thought could be shaped, leaving the final outcome forever in suspense.²³

The fragmentariness of Saussure's writing was a "negative" feature in a purely Saussurean sense. It reflected the inherent impossibility of turning his negative concept of language as "pure form" into a "substantial" narrative. Declaring *la langue* a pure network of oppositions held out the promise of constructing language as a stable model. In adumbration, the inferential chain of postulates concerning language as a logical construct appeared to the author's inner vision with shining clarity; yet the moment he started moving along, he was plagued with irresolvable bifurcations and uncontrollable asides. Fragmentariness was the only way in which he could approach what otherwise remained unreachable.

To the initiated Saussure reader, however, the meaning of his manuscript fragments does not come from the orderly reading of the separate pieces. Judged at face value, each fragment is incomplete, disorganized, often opaque, sometimes to an extent that makes it seem pretty bizarre. However, as the reader proceeds through the relentlessly growing corpus of Saussure's writing, he takes note of numerous "family resemblances" between disparate pieces. Different yet related points raised on various occasions echo one another. While never adding up explicitly to an overall conceptual design, they coagulate into an indistinct yet palpable conceptual "mass." The effect of this manner of writing is cumulative: it depends on the sheer volume of the oeuvre. The further this discontinuous discourse proliferates, the more parallels, variations, recurrences, and periphrases among its disjointed segments come to light. The reader's perception shifts from the often enigmatic abruptness of separate pieces to the growing—yet never definitively shaped—web of their interconnections.

Saussure's occasional comparison of the anagram with Wagnerian leitmotifs can also serve as auto-description of his own writing.[24] The mass of Saussurean fragments is permeated by a web of intellectual "motifs" whose contents echo each other and overlap in many different ways. Projected against this implicit background, each thesis acquires a stereoscopic meaning; a thought manifests itself in a plurality of appearances showing a partial resemblance in which it may be reiterated, qualified, further developed, sometimes even contradicted. The "arbitrary" chaos with which different pieces, or even different statements within one piece, pile one upon another, without either logical or clear temporal succession, in fact contributes to the totality of their interpenetration, which shapes—and constantly reshapes—their meaning. The meaning remains ever in flux, its final outcome endlessly deferred; this is a theory that attains representation through the ceaseless pursuit of itself.

Saussure's notes recall neither the rich French tradition of polished aphoristic writing, from La Rochefoucauld to Chamfort, nor the genre of nineteenth-century philosophical fragments whose most accomplished masters were Kierkegaard and Nietzsche. Saussure's fragments are much more amorphous and impulsive; they are at the same time elliptical and overflowing with the diverse points he strives to make. Numerous lapses in the narrative, amounting even to grammatical incoherence, make each piece manifestly unsustainable without incremental support from other pieces.

The closest analogy to this type of fragmentary writing is that practiced by the Jena Romantics. Among the thousands of fragments written by Schlegel and Novalis between 1795 and 1801, one can find some brilliant aphorisms that—like a few selected passages in Saussure's *Course*—have become etched in the cultural memory. But the overwhelming majority of the fragments that came from the *Athenaeum* circle are written in a manner that is capriciously improvisatorial, paradoxical, and elliptical. In many cases, a single fragment is plainly incoherent, until it is projected on related statements made on other occasions.

There is one important difference between Saussure and his Romantic predecessors. The latter used fragmentary discourse consciously as a vehicle of their cognitive strategy. Saussure for his part never dreamed of treating his frenetic writing as a phenomenon in its own right—his *linguistische Lehrjahre*, to paraphrase the name given by Schlegel to his unpublished compendium of philosophical fragments.[25] Unlike Schlegel, or the late Wittgenstein, Saussure ended up with "piles" of fragmentary notes by default, despairing over the impossibility of shaping them into a consequential discourse.

Saussure's "neo-Kantian" side, longing to see linguistics join the family of the modern sciences, with its object carefully constructed on the basis of universal premises, and his "Romantic" side, which did not allow him to turn a blind eye to the incessant mobility and perpetual elusiveness of the phenomenon, could never be reconciled, leaving him with a sense of helplessness and frustration. Yet it was precisely Saussure's frustration, so different from typical modernist assertiveness (in particular, that of the "Saussurism" of structural linguistics and semiotics), that gave his thought a depth and intensity that had much in common with the early Romantics' cognizing efforts. As Schlegel had experienced a hundred years before, in the wake of Kant's epistemological critique, Saussure found it equally perilous to have a "system" and not to have one.[26]

## READING THE *COURSE IN GENERAL LINGUISTICS*

At first sight, the carefully structured discourse of the published book stood in a remarkable contrast to the "pile" of Saussure's notes. Saussure's scoffing at ideas and opinions he deems wrong occasionally surfaces in the printed discourse, but these potentially disruptive forces are never permitted to grow into uncontrollable outbursts. To some extent, the *Course* probably owed its quiet orderliness to its editors, but, judging by the notes of Saussure's students, this was the predominant mode of his own oral presentations as well. The discourses employed by Saussure in class and on paper belonged to different "speech genres." They evolved each according to its own rules, as if illustrating Saussure's idea of the infinite variety of forms of semiotic expression, each immanent to itself.

The content of Saussure's notes on language and linguistics often stands in striking contrast to the picture of language as a static immanent system, serenely remote from all the disturbances of its real-life usage, which generations of readers perceived in the book, making such a reading itself a powerful convention. The temptation to attribute this discrepancy to the book's nonauthentic character has been strong, particularly in view of the dramatically reduced fortunes of all immanent "systems" in the poststructuralism era. Saussure's notes seemed to answer much of the critique previously leveled at the *Course*, to the effect of an excessive systemic stiffness in the notion of *la langue*. Consequently, considerable efforts have been made to wrest Saussure from Jakobson's embrace, so to speak, and co-opt him into the postmodern world, primarily by citing the evidence of his notes.[27]

And yet—for all the overt differences between the two principal parts of Saussure's legacy, the "substance" of their message was, if not identical, at least related and overlapping to a considerable degree. Giving an unquestioned primacy to one of them while refuting the other results in narrowing the scope of the overall message that emerges from their juxtaposition.

The prevailing attitude toward the *Course* in contemporary Saussure scholarship is that of philological deconstruction. Some scholars dismiss it outright as a fake; a more moderate attitude acknowledges the book's inexorable presence in the history of twentieth-century thought, which would never have occurred without the editors' labor, while deploring their alleged tampering with Saussure's legacy.[28] In any case, the emphasis is on separating Saussure from the book. Every thesis in the *Course* has been compared with existing manuscript sources (not only Saussure's own but also his students' notes), with the general contention that the latter hold unquestionable priority over the former.[29] Consequently, if no direct correspondence to a certain passage in the book could be found in the manuscripts, this passage would be deemed the editors' addition; by the same token, if a certain thesis found in a manuscript is not present in the book, its absence is interpreted as the result of the editors' omission.

Curiously, the "comparative method" used in the book's deconstructing analysis resembles the positivist comparative linguistics of the nineteenth century, which used to be one of the primary targets of Saussure's fury. It bestows the power of absolute reality on any tangible (recorded) "document"—even if it is only lecture notes taken by a student or a single sketchy piece jotted down by Saussure at an unknown time and under unknown circumstances.

As already mentioned, Bally expressed regret that he did not make his own notes of his conversations with the *maître*; it was apparently these conversations that made him eager to give Saussure all the help he might need for realizing his ideas when he was still alive. How many such unrecorded conversations, either between Saussure and his associates or among the latter, constituted an implicit collective memory that underpins the editors' work? Deeming nonauthentic any point in the *Course* that is not directly matched with anything found on paper means ignoring the multiplicity of sources from which the editors drew their compilation of the book.

I find it hard to believe, in view of the evidence of the deference with which Bally approached Saussure's ideas, that he would suppress or add major points in Saussure's presentations at will, simply following his own convictions. Indeed, there were points in Saussure's position that left Bally dissatisfied. Although the *Course* declared "linguistics of speech" to be an equal counterpart of "linguistics of language," this presumable discipline never got its turn to be defined and described in any substantial way in the *Course*. This omission was particularly regretted by Bally, whose interests were centered precisely around issues that could have constituted a "linguistics of speech."[30] The theme of the emotional and individual in language was raised once again by Bally in his inaugural lectures upon assuming the chair in general linguistics after Saussure's death (in the summer of 1913). As for Sechehaye (1908 a), he pointedly declared his attention to subjective factors in language in his article ("La stylistique et la linguistique théorique") in the volume dedicated to Saussure. Saussure, however, remained unconvinced; in his review of Sechehaye's book (1908b), he criticized Sechehaye's argument for "psychologism," expressing the need to build a linguistic model without psychology, on the basis of internal systemic relations—a thesis that would be presented as the cornerstone of his approach in the *Course*'s introduction.

The disagreement between Saussure and his editors surfaced in an editorial note, which Bally appended at the end of part 3, chapter 1 of the *Course* (*CLG*, 197/141), whereby he expressed his regret that Saussure did not find an opportunity in his lectures to explicate his idea of "linguistics of speech" in more detail. Bally was later accused of making the priority of *langue* over *parole*, and of "internal" over "external" linguistics, more categorical in the *Course* than Saussure ever intended. I tend to give Saussure's editors the benefit of the doubt, particularly in view of the fact that the attitude promoted in the *Course* ran against their own convictions. As will be argued in chapter 6 of this book, the idea of linguistics of speech was indeed vexing for Saussure.

The result, perhaps inadvertent, of the philological critique of the *Course* is that when viewed from this perspective it in effect ceases to exist as a coherent book. It dissolves into a plurality of particular points, each appraised according to its correspondence to available alternative sources or the lack thereof. The effect is particularly striking in the critical edition by Rudolf Engler. Engler divided the book into 3,281 segments, each corresponding (or lacking correspondence) to a particular passage in one or another manuscript source, Saussure's own or his students'. The text of the book was then printed alongside Saussure's and the students' notes in several parallel columns in which all the corresponding passages were matched against each other.

The textological and philological work done by Engler amounted to an epoch-making step in assessing Saussure's legacy. The benefits for philological research of having all the versions simultaneously present on one page is obvious. Yet these benefits become a setback when we move from the philological analysis of the text to a critical reading. The reading forced by the critical edition is uncompromisingly "synchronic"; attention is shifted from the way the book's message evolves, often through complex and manifold reverberations between its different sections, to the relations between distinct, "arbitrarily" carved-out parallel passages. In this sense, the critical edition, done with the express purpose of refuting the structural image of Saussure, itself embodied the structural method of textual analysis—what Roland Barthes (1987:chapter 5) ironically described as the method of arbitrary "cutting" and "pasting" of the analyzed text by the critic.

If the book faces the danger of an arbitrary fragmentation, the manuscript sources, on the contrary, face the danger of an artificial structuring. Treating the notes as a more "genuine" expression of Saussure's thought makes it inevitable that they be organized thematically, an organization following categorical divisions established in the *Course*.[31] Consolidated by means of an implicit theoretical scaffolding, Saussure's fragments lose their essential quality, namely, their nonsequential character. The reader of the published notes does not experience the constant jerks and jolts of arbitrary juxtapositions, as the reader of the *Athenaeum* fragments does; by the same token, he is not forced into a recursive reading grounded in multiple superimpositions of separate pieces. Turned into a shadowy "text" with a coherent conceptual narrative (which, ironically, mirrors that of the book), Saussure's "writings in general linguistics" lose, at least to a certain extent, the power of their fragmentariness.

Treating the *Course* as a failure or a fake not only does an injustice to what Bally and Sechehaye accomplished; I am convinced that it undermines the significance of Saussure's manuscripts as well. The partially overlapping mélange that matters most as a representation of Saussure's thought certainly includes the *Course*. Instead of making them compete for "textological" primacy, the *Course* and the notes should be placed in a mutually illuminating dialogue.

If we take a look at the *Cours de linguistique générale*, keeping in mind what we have learned from Saussure's manuscripts, its text loses its presumed homogeneity and sequentiality. Saussure's fragmentariness is present in the *Course*, albeit implicitly. There are discrepancies and tensions between the book's various parts, obfuscated by its neat division into chapters and sections. Paradoxically, it was the physical discontinuity of a lecture course that helped to maintain a rhetorical simulacrum of sequentiality. Every lecture presented a new particular task, introduced a new subject, took a mini fresh start, so to speak; this organizing principle made it easier not to get trapped in excessive scrutiny of how each new step fit with previous ones. The discontinuous sequence of lectures, "arbitrarily" apportioned, made cracks in the logical fabric of the whole imperceptible—or perhaps, if we speak of Saussure himself, bearable. It helped him to "stay the course" (more or less) in his lectures, which he proved unable to do when facing nothing but his own thoughts in the process of writing.[32]

The oral mode of communication did not leave time for procrastination. The moment a certain thesis had been expressed, it inexorably receded into the past, leaving no time for musings about its manifold consequences that might have proven disruptive. What would emerge later in the flow of the course's narrative might in fact contradict some earlier points, but those contradictions appeared smoothed out by the inexorable linearity of the sequence of lectures. Yet, in the third course, this appearance of unperturbed coherence had already started to crumble. At some point, Saussure had to stop the train of his "theorems," making a fresh start in a way reminiscent of his notes. The second half of the course was superimposed upon the first via a reexamination and redefinition of its content, a process involving introducing alternative terminology. The same problems were presented anew, by way of a variation on what had been said about them in the previous semester. Near the end of his last course, we see Saussure drifting toward the strategy of a nonlinear, incremental presentation that dominated his notes.

In their compilation the editors had to abandon the plurality of narrative and content of Saussure's courses and make a definitive picture, without which the book could not have come into existence.[33] Still, the *Course* did not completely abandon the implicit discontinuities that were inherent in Saussure's representations of his ideas. In different chapters of the book its intellectual edifice undergoes incremental changes. At one point, "arbitrariness" is proclaimed to be the absolute principle; at another, its absoluteness seems to be undermined by the concept of "relative arbitrariness"; at yet another it is suggested that different languages—such as Indo-European and Chinese—may feature relative arbitrariness to a different extent, with the consequence that absolute arbitrariness also assumes a different relative weight in such languages; still later, any hierarchy of different structural types of languages is resolutely rejected: no structural principle is superior or inferior to any other, Saussure proclaims with vehemence. Some issues whose relevance for the whole remain unclear are discussed at length; this happens, for example, when Saussure indulges his lifelong fascination with classifying speech sounds according to their physical properties, putting aside for a while his theoretical claim of the irrelevance of the physical aspect outside its relational value in the sign. Finally, there are subjects that never receive any development beyond an initial mention—first and foremost, the notorious issue of the linguistics of speech.

These tensions are genuine; they emerge in the corpus of Saussure's notes as well. In this respect, bringing in the notes can illuminate the reading of the book.[34] However, the book in its turn is needed to read the notes. One can see in Saussure's lectures his efforts to consolidate the subject of his inquiry; we are made witnesses of Saussure's insistent search for a feasible way "whither to proceed" in the face of his awareness of the fact that there exist many possible ways of proceeding, each of which could be as good, or as bad, as any other. The full value of what Saussure expressed in his written fragments comes to light only in the face of what he has managed to achieve—albeit not without vacillation—in his lectures.

It should not be forgotten that the image of the *Course* that prevailed through the first two-thirds of the twentieth century—that of an immaculately logical model of language in which the primacy of the "structural" element was highlighted to such an extent that it made even some adepts of "Saussurism" complain—was not an objective quality of this "text" but the result of a reading done in a certain context or contexts and answering certain intellectual purposes.[35] If the perception of Saussure's theory has eventually undergone radical changes, it was primarily due to the change of intellectual perspectives and goals that occurred beginning in the late 1960s. If read from a different perspective, the *Course in General Linguistics* reveals the features of discourse and content that immediately strike one upon reading Saussure's notes.

The controversy surrounding the famous concluding phrase of the *Course* will serve as a case in point. Godel unequivocally dismissed, citing its absence from the manuscript sources, the authenticity of the concluding aphorism in which "language viewed in itself and for itself" was proclaimed to be "the only and true object of linguistics." The sentence in question, soon to become proverbial, seemed to suggest primacy of "internal linguistics," an attitude that constituted a veritable mantra of the structural approach. In De Mauro's formulation, "the addition of the final phrase is a hallmark of the editorial manipulation of the Saussurean argument, which should be held partly responsible for the exclusivist bend of structuralism, particularly its post-Bloomfieldian breed in the USA."[36]

The sentence's origin was attributed to various sources, even such farfetched ones as Franz Bopp's (1816) foundational book on Indo-European linguistics—a work to which Saussure often referred negatively, which made Bally's presumed editorial "violation" of his teacher's thought look particularly egregious.[37] An expression close to the concluding phrase of the *Course* was found in Bally's own paper at the Congress of Neophilologists in Zurich (1910), in which he cited as a major achievement of modern linguistics the fact that "a state of language can be perceived in itself and for itself, ignoring its past" (Lepschy 1979:27–28). As a matter of fact, one need not dig so deep, since a similar expression appears on the first page of Bally's *La langage et la vie* (1926 [1913]): "One can say that until the beginning of the twentieth century language had never been studied in and of itself, in its true function." Given the fact that the entire narrative of Bally's book was permeated with allusions to Saussure's ideas, it seems at least as plausible to conclude that his statements to this effect were in fact an echo of Saussure.[38] Yet another putative source of the notorious sentence can be found in Adrienne Necker de Saussure's *Progressive Education*, wherein she defines the essence of her method as seeking the inner perspective of the child "lui-même," instead of observing his behavior from the outward point of view of the educator.

The virtually unanimous dismissal of the sentence about language "in itself and for itself" as apocryphal does not take into account the possibility that Saussure might have actually said it, or something close to it, on certain occasions.[39] Indeed, as a less heated examination of the rest of the book, as well as of Saussure's own manuscripts, shows, the concluding sentence was in fact far from being as isolated in the Saussurean corpus as some critics of the *Course* asserted. Words about the "true and veritable object" of linguistics, or about language "envisioned in itself," appear literally dozens of times in Saussure's notes as well as elsewhere in the *Course*.[40] It would not be an exaggeration to say that expressions like these were characteristically and typically "Saussurean." This does not mean, however, that the categorical assertion of the concluding phrase of the *Course*, like so many others of a similar kind made by Saussure on the spur of the moment, contained the whole truth and nothing but the truth of his approach to language. In fact, if checked against numerous occasions in Saussurean texts in which the "true" and "unique" nature of language was invoked, the meaning of this expression turns out to be not as unambiguous as it appeared either to the *Course*'s champions or its critics.

The most natural context that helps to explain this contradiction and, at the same time, allows a glimpse at the sensibilities and concerns that stood behind it is offered by the last chapter of the book, at whose tail end it appears. It is precisely this context, however, that has been lacking in its alternative reading, either as the declaration of the principle of "structure" or as a fake. Indeed, the chapter's title, "Families of Languages and Linguistic Types," does not invite any association with that highflying statement; what it seemed to suggest was a straightforward discussion of the two kinds of language classification that had been in broad circulation in linguistics since the previous century, a topic that continues to be taught, essentially in the same way, in courses on "general linguistics" in our day.

Saussure's chapter deviates from this promised generic content from the very beginning. It starts with an emphatic reiteration of the principle of the arbitrariness of linguistic structure, which is now formulated as the principle of the unlimited variability and unpredictability of different structural types of languages. Suddenly, the narrator's voice is gripped by a seething emotion that erupts in an outburst of righteous rhetoric, all of it seemingly totally unwarranted by such an innocuous empirical issue as linguistic typology. The *Course* comes forward with an assertion—using expressions whose emotionally charged, angry tone sounds distinctly Saussurean and could by no means be attributed to the editors—that no single family of languages "obtains the right" to the exclusive representation of a certain linguistic type; moreover, no permanent association between a certain language and a certain structural type is guaranteed. "In whose name," the book's narrator exclaims, could one pretend to impose such a limitation on a phenomenon that knows no limitations whatsoever? (*CLG*, 313/227). The development of a language is arbitrary, i.e., totally independent of any human affairs and intentions; in the final analysis, it is only pure chance that can claim its "rights" over the particular way a certain language evolves and is shaped (*CLG*, 313/227).

Armed with this general principle, Saussure then turns to examples of various languages and to the ways their structures change over time. It turns out that neither structural permanence nor a predictable direction of change can be sustained as a general principle: "There are no immutable traits;

permanence is the effect of an accident" (*CLG*, 316/229). A smirk at "laws" (a jab transparently aimed at the Leipzig school), in which some try to capture the essence of a certain structural type, is followed by another iteration of the principle of "blind evolution" that reigns in the domain of language. Yet another vehement rhetorical gesture is directed toward Schleicher—that habitual *bête noire* of Saussure's notes—and other proponents of the concepts of the "organism" or "genius" of a language. There is nothing in language that belongs to it constitutionally. Whatever chimera of order may emerge for a time, it can dissolve or be transformed at any moment.

It is at this point of total negativity, into which the narrator has been drawn by his own polemical vehemence, that the concluding phrase of the *Course* appears. It deserves to be quoted in full: "What transpires from the incursions we have made into the frontier domains of our science is a lesson that is purely negative but the more interesting for that, since it agrees with the fundamental idea of this course: *linguistics has as its unique and true object the language envisioned in itself and for itself.*"[41] The improvisational incoherence of the meaning of the concluding sentence (whose second part seems to contradict its first) betrays its oral origin. Saussure's all-pervasive "negative" exploration of the issue of structural typology destroys not only the prejudices that accumulated at this "frontier domain" of linguistics; it proves just as destructive to his own key notion of *la langue* as a system of signs. What kind of a system is it, which at any moment can be "dissolved (*défait*) or transformed by chance"? How viable is the vision of such a system, if in fact it amounts to no more than a point within a line whose curvature no one can predict? The situation is saved by rhetorical assertiveness, which, according to a peculiar law of Saussure's writing, is a sign of his inner sense of losing ground. The seemingly upbeat, slogan-like pronouncement that was taken by so many to be the banner of a new linguistic science recalls numerous points in Saussure's notes where he reaches a stalemate and responds by stopping abruptly.

We should reconcile ourselves to the fact that the definitive or "genuine" representation of Saussure's ideas does not exist, nor has it ever existed. A plurality of representations, freely evolving in different directions, was constitutive of Saussure's thought and essential for the conceptual vision he pursued. It corresponded to the central principle of his approach to language, which, in the end, has made any systemic and definitive picture impossible: the principle of the unfettered freedom of language, resulting in the infinite plurality of forms that language assumes and the infinite diversity of the directions in which they may evolve.

# PART 2

Postulates About Language and Their Demise

Antinomies of the Sign | **THREE**

## LINGUISTICS IN SEARCH OF ITS SUBJECT

The *Course* begins (after a brief historical survey) by addressing the key issue that makes linguistics as a discipline methodologically problematic: the lack of a clear definition of its object of study.[1] To say simply that a linguist studies "language" is not to address the problem at all, since a variety of other disciplines also deal with language. Language figures, one way or another, within the framework of anthropology, sociology, psychology, acoustics, physiology, history, philosophy, philology, cultural studies—a deceptive richness that in fact leaves language without an epistemological home of its own: "In fact, the whole world is occupied with it to a greater or lesser extent; but—a paradoxical consequence of the interest it has attracted—there exists no other field that germinates more absurd ideas, prejudices, mirages, and fictions" (*CLG*, 21–22/7). Barely disguising his irritation under the terse rhetorical veneer of his lectures, Saussure declares it the "first and foremost" duty of a linguist to "denounce" all these untruths, making them "dissipate as completely as possible" (*CLG*, 21–22/7).

Saussure's epistemological critique of the foundations of linguistics in his lecture courses reflected pressing concerns he had had since the early 1890s. In the now famous note beginning with the words "Unde exoriar?"

(Whence to begin?)[2] and elsewhere,[3] Saussure persistently reiterated his thesis that a snapshot of language could be taken from an indeterminate plurality of possible angles. Consequently, he spoke of the "grand necessity" of separating linguistics from other sciences dealing with language.[4] We read in the notes that any idea concerning language can be subjected to "twenty kinds of analysis" (*ELG*, 232/164); this point is echoed in the introductory section of the *Course,* which emphasized that linguistics should be "carefully distinguished" from the way language is treated by other disciplines (*CLG*, 21/6).

Saussure's position was consistent with the antipositivist revolution in contemporary epistemology. The spirit of the times, with its rising skepticism about positivist "facts," which only recently had seemed irrefutable, coupled with the quest for an explicit methodology, can be perceived in Saussure's notes when he remarks, for instance, that "the past of linguistics consists of a general doubt about its role, its place, and its value, accompanied by a colossal acquisition of facts."[5] This is what distinguished Saussure from virtually all of his colleagues—"pure" linguists whose "exceedingly amusing" lack of awareness of the cognitive abyss over which they trod, as if they were in possession of the truth itself (*ELG*, 116/81), was a constant source of consternation for him.

Proponents of the new trend in epistemology and philosophy of science emphasized that any object of study always appears to be a mental construct that rests on certain postulates, whether consciously formulated or tacitly implied. By explicitly outlining the categorical boundaries of its subject, a discipline is prevented from drowning in the intellectual muddle (the Saussurean "twenty kinds of analysis") that occurs when such boundaries remain vague.

Even before major modernist philosophical schools, such as neo-Kantianism, empiriocriticism, phenomenology, and the Bergsonian concept of duration, emerged at the turn of the century, the new trend could be seen in the natural sciences, notably in the works of Hermann von Helmholtz. In a popular summation of his studies of optics, Helmholtz (1996b [1895]) proclaimed that there is no such thing as the "natural" appearance of objects. What we perceive as visual snapshots of objects are in fact signs whose apprehension involves certain skills. As if anticipating one of Saussure's central postulates about language, Helmholtz points to a "striking analogy" between visual perception and "another system of signs which is not given by nature but arbitrarily chosen"—namely, "the words of our mother tongue" (Helmholtz 1996b [1895]:274–276). In another work,

Helmholtz applied the same principle to sensory experience in general: "our sensations are, as regards their quality, only signs of external objects, and in no sense images" (343).

Saussure's use of the metaphor of "vision"—that is, of the need for linguistics to learn how to identify its object among the plurality of projections in which it appears—might have been directly adopted from Helmholtz's optical studies. Saussure's identification with the methodological premises of the "new physics" (and also, perhaps, the "new chemistry" of Ostwald and Mendeleev) was just the flip side of his scornful rejection of the old-fashioned scientific claims of the Neogrammarians (the *Junggrammatiker*). The irony of the situation was that while the Neogrammarians envisioned language as a positively given object that could be described by the methods of the (positivist) natural sciences, the new trend in science sought an analogy with the "arbitrary signs" of language for explaining the phenomena of nature in their relation to cognizing consciousness.

If the "fundamental truth" about language cannot be simply pointed out, the only way to "retrieve a firm terrain" for linguistics lies in a "comparative critique" of different points of view on language (*ELG*, 199/137). This "comparative critique" is essentially a reductive task: it constructs an object by subtracting from it what lies beyond its postulated boundaries. Edmund Husserl's *Ideas of Pure Phenomenology and Phenomenological Philosophy* appeared in 1913, the year Saussure died. Yet, setting aside the question of any direct influence, one can detect a pronounced parallel between Husserl's phenomenological reduction and Saussure's negative epistemological strategy—a parallel that attests to the extent of Saussure's awareness of the philosophical culture of his time in general. Like Husserl, Saussure proceeds by taking away all of the substantial features of language, both "objective" and "subjective": on the one hand, its material fabric (sounds), and on the other, the perceptions language evokes in the mind of a speaker. Demonstrable as they are when one observes how people speak, the substantial material and psychological features of language are not transcendental, in the sense that they do not exist as a priori (in Saussure's term, *veritable*) dimensions of language outside the manifold conditions of its usage which, if taken into the picture, "open the door immediately to thousands of contestations" (*ELG*, 81/55).[6]

Saussure calls the transcendental object that emerges out of this reductionist critique *la langue*, to distinguish it from *le langage*, i.e., speaking activity in general whose various dimensions could be studied from a number of perspectives. *La langue* is a construct in which language is reduced to its inalienable features, the ones that belong to it unconditionally. It is a product of an immanent vision that considers language for its own sake, ignoring what language may be used for or how it is related to various human faculties and institutions.

While on the one hand postulating a priori features defines an object in its own right, by the same token it also points to its place among other similarly constructed objects. When, however, after constructing "the true and unique" (i.e., a priori given) object of linguistics, Saussure turned to defining its place among other disciplines, he encountered insurmountable difficulties that undermined the results of his epistemological labor. For *la langue,* as it was postulated, showed itself to have certain features that set it apart from all the known phenomena, natural and social alike.

## THE DOUBLE NATURE OF THE SIGN

The fundamental units of language, its inalienable property, are signs. A sign is a bipolar phenomenon: it couples a material representation with a content that is represented. That in itself, of course, has been common knowledge since Aristotle and St. Augustine. What Saussure realized was that for the sign as a linguistic phenomenon, its substantial physical shape and content are irrelevant. As a matter of principle, any physical shape can be coupled with any domain of meaning to form a sign. How many distinct signs cover a certain domain of content in a given language, and how the forms of those signs are related to each other, is a matter that rests solely on the composition of that language, which is shaped by blind convention. What matters for a sign is the bare fact of interconnectedness between some physical shape and some content and not the nature of what is connected.

That the connection between the form and the meaning of a sign is a matter of social convention—a *contrat social* between speakers of a language—was an idea introduced by French philosophers of language of the Enlightenment (to whom Saussure usually referred generically as *les philosophes*), particularly by Rousseau and Condillac, and applied to linguistics proper by Whitney. Saussure praised these thinkers on numerous occasions for emphasizing the social factor in language. However, he found missing from the argument of his predecessors a crucially important point, which ensued from the peculiarity of the double nature of signs.

When stripped of any substantial outward properties, the two sides of a sign turn out to be inseparable; they are "united in an absolutely indissoluble way" (*ELG*, 73/48); both sides exist only vis-à-vis each other, correlatively (*CLG*, 99/67). A sign has nothing to show but the fact of correlativity between its two sides. Its content is contingent on representation, while the representation is contingent on the content it represents (*CLG*, 144–145/101–102). The moment one side is separated from the other, it simply ceases to exist as a phenomenon of language. If we listen to speech without recognizing its meaning, what we hear is a continuum of sounds; speakers' ability to apportion this continuum into distinct units rests on their realization of the meaning attached to them. Yet while the continuum of speech owes its segmentation to the meaning carried by distinct sound combinations, the continuum of meaning turns into tangible concepts by virtue of its representation through distinct physical entities. Meaning is like hydrogen filling a balloon: it is what makes the balloon fly, but without the balloon, it would dissipate without a trace (*ELG*, 115/78). "The two chaoses yield an order by uniting. Nothing could be more futile than to try to put them in order separately" (*ELG*, 51–52/32).

Again and again, Saussure comes out with thunderous denunciations of the traditional view—he calls it "nomenclaturism"—according to which words are nothing more than the labels pasted on certain ideas, assigned to a content that is already "there." Saussure finds the idea "most vulgar" (*ELG*, 106/70). He does not mean, of course, that no thinking is possible outside language. But "without resorting to signs, we would be incapable of distinguishing two ideas in a manner that is clear and consistent" (*CLG*, 155/110). Human thought would be "nothing but an amorphous and indistinct mass" but for the fact that it is apportioned into distinct entities of meaning by being represented by distinct material carriers (*CLG*, 154/109).

Saussure rejected the traditional terms "form" and "meaning" for precisely the reason that they implied the possibility of observing the two sides of a sign as separate phenomena, apart from their mutual relations. In early notes, he suggested composite terms instead: "vocal figure" (*la figure vocale*), i.e., a configuration of sounds shaped by its correlation with a meaning, and "form-sense" (*forme-sens*), i.e., a configuration of meaning shaped by its correlation with a sound (*ELG*, 17/3). It was only in the second, revisory part of his last lecture course that Saussure abandoned awkward composite denominations in favor of the terms *signifier* and *signified* (*signifiant* and *signifié*), whose etymological kinship reflected their interdependence; emerging at the very last moment, they nevertheless eventually became standard items of Saussurean terminology—one of his terminological signatures—thanks to the published *Course*.

Thus, although the dual configuration of signs is based on a social convention, it is a convention of a peculiar kind. Conventions of social behavior, while a matter of social acceptance, are never totally unrelated to the primary experiences of those who accept them. That one is supposed to fall prostrate nine times when facing the Chinese emperor is, of course, a conventional act, as far as the number of the bows is concerned; but the gesture of prostrating oneself as an expression of submission and awe has a certain experiential ground (*CLG*, 101/68). Compared with this, the linguistic "gesture" of moving one's organs of articulation in a certain way to express submission and awe has nothing to do with the experience of submission and awe. Language as a social institution is not merely a convention but the empty shell of convention; in this sense, it can be called a "pure institution" (*ELG*, 211/147).

It is in this sense that the *Course* proclaimed the inner structure of signs to be "arbitrary." Speakers accept the signs of their language as they are, without asking for any logical or empirical justification of their dual configurations. True, the configurations themselves may change as time passes. These changes, however, are also arbitrary. A particular change can be justified after the fact: a sound change may eliminate an awkward sound combination; a new word, or a new meaning of a word, may emerge to fill a conspicuous gap in naming certain phenomena. But language development at large knows no teleology.[7] The inner structure of a language at any particular point in time is a matter of pure "chance" (hazard); it reflects nothing but the blind vicissitudes of the tradition that maintained the transmission of the language over millennia, a process in which it shed and acquired features unpredictably (*ELG*, 262/188).

Just when Saussure succeeded in postulating the constitutive property of language, he came to realize the peculiar predicament faced by the discipline due to the unique character of its subject. Although Helmholtz declared all sensations to be a result of learning rather than direct experience, he did not deny the existence of an inherent connection between an object and its representation: "an image must, in certain respects, be analogous to the original object."[8] Even though a natural phenomenon has to be mentally construed in order to be properly cognized, its primary perception, at least, is given directly in experience; there are limits, set by the primary experiential features of an object, that its mental presentation does not overstep.

Saussure agrees: he is convinced that all descriptive disciplines except linguistics have in their possession primary "facts," either material or social, that are given, at least as an initial approximation, in experience. Zoology is occupied with living organisms, physics with physical bodies, chemistry with chemical elements, history with historical events and actors, sociology and anthropology with social institutions and cultural rites. How these facts are viewed, how their properties are explained, depends, of course, on their conceptualization. But the primary apportioning of experience into entities to be conceptualized is more or less evident from the beginning.

In this respect, language is dramatically different. The "facts" that speakers experience are inherently heterogeneous: "neither sounds nor ideas" (*ELG*, 250/178), but rather, "signs-ideas" as symbiotic unities (*ELG*, 20/5). A particular apportioning of meaning among signs in one language may prove totally alien to another language; as a matter of fact, symbiotic entities constituting signs never repeat themselves precisely within the frameworks of different languages. We would search in vain for a common principle that could serve as a basis for comparison for all the varieties of sound-cum-meaning combinations to be observed in various languages.

A scholar dealing with metals, minerals, or biological species can rely on a primary set of observable phenomena as his starting point; however, the configuration of signs in one or another language is "strange and perplexing"—pure "play" that finds no support among perceptible phenomena (*CLG*, 149/105). An anatomist does not dissect a cadaver indiscriminately, he follows the natural joints of the body; yet nothing indicates in advance to a linguist where he must "cut" an amorphous "band" of sounds or a cloud-like conglomeration of meanings flowing in speech (*ELG*, 257–258/184). How can one classify "objects" consisting of two totally heterogeneous components that are brought together in a fashion so capriciously idiosyncratic as to defy any common logic? Imagine, Saussure remarks in frustration, a scientist given the task of sorting out "species" that present themselves as a cross between a horse and a "bizarre" iron plaque or a sheep whose body is extended with a brass ornament; no doubt he would reject such a task as absurd. Meanwhile, linguists occupy themselves with such absurd "species" with unperturbed assurance, as if they were only natural (*ELG*, 18/3).

A symbiotic conflation of the material and the spiritual makes language into an object for which any epistemological analogy turns out to be imprecise. In a passage in the *Course*, Saussure speaks of the "mysterious" phenomenon of the "thought-sound" (*pensée-son*), which is neither the "materialization of thought" nor the "spiritualization of sound" (*CLG*, 156/111). It is concrete and abstract at the same time: concrete, because it always deals with particularly apportioned entities of sound and meaning;

abstract, because it deals not with the sound and the meaning as such but with their interplay.

According to Saussure, linguistics, together with studies of other systems of conventional signs—among which he lists certain social rites, forms of politeness, military signals, games, and so forth—should form a peculiar domain of study that belongs to neither the natural nor the social sciences.[9] He proposed calling this new discipline semiology (*CLG*, 33/15).[10] This decision, however, does not remedy the fact that a linguist cannot rely on established methods that are valid for other disciplines. Saussure's postulate of the arbitrariness of the dual configuration of signs excluded the possibility of anchoring language either in natural laws (as claimed by the Neogrammarians) or in universal logical categories (as would be done later by generative grammar). The whole field of "semiology," of which linguistics obviously constituted by far the most important part, had to be invented anew as a domain of cognitive activity belonging to a class of its own.

It was in this sense that Saussure spoke of the "fatality" of the science of language (*ELG*, 227/159). The conclusion he arrived at is aporetic: it is the very process of the cognitive construction of language that makes it a phenomenon that defies any firm theoretical basis for such construction. This leaves language totally at the mercy of the point of view from which one views it. "Far from the case of objects preceding a point of view, one can say that it is the point of view that creates an object [of language], while nothing tells us in advance that one of the ways of considering the facts in question should precede or would be superior to the others" (*CLG*, 23/8). Paradoxically, language "in itself and for itself" turns out to be a phenomenon about which one has to ask oneself whether there is anything there but "our points of view multiplying without limit" (*ELG*, 67/44).

## ARBITRARINESS AND NEGATIVITY: LANGUAGE AS PURE FORM

### Arbitrariness: The Categorical and Empirical Dimension

Saussure's understanding of language as a phenomenon of a peculiar kind rests on the core assumption that the relation between the two sides of a sign is arbitrary, i.e., not grounded in any natural order of things or logical pattern. The absence of any rationale, save blind convention, for any particular signifier and signified to be coupled in a sign makes its duality irreducible. The infinite variety of signifier-signified constellations that can be observed in languages never coalesces around an ultimate general principle; the structure of a sign system as a whole remains essentially unpredictable as it emerges from one case or another, one language or another, one historical moment to the next. Any emerging patterns prove, under scrutiny, to be merely local patches of orderliness that never become a general rule. The idea of the ultimate unruliness in the manner by which signifiers and signifieds are tied together by convention stands at the core of the radical novelty of Saussure's view of language, setting it apart from the conventionalist approach of his predecessors.

Yet for all the enormous weight Saussure gave to the concept of arbitrariness,[11] he never expounded it in a definitive and unambiguous way. Paradoxically, it was perhaps Saussure's eagerness to explain all the consequences of arbitrariness, which indeed are formidable, that compelled him to skip over the concept's definition in haste, leaving it, both in his notes and in the lectures, barely outlined, often by pointing to random examples that proved more confusing than helpful. In his typical manner of resorting to emphasis whenever he sensed holes in his representation of an issue, Saussure admonished his listeners that the consequences of arbitrariness are "innumerable"; however, not all of them could be made immediately evident: large exploratory "detours" were needed for the "primordial" importance of the principle to be appreciated (*CLG*, 100/68). If he had hoped that the concept could be wrested from the danger of trivialization solely by virtue of those "detours," it was long before such hopes were realized.

It is easy to mistake arbitrariness for something no more significant than a scholastic paraphrase of Shakespeare's "What's in a name? That which we call a rose / By any other name would smell as sweet."[12] One need hardly be a linguist to realize that the sound shape of the word *rose* has nothing to do with the object it "names."[13] The situation recalls what Saussure once said about language in general: it seems obvious to everyone what "language" is, yet it is precisely the deceptive clarity of the quotidian perception that plunges the matter into a fatal confusion. Saussure himself gave "aid and comfort" to this kind of trivialization of the issue by illustrating arbitrariness—perhaps on the spur of the moment in a lecture—with a seemingly obvious yet in fact misleading example: namely, that there is no reason why a certain animal species (bull) needs to be represented either by the signifier *b-ö-f* (*boeuf*) or by *o-k-s* (*Ochs*[*e*]); this just happens by convention "on either side of the border" (*CLG*, 100/68). As Jakobson rightly pointed out, this passage in the book succumbs to the "nomenclaturist" understanding of the issue that Saussure himself never tired of fighting: it implies that there is a ready concept waiting to be given one or another "name" by convention.[14] To claim that "the same" animal is named differently on either side of the Franco-German border obfuscates the fact that the signifieds represented by *boeuf* and *Ochse* only partially overlap; their overall semantic spaces are as incompatible as their sound shapes.[15]

This lack of precision in defining the concept opened the way to the criticism that, on several points, it seemed to contradict empirical observations of linguistic data.

First, arbitrariness as a universal principle seems to be undermined by the existence of so-called iconic signs, such as interjections and onomatopoetic words, in which the physical shape of the signifier is homomorphous to certain features of the concept it represents. Saussure tried to refute the menace from this corner by asserting that such cases are few and that they are all "semi-conventional" anyway (*CLG*, 102/69).[16] This rather feeble defense could only provoke accusations that he "exaggerated considerably the role of arbitrariness and underestimated sound symbolism."[17] As later studies—notably by Jakobson, who consistently expressed hostility to the Saussurean idea of arbitrariness—suggested, iconicity in language seems insignificant only to those who adhere to an extremely narrow definition of the issue. A more inclusive approach not only reveals the much wider presence of iconicity in the vocabulary,[18] but shows its manifestation in numerous morphological and syntactic patterns whose structure reflects certain features of the concept they express. Crossing into the domain of the linguistic ideas of Russian futurist "transrational poetry" (Khlebnikov 1987 [1913]), with its intense quest for universal sound symbolism, Jakobson suggested that it is iconicity rather than arbitrariness that underwrites language as a universal principle (Jakobson and Waugh 1987:chapter 4).

But even setting aside the contentious issue of iconicity, a second formidable empirical challenge to the universality of arbitrariness comes from a widespread phenomenon that Humboldt called the "inner form." As Humboldt pointed out, in many cases the form of a word represents its meaning not directly but by referring to another meaning. In such cases, the coupling of a signifier and a signified acquires a rationale because of its reference to another sign. We recognize that the signifier *teacher* represents the meaning "he/she who teaches" because of its relatedness to the verb *teach* and the agentive suffix *-er*; the meaning of *housekeeper* emerges out of its reference to *keeper* (in its turn referring to *keep* and *-er*) and *house*; or as Saussure himself pointed out, while there is no reason (at least, as far as modern French is concerned) why the sound combinations *deux* and *vingt* should signify "2" and "20," respectively, the relation of *vingt-deux* to its meaning "22" is motivated by its reference to the primary signs from which it is derived. In words with an "inner form," the relation between the signifier and signified is constructed rather than arbitrarily declared.

Saussure's response to this problem, once again, was not convincing. To cover cases such as *vingt-deux*, he introduced the notion of "relative arbitrariness." He even suggested that some languages, notably Chinese, due to the sparsity of its derivational patterns, may feature relative arbitrariness to a lesser degree (and, by the same token, show a stronger propensity for "absolute arbitrariness") than languages such as Indo-European and Finno-Ugric, while Semitic languages occupy an intermediary position between these polar types (*ELG*, 301–302/210). Introducing "relative" arbitrariness invalidates the concept as a universal principle, turning it into an empirical feature that various languages possess to different degrees.[19]

Perhaps the most serious objection to the concept of arbitrariness arises from the issue of "reality," whose implicit exclusion as something irrelevant to the sign led to Saussure being accused more than once of championing a modern version of medieval realism (Furton 1995:48). Ogden and Richards (1923) considered Saussure's avoidance of the notion of the symbol (whose traditional interpretation presumes a real-world phenomenon represented in it) as a sign of his theoretical "naïveté."

By far the most persuasive ("beautiful," in Jakobson's estimation) critique along this line came from Benveniste (1966a). It stemmed from Saussure's own thesis of speakers' blind acceptance of the convention that holds a signifier and a signified together. As Benveniste pointed out, if speakers accept their language unquestioningly as a phenomenon whose features need neither logical reasoning nor empirical justification, "le lien entre signifié et signifiant n'est pas arbitraire, il est nécessaire." Benveniste saw in Saussure's emphasis on arbitrariness a token of his adherence to the modernist "philosophical relativism" of the turn of the twentieth century.

Perhaps as a result of this critique, scholars in the last half-century mostly felt reticent about this aspect of Saussure's theory. One can detect a defensive note in Joseph's (2004:69) assertion that championing arbitrariness was Saussure's way of taking a stand against the proliferation of artificial languages, on the one hand, and "wrong-headed" concepts of language as a carrier of collective mentality, with its nationalist and racist implications, on the other. To many, the principle of absolute arbitrariness signified an excessive relativist rigidity that contradicted the general "spirit" of Saussure's teaching.

A notable exception to this trend was a work by the literary theorist Jonathan Culler (1986 [1976]). Contrary to the predominant tendency to marginalize or trivialize the issue, Culler argued that arbitrariness constituted the very core of Saussure's approach to language because of its inalienable connection to the principle of the duality of the linguistic sign. He refuted the view of arbitrariness as a heuristic instrument of excessive systemic rigidity; far from that, Culler claimed, arbitrariness, understood as the direct consequence of the unbreakable link between the signifier and the signified, means the total volatility of the sign, its openness to incessant and multiple challenges that make it unable to sustain whatever state it finds itself in at any given moment.

Culler's is a brilliant theoretical insight; what remains to be clarified is the specifically linguistic side of the problem, namely, how to maintain the principle of total freedom, signified by arbitrariness, in the face of the many instances of iconically or etymologically "motivated," i.e., not fully free, semiotic units that can be observed in any language. One can agree with Gadet (1987:40–41) that arbitrariness "in a banal sense" does not explain the double nature of the linguistic sign. The question remains: how to interpret the relevant linguistic data beyond the "banal"?

To appreciate the full scope of Saussure's concept, it is necessary to distinguish two different levels on which arbitrariness can be understood: on the one hand, as a founding principle of philosophy of language and, on the other, as an empirical feature that can be observed in vocabulary. The identification of the arbitrary with the unmotivated misses this distinction and, as a result, paves the way for the idea that there can be different kinds and degrees of motivation and arbitrariness. Meanwhile, the universality of arbitrariness as the constitutive principle of language is not contradicted by the empirical fact that in certain words the signifier-signified relation appears to have a rationale of one kind or another.

The difference between the postulated principle and the observable data becomes reconciled when we note that even in cases where the relation between a form and a meaning could be inferred from a derivational pattern, this inference alone is never sufficient to predict the exact character of the sign as it is known to speakers. True, the composition of a derivative sign can be inferred from its relation to the base. But there exists an infinite variety of potential paths of inference by which a sign could be constructed out of its semiotic antecedent; there is no way to predict which of those infinite possibilities will be employed by language in one particular case or another. Although we understand how a derivative sign has been constructed, we understand this only after the fact of our knowledge that it has actually happened this way and no other.

Looking at words with clear derivational patterns, one can easily be lured to the conclusion that, even if one had no knowledge of the value assigned to them by convention, one would still be able to grasp it by inference. This conclusion, however, is illusory. Both the form and the meaning of *housekeeper* stem from *house* and *keeper* in a way that seems perfectly logical. Imagine, however, someone trying to infer the meaning of *housekeeper* from its ingredients, without knowing that meaning for a fact. Does *housekeeper* mean a person who guards the house, or owns it, or retains it temporarily, or occupies it as a squatter—or perhaps not a person but a device that prevents the house from collapsing? The only way to know that our educated guesses are wrong is to know the meaning of *housekeeper* as determined by convention—that is, to treat it as arbitrary.

Even in such seemingly trivial cases as that of twenty-two, the situation is not as simple as it looks at first glance. How can one know beforehand whether the signifier for "22" should be *twenty-two,* or *twenty-and-two,* or *two-and-twenty* (German *zwei und zwanzig*); or perhaps it should be altogether different, say, *two dozen minus two*?[20] The assortment of possible alternatives is potentially infinite since it knows no logical limit.

Language seems to invite speakers to reason with it—to build explanations based on patterns that, at first glance, seem logical and quite transparent. Such partial inferential patterns, seemingly suggesting an ultimate logical organization of signs, may be forthcoming for all eternity without ever coalescing into a coherent universal order. They are doomed ever to remain isolated pockets of order whose extent remains undetermined. In the end, any rational procedure capitulates in the face of blind convention.

Empirical knowledge about the world is of no more help in grasping the value of a sign than are logical patterns of inference. Again, it seems obvious that the words of a language reflect the experiences of its speakers; trivial examples to this effect, such as the proliferation of words describing various kinds of snow in the languages of inhabitants of the far North, abound in popular linguistic literature. But it would be futile to try to predict how many such words would emerge in one northern language or another and what semantic space would be allotted to each of them. When one encounters the Finnish word *ahava*, which means, approximately, "a piercingly cold damp wind in early spring," one can easily picture the natural conditions that make this word a useful item of the Finnish vocabulary. But it would be manifestly absurd to try to infer the whole repertory of words in Finnish related to bad weather from observations of the habitat of its speakers.

To sum up, arbitrariness does not mean that the relation between form and meaning must be totally fortuitous in all empirically observable cases. What it means is that, although an external rationale, of one kind of another, for the given character of a sign does exist as an empirical feature of the vocabulary, such a rationale is never sufficient either for determining the value of signs or for predicting the direction of its further development. In the final analysis, the status and the destiny of every sign, be it "iconic" or purely "symbolic," "relatively motivated" or "simple," is a fact of convention.

It is in this sense that arbitrariness can be understood as a truly universal, a priori given property of signs. It is a foundational principle of language, its constitutionally given transcendental feature, rather than an empirical yardstick more or less applicable to various domains of the vocabulary. The absoluteness of arbitrariness is grounded in the fact that the signifier and the signified, as they are defined by being linked together in a sign, do not exist outside that linkage. Strictly speaking, no justification of the "relation" between the two sides of a sign is possible outside the bare fact of its existence at a given moment in a given language; they are nothing but "sides" of a bipolar phenomenon—not phenomena in their own right that could be "related" to each other.

### Negative Implication: The Irrelevance of Substance

Saussure's insight had overwhelming methodological consequences whose scope no one could appreciate better than himself. Since neither the signifier nor the signified of a sign can exist outside their arbitrary interconnectedness, it is impossible to speak of either of them in positive, substantial terms. The moment we focus on either side of a sign in an attempt to describe it, the phenomenon of the sign is lost. Saussure's idea undermined the traditional understanding of the sign as something standing for something else, suggested by Aristotle, canonized by medieval scholasticism and universally accepted ever since.[21] Under Saussure's approach, neither that "something" (i.e., the sign's form) nor the "something else" (the meaning) exist prior to and outside of their encountering each other in a sign. Defining the meaning of a sign by referring to its content does not render "a linguistic fact in its essence and all its scope" (*CLG*, 162/116). By the same token, the classification of its speech sounds, useful as that may be as an empirical tool, cannot be taken for a linguistic description of the signifier. Saussure even suggested that the excessively precise acoustic or articulatory description of sounds is counterproductive, as far as linguistics is concerned, since it puts too strong an emphasis on substance.

If the sign literally cannot be "grasped," either from its material or its semantic side, how can one approach *la langue* as a system of signs? The key to the problem lies in the notion of the "system." Unsustainable on their own, the signs of a given language exist only together, in mutual relations. It is a "grand illusion," Saussure forewarns, to think that one can describe a sign as a single instance of union between a form and a meaning, since that would mean referring to them in substantial terms; signs can be reached only in a system in which they are positioned vis-à-vis each other (*CLG*, 157/112).

The total dependence of the form and meaning of signs on their intra-systemic relations is captured in one of Saussure's key terms: the "value" (*valeur*), in the notes sometimes also called the "differential value" (*valeur différente*). The "value" of a sign is what distinguishes it from other signs. It characterizes signs as "oppositive, relative and negative entities" (*CLG*, 164/117). The word in itself is an empty shell whose values, on the side of both its signifier and its signified, are determined by its oppositions to or distinctions from what it is not (*ELG*, 74/50). Two signs "are not different, they are only distinct; there is nothing between them but an opposition" (*CLG*, 167/119). A sign has neither "form" nor "meaning" in a traditional sense; it does not possess a secure semiotic space allotted to it but, rather, occupies as much space as other signs in the same language allow it to have. The meaning of *supplice* is defined not by its relation to certain experiences, historical realities, images, and so forth, Saussure explains, but solely by its differentiation from *martyre, tourment, torture, affres, agonie,* and other related terms. The *Course* seconds the point by stating that the meaning of *redouter, craindre,* and *avoir peur* are determined by nothing but their mutual opposition; it is impossible to understand the meaning of any of them without referring to "its competitors" (*CLG*, 160/114). (One cannot help sensing, in those ostensibly random examples, the depth of the depression into which Saussure was plunged by his own discovery.)

According to Saussure, a typical mistake which *les philosophes* shared with common users of language consists in treating language as a "vehicle of thought." The point is that language is not about whatever referential content it may evoke in the minds of its speakers. The primary characteristic of language is negative: language is a pure (i.e., defined negatively in oppositional terms) form; it consists of differences and nothing but differences (*ELG*, 264/189)—a crucial point that is aphoristically formulated in the *Course*: "Dans la langue il n'y a que des différences sans termes positifs" (*CLG*, 166/118).[22]

Taking a jab at Humboldt's vision of language as the carrier of the collective experience of a nation, Saussure speaks with pointed sarcasm about those who think that all the richness contained in the meaning of a word "could not have happened otherwise than as the fruit of reflection, of experience, of a profound philosophy accumulated in the depth of the language by generations of those who used it." What happens in and with a language is just the opposite: "no sign is delimited by the sum of positive ideas on which it is focused at the given moment; it is never delimited otherwise than negatively, by the simultaneous presence of other signs" (*ELG*, 78/52).

The lack of any substantial quality makes the integrity of a word, as it is laid down in a dictionary, "imaginary" (*ELG*, 83/56). The different meanings of a "polysemous" word emerge from the different oppositions in which this word finds itself in a language. For instance, the word *moon* has one signification in opposition to sun, another in opposition to day or year (as a time measurement related to an astronomical cycle), yet another in opposition to stars as a source of light in the night, and so on. There are no positive substantial features that would "coordinate" all those meanings; they all arise in a random way, negatively, i.e., each by being differentiated from something else (*ELG*, 88/60).

I believe that Saussure goes further than any twentieth-century theoretician of meaning in exploring the depth of negativity in language. In particular, Saussure's understanding of polysemy as "an allegorical picture" whose various components are conjoined in an arbitrary fashion (*ELG*, 112/76) was more radical than Wittgenstein's idea of family resemblances. The latter, while rejecting the idea of a common denominator or "invariant" of meaning, still considered the relations between particular meanings in positive terms, as a matter of their "familial" similarities and overlaps.

The immanent character of the system of semiotic differences in each language makes it impossible for signs in different languages to have identical semantic values, no matter how close they appear to be with respect to their overt referential content. Projecting the signs of one language onto the signs of another never yields a perfect fit. Each language presents a labyrinthine maze of semiotic spaces held together by no other principle than their mutual support through a mutual delimitation "in a complicated interplay resulting in an eventual balance" (*ELG*, 66/43).

The purely oppositive character of linguistic values renders void the question of the "origin of language" with which eighteenth-century philosophy of language was much preoccupied. Saussure's vision of language as a network of pure differences makes the question of its origin logically unsustainable. Language cannot have originated from the absolute unity of an imagined "first sign." It would be vain to attempt to construe some absolutely unified point of departure from which language ostensibly started to evolve—the kind of speculation of which the age of Enlightenment was so fond. Language begins when something is distinguished from something else—which means that language can never "begin" as a single step from nothing. No fact of language is elementary (*ELG*, 20/5); from the very first moment in the existence of language there has already been a differentiation.

By the same token, language evolution has nothing to do with "development" in a conventional sense. The signs of a language are "always adequate" to what they express (*ELG*, 102/67) because they express nothing but mutually defined values. Saussure once suggested that if there were a language that had just two distinct signs, it could still accommodate everything in the world; in such a language, a certain plurality of objects would be identified with sign A, while another plurality would receive their identity from sign B.

The radicalism of Saussure's negativity was always a sticking point even for those who were otherwise positively disposed toward his theory. As has been pointed out more than once, the world as perceived by human consciousness is not an empty space waiting to be filled by language in some fashion or other. Thought prior to the sign is not totally amorphous: it already presents experience organized into "proto-concepts" (Mazzone 2004). Such a critique misses Saussure's point, which is not to deny that perception has any experiential basis or that consciousness is able to organize perceptions into broader categories. Neither does the Saussurean approach deny any link between those perceptions, on the one hand, and patterns of their semiotic representation in language, on the other. What the principle of negativity means is that this link is never consistent. Any threads of connection that can be discerned between our experience of the world and its reflection in our language are doomed ever to remain no more than spurious and coincidental. Whatever people's "proto-concepts" about the world may be, the structure of their language cannot be derived from them. In their perception of the world, people rely on prototypes grounded in experiential features of phenomena. But once this reflection of the world by consciousness enters the realm of signs, it undergoes incessant arbitrary reconfigurations, making it impossible to rely on the experiential basis when dealing with language. Whatever we think in connection with or alongside language, in the last count the language remains subject to no rules but the fact of its existence.

## IMMUTABILITY AND MUTABILITY OF SIGNS: AN INDISSOLUBLE ANTINOMY

Whether Saussure's commentators adhered to his concept of the arbitrariness of signs or tried to contest it, the idea itself, based primarily on the way it was presented in the *Course,* was almost universally understood as an emphatic assertion of the necessity, or even compulsion, for speakers to use language as it is. This understanding was largely responsible for the strong determinist bent in structural linguistics and, by the same token, for the subsequent critique of its (and, along with it, of the *Course*'s) deterministic "authoritarianism."

Indeed, the *Course* paints a striking picture of a speaker deprived of any tools of reasoning or worldly experience when facing the conventions of his language, to whose inexorable arbitrariness he has no choice but to succumb. The speaker faces the imperative of the inner structure of the language, which has no other justification but that it is the way it is: "A signifier chosen by *la langue* cannot be replaced by another. . . . No society knows or has ever known its language otherwise than as a product inherited from preceding generations and taken as it is" (*CLG*, 104–105/71–72).

Saussure's notes, however, offer a picture that at first sight seems to be diametrically opposed to the one presented in the *Course.* Here, the principle of freedom, which the *Course* seemed to deny completely, emerges with the utmost emphasis. Not only does language change, but it cannot exist otherwise than in a state of spontaneous change; it evolves inexorably, like a stream running down a mountain (*ELG,* 94/73). *La langue* as a semiotic system is not a ship at anchor, Saussure remarks, but a ship at sea: "The moment it touches the sea, it is vain to think that one could predict its course by projecting it from one's knowledge of the material out of which it has been made, and of its interior construction" (*ELG,* 289/202).

It is fascinating to see how Saussure applies Durkheim's concept of "social facts" to opposing ends in the *Course* and in the notes. In the former, language is presented as a "social act"[23] because it compels the speaker to conform; any individual effort, either by a single speaker or by a collective, succumbs to the imperative of social convention: "No individual, even if he willed it, could modify in any way whatsoever the choice that has been made; and what is more, the community itself cannot control so much as a single word; it is bound to the existing language" (*CLG*, 104/71). But in the notes, the seemingly helpless, conformist "community" becomes an uncontrollable "mass" of speakers. Here Saussure sounds more like Bakhtin: "From the instant at which a symbol becomes a symbol, which is to say, from the instant at which it becomes immersed in the social mass that establishes its value at any given moment, its identity can never be fixed." The "social collectivity" is heterogeneous—language evolves "between many" speakers (*ELG*, 290/203); all the changes are produced in a chaotic and improvised fashion, in the process of spoken exchange (*ELG*, 95/64–65).

How can one assess this glaring contradiction? The habitual explanatory path taken by "Saussurology" is to assign the superior value to the notes while blaming the book's editors for distorting or misunderstanding Saussure's thought in their "vulgate." And yet, Saussure himself was aware of the contradiction. The *Course* speaks about the two main principles according to which signs exist, calling them "immutability" and "mutability." Typically for the book (which in this respect probably reflects the rhetoric of Saussure's lectures), there is a vague protestation to the effect that these two principles are not as contradictory as they look and can be reconciled (*CLG*, 108–109/74), which, however, is left hanging in the air without any further elaboration. The fact of the matter is that the immutability and mutability of signs represent two complementary facets of the most general a priori feature of language, which is its arbitrary constitution. Both principles are logical consequences of the fact that, insofar as they are considered within the inner arrangement of language, signs turn out to be devoid of any substantial support.

The "immutability" of signs stems from their inner emptiness, which makes them unsustainable otherwise than as a system in mutual relations. Speakers cannot willfully target any single sign for adjustment, since there is no such thing as a solitary sign to be targeted; each time a speaker deals with a particular entity he faces a whole network of oppositions. The "social contract" between speakers concerning their language has a wholesale character. One cannot perform "surgery" on a language by purposefully assigning a new meaning to a particular word without causing incalculable side effects to ripple through the system as a whole. The same principle applies to the sign's material representation: any tampering with one signifier would affect other signifiers by tipping the balance of their distinction.

And yet, in an astonishing paradox, it is precisely the lack of substance that makes the sign, immutable when looked at from one point of view, also mutable, and moreover, unsustainable. The lack of any solid ground behind the sign's value makes it vulnerable to arbitrary change. One cannot defend a sign's integrity on the ground that it corresponds well to a certain logical pattern or certain quanta of worldly experience. Since the convention that supports the sign is "pure"—i.e., empty, groundless—it turns out to be unenforceable; any mutation goes, insofar as it is spontaneously accepted and adopted by speakers in the process of language use.[24]

Culler was the first to note that the idea of oppositive values, predicated on the principle of arbitrariness, makes the system of such values open to uncontrollable and unpredictable changes.[25] Having plunged into an open "sea" of usages, with its infinite variety of voices and intentional vectors, the system of purely oppositional values has nothing to shield it against the pressures that come at it from all sides in a chaotic and volatile fashion. Nothing prevents it from being pushed in any direction at any moment.

For all their apparent polarity, the thesis foregrounded in the book, that nobody and nothing can institute a change in *la langue,* and that in the notes, that nobody and nothing can control the inexorable process of its change, stem from the same fundamental vision of the elemental nature of language.

The notes that depict language as moving precipitously, like a stream rushing downhill, totally at the mercy of the "mass" of heterogeneous social forces, in fact elucidate the meaning of the emphatic assertions in the *Course* of the powerlessness of both the individual and the community to change anything in their language. Speakers are indeed powerless, but only in the capacity of purposeful, teleologically minded agents. Language does not yield to any deliberate attempt to amend it in a certain "desirable" direction, because no particular entity in it can be exempted from the whole for a targeted operation. A purposeful "language policy" may achieve certain local results, but, in the long run, consciously instituted changes always bring with them unintended consequences, leaving language as unyielding to deliberate control as ever. A "fundamental error" of *les philosophes* of the eighteenth century was their failure to understand that, as a social phenomenon—precisely because it is a social phenomenon—language cannot be either constructed or revised in a rational manner (*ELG,* 94/64).

However, when speakers act unconsciously, just by using language on the spur of the moment, they provoke imperceptible and uncontrollable changes—in fact, cannot help inflicting them. Each time a speaker applies a certain expression to the unique circumstances of a given moment of speech, he opens the way to inflecting its meaning. To say "adopting an idea," by analogy with "adopting a child," or *fleur de la noblesse* by analogy with *fleur du pommier,* is to affect not just a single utterance but the whole state of linguistic values (*CLG,* 151/107). Likewise, each time a speaker produces a given expression with a particular unique combination of pitch curve, tempo, dynamic, and vocal timbre—responding, with the help of these tools, to the demands of the moment—he affects the balance of established signifiers.

The principles of the immutability and mutability of signs coexist, and moreover, are complementary, two different perspectives from which language can be viewed. To the uninvolved observer who posits himself outside language, it looks like a stream of uninterrupted and uncontrollable transmutations. No single instance of language use is ever an exact repetition of a previous one, with regard to both its signified and its signifier. Defenseless against the incessant and spurious forces that press on it, because of its inner emptiness, language proves incapable of maintaining itself in this volatile environment. Far from the solid geometry of a crystal lattice, its network of oppositions behaves like a "gaseous" entity, no more capable of resisting outside forces than a cloud at the mercy of the wind.

When, on the other hand, the observer acts in the capacity of a speaker, his consciousness of his language moves together with the movement of the language itself. From this inside perspective of the speaker—or, if we use Saussure's expression, from the point of view of *la langue en lui-même*—language appears immutable. No matter how many changes in a language could be noted by an outside observer, its speakers always face it as a "state"; whatever spontaneous change arises at a given moment causes the whole system to adapt to it, thus remaining in perfect harmony with itself. As Saussure pointed out on several occasions in his notes, the differences between "old," "middle," and "modern" French, or the idea of French as an offspring of Latin, are no more than abstractions constructed by linguists (in their capacity as outside observers). As far as speakers were concerned, they could never have known—without an outside prompt—that their language had ceased to be "old French" and become "middle" or that the language they spoke was not "Latin" anymore but "French." Had there been a speaker whose life span comprised two thousand years, he might have thought of himself as still speaking the language of Cicero—with perhaps a few "generational" changes in it—while in fact speaking modern French or Italian.

Saussure's depiction of a speaker whose every choice is being made for him by his language addresses the speaker's linguistic consciousness, not his linguistic behavior. The latter, on the contrary, involves a constant meddling with available linguistic resources, to which language always yields, most often imperceptibly.

## FREEDOM AND APORIA

To part with any external support, from empirical "common sense" to universal categories of reason, while dealing with language in its purest essence, did not prove easy. As Saussure notes, we tend to assign "precipitously" some positive existence to what is in fact purely negative and purely differential. And yet, Saussure adds, "perhaps, I admit it, we are called to recognize that without this fiction, the spirit would find itself literally incapable of commanding this sum of differences, in which no single shred of a positive and firm signpost appears at any moment" (*ELG*, 65/42).

The lack of any substantial anchor makes language fleeting and volatile. It never stands still—the moment you have grasped it in a certain state, another state emerges that refutes the previous one. For instance, take any notion of a grammatical category, "for example genitive," Saussure remarks (apparently recollecting his experience with classifying cases of the "genitive absolute" in his dissertation). The notion of the genitive is "completely ungraspable" (*insaisissable*), "a word literally devoid of any sense," since the meaning of *genitive* is always "extending, from one moment to another, one page to another, one line to another." To speak about the genitive as a category implies that there is an idea "superior to signs, exterior with regard to signs, independent of signs" (*ELG*, 55/34). Language has no firm "signposts," as the conventions of grammatical description suggest; in reality, there is nothing but a continuum in which the relational network remains ever in flux.

The fundamental error of both the structuralist and the generativist approaches was that they gave ontological value to such "precipitous" acts. Structural patterns and algorithmic rules imposed on language become a second reality, acquiring a life of their own. By proceeding in this way, twentieth-century theoretical linguistics continued to revel in what Saussure perceived as the codification of "phantoms." It was that complacent "illusion" Saussure rebelled against and desperately sought to escape—even though each escape attempt left him empty-handed, peering into a void.

A close reading of the *Course* reveals the same anxieties lurking behind its aphoristic facade, occasionally erupting onto the surface. In "ces gants sont bon marché," is *bon marché* an adjective?—Saussure demands of his audience. Apparently it is not, since it does not correspond to many features of a "normal adjective"; on the other hand, simply declaring *marché* a "noun" would mean ignoring constructions like this one (*CLG*, 152–153/108). If one reads the *Course* as a theoretical "grand narrative," it is easy to overlook this passage as an incidental aside. Yet the discussion of this example leads Saussure to a conclusion that reverberates with the central concern of his notes: "Thus, linguistics labors without respite over concepts forged by grammarians. . . . And if they are phantoms, with what realities could they be matched? In order to escape from illusions, it is necessary to become convinced from the start that concrete entities of *la langue* are not presented to our observation by themselves; that one strives to grasp them, and by doing this, one comes into contact with reality" (*CLG*, 152–153/108).

When Saussure was writing the initial corpus of his notes in the mid-1890s, he was still hopeful that eventually he could succeed, through an ardent labor of inferential thinking, in getting past all the "phantoms" and touching the essential core of language, thus establishing a solid objective foundation for linguistic studies; hence his notorious hesitation to give any finalized shape to his thought, a step whose arbitrary relativity—that is, the fact that it could always be reshaped in innumerable ways—he immediately realized once he tried to take it. But in the second half of the 1900s Saussure came to realize the epistemological impossibility of this goal. Language is not an abstraction; nothing in language exists outside and beyond representation. Yet its palpable reality remains perpetually elusive as a result of the absence of any general ground on which one could establish reliable connections between the representational surfaces and the values they represent—no foundation, that is, except the negative one of their arbitrariness. The principle of negativity, based on the arbitrary duality of linguistic signs, becomes the "irreducible" fact of language (*ELG*, 39/22). *La langue* is not merely an inner knowledge ("competence") stored in the minds of its speakers, as Saussurean linguistics often claims. It represents no empirical reality at all, even an ideational one. Rather, *la langue* as a pure (negative) form is a notion of the metaphysical state of language.[26] Consequently, *la parole* cannot be understood as the "manifestation" of *la langue* in the outward reality of speech; it is separated from *la langue* by a metaphysical abyss.

Yet discovering arbitrariness, despite its devastating methodological consequences, was not a purely negative outcome. By wresting language from any empirical or logical order, Saussure's principle of arbitrariness revealed itself as the principle of freedom—a linguistic manifestation of the metaphysical principle of free will that people exercise in their capacity as speakers. Challenging arbitrariness through examples of more or less extended local patterns of reason in the composition of its signs is as futile as challenging the principle of free will through examples of human behavior that are more or less obviously caused by logical reasoning or empirical necessity. In both cases the essence of the matter is not the possibility of a local causality but the ultimate impossibility of deriving human behavior at large from any comprehensive causality pattern.

The fundamental freedom of language, grounded in arbitrariness, shows itself in the unlimited diversity of forms different languages, or even one language in the course of its development, may assume. No logical or empirical restrictions exist that could determine the playground of values that is language or set limits to its transformations. For Saussure, the structural diversity of languages is more than an empirically known fact—it is, rather, "primordial reality," reflecting the very essence of language. The question "whence to begin?" is a question without a definitive answer when one approaches "the slippery substance" of language (*ELG*, 281/197). The truth about language lies not in ultimate generalizations but, on the contrary, in the unceasing comparative analysis of its diverse manifestations.[27]

This makes language a fundamentally "human" phenomenon in the most general sense that its metaphysical essence reflects the nature of those who speak it. The principle of the linguistic "free will" of speakers leaves language on its own amidst all the phenomena of the world subject to physical and/or logical causality. The Kantian subject faces a world that is shaped by a priori categories he cannot transcend. Yet the subject is endowed with the gift of "genius," which makes him never tired of challenging the boundaries of a world circumscribed by pure reason. It is this gift (or curse, as some Romantics would say) of free creativity that sets him apart from the rest of the world. In a striking parallel, the Saussurean *langue* emerges as endowed with a quality that sets it apart from all other phenomena of the world. Like human consciousness itself, it is "conventional, nay arbitrary, totally devoid of a natural rapport with objects, absolutely free and lawless in rapport with itself" (*ELG*, 202/140).

Fragmentation and Progressivity | **FOUR**

*Saussure's Semiotics in the Mirror*
*of Early Romantic Epistemology*

## IN SEARCH OF SAUSSURE'S INTELLECTUAL ROOTS

Tracing Saussure's intellectual roots is not easy. In his writing, including the notes, he rarely referred to ideas or authors outside technical linguistic studies. Saussure's personal library, eventually bequeathed to the University of Geneva, consisted exclusively of books on linguistics (it is possible, however, that what his family decided to give away was only part of his library: Stancati 2004). Whenever Saussure delves into general issues of methodology, his references typically become generic, even sweeping; he fights with "prejudices" and "stupidities," and often qualifies and differentiates without specifying the target of his argument. Many of those who knew Saussure marvelled at his erudition in matters of philosophy, literature, art, and music,[1] yet in his writings one can find only occasional clues hinting at this background. For instance, we would never have known that he was interested in music at all, if not for some cursory yet sharp remarks in the notes about Wagner's leitmotifs and Bach's sound symbolism.[2] Saussure's ability to raise fundamental epistemological questions concerning the subject and method of linguistic studies show him to have been abreast of contemporary epistemological ideas, without giving any tangible evidence about which authors and works he may have been aware of or familiar with.

For instance, his treatment of the evolution of language reads at times like a linguistic incarnation of Bergsonian duration—without any sign of Bergson's presence on his intellectual horizon. To use Saussurean terms, we can say that what surfaces as the outward representation of his ideas is only a set of "differences" by which his thought seeks to determine its place among a variety of concepts and approaches concerning theory of cognition, philosophy of language, sociology, anthropology, psychology, studies of myth, and modernist poetics. As to the "substance" of those differentiations, it remains almost entirely tacitly implied.

Much has been said about the Saussure family's hallowed tradition of excelling in the natural sciences. This background, resounding with Saussure's own supreme aptitude for pattern building (of which his book on Indo-European vowels is a prime example), could suggest that Saussure's approach to "general linguistics" was inspired by the natural sciences and mathematics, an assumption reinforced by his own occasional declarations of the need to present language as a chain of "theorems." This assumption reinforced the perception of timeless structural orderliness in which Saussure's linguistics was cast by subsequent generations. What this perception missed was the irreconcilable contradiction inherent in *la langue* that set it apart from natural sciences—a contradiction stemming from the heterogeneous yet symbiotic duality of the linguistic sign. The Leipzig school's straightforward conviction that the laws of language are equivalent to natural laws and can be described accordingly evoked Saussure's scorn.

Saussure was one of the world's foremost experts on Sanskrit. Sanskrit stood at the epicenter of his teaching curriculum in Geneva and (together with the classical languages) of his Indo-European studies. It is natural to presume that the famous Panini grammar of Sanskrit—a formidable compendium, written in the fourth century BC, of about four thousand rules or *sutras*[3]—must have played an important role in shaping Saussure's approach to language. Panini's striking ability to focus on linguistic forms and their mutual distinctions, a feature quite a few modern scholars have perceived as protostructuralist or even protogenerativist (Kiparsky and Staal 1969; Misra 1964), invited analogies with Saussure's *Course*.

One of trademarks of Panini grammar was its precise and detailed description of speech sounds and their alternations at the boundaries of words and morphemes. This topic clearly fascinated Saussure. Even in the second and third lecture courses on general linguistics, with their heavy slant toward philosophical problems of language, substantial space was allotted to descriptive phonetics; consequently, a chapter on the subject appears in the *Course*. Yet this elaborate excursion into empirical matters stands isolated in a book whose central theoretical nerve asserts that the physical quality of speech sounds is irrelevant. Saussure's occasional profession that he "had no taste for phonology" (*ELG*, 244/173), while consistent with his theoretical convictions, was hardly sincere. As happened more than once in situations when Saussure became aware of contradicting himself, he tried to explain it away on didactic grounds: one had to take on phonological matters in order to correct errors in existing views (*ELG*, 244/173).

Panini's influence on Saussure's dissertation on the genitive absolute construction (1881) was unmistakable. Saussure's double classification of the data—according to both its formal features and its meaning—reflected the way Panini described the Sanskrit case system. Yet one can see Saussure's doubts about the viability of his own description (which he was careful enough to voice only in the dissertation's "supplement"), later coming to the surface in his statements to the effect that all grammatical notions ("as, for example, genitive") are no more than conventions of descriptive metalanguage, valid only insofar as one is willing to play along with them.

During the last twenty years of Saussure's life, when he was striving to define his philosophical approach to language, we see no evidence of his involvement with Panini as a theoretical work, despite the fact that for all those years Sanskrit remained the centerpiece of his teaching load. At that time there was a vivid polemic among scholars concerning the provenance of Panini's compendium and its possible predecessors. Saussure remained uninvolved, even though some scholars, to whom he felt intellectually or personally close, such as Whitney and Wackernagel, played a prominent role in the debates. Saussure's name does not appear in the extensive modern bibliography of works about Panini (Cardona 1976). It could be said that Saussure tried, but eventually rejected, the pattern-building approach to language for which Panini presented a protomodel.

Saussure's repeated praise of Whitney and, less specifically, of the French *philosophes*, for their emphasis on the social conventionality of language is one of the rare instances when we can see him referring to general philosophical ideas about language in a positive mode. These positive judgments are often pronounced in conjunction with ferocious diatribes against the "German" approach to language as an organism (an attitude exemplified to Saussure in particular by Schleicher and to a lesser extent by Humboldt).[4] As Saussure turns to defining his own approach to linguistic conventionality, however, he does so by distancing himself from his predecessors. What one observes in language is empty or "pure" convention, the arbitrary confluence of accidents of usage. This exempts language from social "institutions" grounded in substantial social practices. Saussure's emphatic assertion that language knows neither "beginning" nor teleological ends sets him apart from the French Enlightenment philosophy of language and its modern echoes, exemplified in utopian plans for an artificial "universal language." On this issue, Saussure stands on the side of Herder and Hamann and against Rousseau and Condillac, though he never mentioned either pair directly.

This last point brings us to an issue that further obfuscates the discussion of Saussure's intellectual roots—his peculiar relationship with Germany and her intellectual world. Saussure's entire adult life took place under the shadow of the catastrophic consequences of the Franco-Prussian War. When in his lectures he cites a seemingly random example of a certain animal species being called either *boeuf* or *Ochse* on "this and that side of the border," one can sense that the issue of that contentious "border" (with its personal dimension, due to his own Lotharingian roots) is never far from his mind. Lingering animosity toward "Germans" can be seen in the especially shrill vituperations in Saussure's notes against the "idiocies" (*bêtisses*) of certain German ideas concerning language and linguistics. The French-German frictions that surrounded Saussure's career erupted after his death in a controversy about who was to publish his papers in Indo-European linguistics. In a way, this pattern persisted in later (predominantly Swiss and French) Saussure scholarship, which rarely even glances at "that side of the border" in search of Saussure's intellectual roots.[5]

Nonetheless, Saussure's deep involvement with German language and culture was evident throughout his life. Not only did he receive his linguistic education there, but, together with Sanskrit, Germanistics comprised the core of his profile as a teacher. The full depth of Saussure's involvement in the field is attested by his extensive studies of the Nibelung epos in the 1890s and 1900s.

It should be noted that Saussure's ferocious critique of the hyperpositivism of the Leipzig school was done from methodological positions that bore the unmistakable imprint of the German philosophical tradition—from Kant to early Romantic philosophy of language and history (from Herder to Novalis) to the contemporary neo-Kantian, logical (Frege) and phenomenological critique of positivism. Explicating this tacit yet palpable background might have a considerable impact on the way Saussure's pronouncements—often elliptical, aphoristically terse, and riddled with seeming contradictions—can be interpreted. Perhaps most importantly, it could help to resolve many of the apparent contradictions between the *Course* and Saussure's notes by offering an intellectual framework in which they can both be read.

The question is, of course, how these analogies could be substantiated. For instance, the parallels between Saussure and Novalis in their approach to some fundamental properties of the sign are striking. Saussure seems to share with Novalis the idea of the inalienable duality of the two sides of the sign; the idea in itself is so original, so removed from conventional perceptions of the sign's form and meaning, that no convincing analogy to it can be found anywhere else. Yet however much or little Saussure may have been aware of the *Athenaeum* metaphysics of sign and language, it left no explicit trace among his scarce references, although it is hard to imagine that he was not familiar with at least some of Novalis's writing, various collections of which had appeared throughout the nineteenth century (including a very substantial two-volume edition in 1901).

Saussure's reserved, even somewhat dour public persona presents a stark contrast to what we conventionally think of as a "Romantic personality." Not only the generic image of the dishevelled "romantic," but even its more dignified versions—Novalis's passionate quest for the absolute or the young Schlegel's irreverent wit—seem remote from Saussure's personality or at least from its outward appearance. Thanks to Saussure's private papers, we know about the passions, anxieties, and outbursts of anger and sarcasm that were hidden behind that reticent facade. Yet judging by the *Course's* rhetorical attire, as well as the memories of his disciples, Saussure always projected an outward image of total intellectual composure, even though upon scrutiny it might turn out that what he was saying in his imperturbably lucid manner didn't quite hang together.

Saussure's declared goal was to lay out the foundations of linguistics with shining rationality, as a sequence of "theorems"—an achievement that would gain it entry into the compendium of modern sciences. Yet he was never able to come to terms with the intellectual compromises necessary to give "the science of language" an orderly rational shape. One could say that the wrenching contradiction between the clearly envisioned ultimate goal and the equally clear awareness of its unattainability revealed a state of mind akin to that of the early Romantics in the 1790s, before Romanticism succumbed to sweeping utopianism and flamboyant rhetorical postures. The predominant tradition of Saussure's reception in the twentieth century highlighted his rationalist side while ignoring (or simply being ignorant of) the intellectual drama behind his seemingly unwavering if sometimes contradictory logic.

Exploring the philosophical ground from which Saussure's ideas emerged could lead to a considerable reconfiguration of his entire intellectual landscape. In particular, it could help wrest Saussure from the utopian constructionism of the high modernism of the 1920s–1950s, while reaffirming, and casting a new light on, his connections with the epistemological revolution of early modernism (1890s–1900s) and its early Romantic antecedents.

## A MISSING LINK? FROM "PROGRESSIVE EDUCATION" TO "GENERAL LINGUISTICS"

### Hidden in Plain View

It is time to explore clues that link Saussure's idea of the unique epistemological predicament involving language with early Romantic philosophy of cognition and meaning. In purely personal terms, those clues look neither vague nor remote. In all probability, it was a tangible human continuity with roots in his family that underlay Saussure's "elective affinities" to the world of the *Athenaeum*. That this line of the family tradition has remained hidden in plain sight for so long can be explained only by the blinding glare of the spirit of Enlightenment rationalism and scientific exploration embodied in generations of the Saussure family, which seemed to highlight Saussure's scholarship and personality—as it was seen in the age of structuralism—in the most flattering way. By the same token, the early Romantic lineage of Saussure's intellectual genealogy was doomed to remain in the background. I mean, of course, Saussure's great-aunt, Albertine Adrienne Necker de Saussure (1766–1841), and her renowned—albeit not within the domain of Saussure studies—concept of "progressive education."

A cousin (on her husband's side) and a close friend of Germaine de Staël, Necker de Saussure had close relationships with such key figures of French and German early Romanticism as Benjamin Constant, August Wilhelm Schlegel, and Friedrich Schleiermacher. She was a frequent guest at Chateau Coppet, the Swiss residence of Mme. de Staël and a frequent meeting place of the early Romantics, which emerged in 1790s as an important center of the movement together with Jena.

At that time, following the birth of her four children, Necker de Saussure began noting down her observations of their behavior, beginning from the earliest stage. She was convinced early on of the necessity of turning her reflections into a book. However, it took her a long time to realize this project. In the course of the more than three decades that separated Necker de Saussure's initial design from its completion, she translated and published A. W. Schlegel's *Course of Dramatic Literature* and wrote a (rather hagiographic) book about de Staël's life and work after her friend's death in 1819.[6]

Upon its appearance, *L'éducation progressive* (vols. 1–2, 1828–1832, supplemented by *Étude de la vie de femmes*, 1837) enjoyed broad recognition. Several subsequent editions followed promptly in France (vol. 1, 1836 and 1843; a revised new edition of vols. 1–2, 1847) and in Germany (vols. 1–2 in 1838, followed by yet another translation in 1842; vol. 3 in 1839), where the book elicited a particularly wide response, perhaps because of its close intellectual kinship with German early Romantic philosophy (Maurer 1938:90).

A vivid interest in Necker de Saussure's work and personality persisted well into the twentieth century.[7] This recognition, however, never spread across the compartmentalizing barrier separating the field of child psychology and education from theoretical linguistics. We find no mention of her grand-nephew in books dedicated to Necker de Saussure, while she receives only a few vague, sometimes condescending remarks in the literature about him.[8]

Saussure's great-aunt died sixteen years before he was born. True, her library, containing a large collection of works of Romantic literature and philosophy, remained at Vufflens; true, in his youth Saussure's teacher Pictet was a close friend of hers. But while Saussure's familiarity with Necker de Saussure's intellectual heritage seems highly probable, it cannot be stated for a fact.

Still, upon reading *L'éducation progressive* one cannot fail to discern numerous threads leading to Saussure's thought and writing—from the general philosophical perspective to some key concepts and even certain favorite turns of speech. Moreover, as I will try to show, some aspects of Necker de Saussure's work can be seen as occupying an intermediary position between early Romantic epistemology and Saussure's philosophy of language. This makes Necker de Saussure an important albeit hypothetical link between Saussure and early Romantic metaphysics.

### The World of a Small Child: Pure Differentiation

Necker de Saussure's book, particularly the first volume, was focused on the child's development beginning from the first few weeks of life. At this stage, the book asserts, the child does not yet possess the faculty of reflection, at least not as he begins to after the age of five (1:2–3). For the first eight days of his life in particular, a child is unable to differentiate between his inner sensations and outward impressions. Since he cannot externalize his impressions as if they were something that lay outside his self, he is unable to distinguish among them, since the act of distinguishing one impression from another is possible only through their externalization (1:142). All the child perceives is perceived as his own sensations, as in a dream. The newborn child is a "direct creation of God" (*oeuvre immédiate de Dieu*) (1:9): his state is that of an absolute wholeness which is, by the same token, a blank state of total indistinction.

When, from that very first moment on, the child moves toward cognizing the world around him, he does so by making *distinctions*. It is not a process based on preset categories, which in any case the newborn child is as yet unable to employ. Instead, he proceeds by groping for cognitive experiences in an arbitrary, random succession.

Concentrating on the reactions of small children allows Necker de Saussure to make a discovery whose significance goes beyond the domain of child psychology: namely, that the process of signification evolves as pure differentiation, i.e., as a sequence of acts of distinguishing one signified entity from another rather than as a "substantive" grasping of the content of particular phenomena. The child perceives a difference and seeks to express it: he calls all fruits "apricots" (thus distinguishing them from other samples of food), before arriving at differentiating between, and acquiring names for, pears, prunes, grapes, and cherries (1:212–213). The child does not proceed logically, from a general idea to its species; he does not think of "fruit" as a general concept. The fact that the first act of differentiation involved the name *apricot* and not, say, *apple* was a pure accident. The sign *apricot*, once distinguished from some adjacent semiotic domains (say, *candy* or *ball*), suits the child perfectly well as the designator for a number of things, until the child arrives at a further differentiation. We can recall Saussure's argument that if one encountered a language whose vocabulary consisted of just two words, one would discover that for the speakers of that language the whole world was divided into two classes of phenomena corresponding to these two words. As a matter of fact, Necker de Saussure was aware that the principle of comprehending phenomena through differentiation does not apply only to infants. As a curious parallel to children's strategy of signification, the book cites a "prince Lee Boo of the island of Pelew" who, upon arriving at Macao, saw a horse and called it *dog*.

Another variation of the idea of cognition as a chain of differentiations can be seen in Necker de Saussure's observations, in her diary, of the evolving characters of her children. From a very early stage, she remarked, their behavior pointed in different directions, showing no uniform pattern of development. In this situation, it seemed more feasible to her to describe her children by pointing to differences between them rather than by trying to characterize each child separately (Mestral Combremont 1946:71).

The fact that one concept is cognized by being differentiated from another by means of representation makes a concept and its representation inseparable. Our soul is "condemned not to employ its activity otherwise than through impressions" (i.e., outward representations), the book argues (1:356). As if in anticipation of Saussure's semiotic terminology, the book refers to the small child's psychology as characterized by a "double nature." Since the outward stimuli the child receives and his responses to them are unmediated by learned patterns of reason, Necker de Saussure claims, they stand in a kind of symbiotic relationship in which they simply cannot be considered separately. In the context of a small child's world, what a certain phenomenon "means," that is, what response it elicits in the child, has no direct connection with that phenomenon's established values as they are known to us. It is impossible to determine with certainty what impression a certain event has left in a small child, nor upon what inner impulse he acted in a certain way. All one can observe is a symbiotic connection between a phenomenon and the meaning it elicits.

For Saussure, the duality of the linguistic sign marked the uniqueness of language among all material and spiritual phenomena. Much in the same way, Necker de Saussure argued for the uniqueness of the human infant among all living creatures. The world of an infant finds no analogy either in the spirit of a more developed human being, which has been imprinted by an increasing recognition of uniform patterns of reason, or in that of an animal, which is guided by natural instincts. From the moment of birth, the attention of an animal is directed by instinct toward phenomena related to the necessities of its survival; it seeks signs of food and shies away from signs of danger in its environment. In a maturing human being, a similar predictability of reactions to external phenomena is brought about by experience and the guidelines of education. But the attention of an infant is directed neither by reflection nor by any "natural" interest. The peculiar characteristic of the child's behavior is its lack of any predictable sequentiality, grounded in the child's ability to be engaged by "alien objects" (1:362)—"to act, not to obtain a result from his action" (1:365).

The idiosyncratic inseparability of external stimuli and internal responses in the small child's "double consciousness" has two fundamental consequences. The first finds a close parallel in Saussure's principle of the "mutability" of language. The lack of any constant ground or pattern for connecting what is going on "inside and outside us" (*en dedans et en dehors de nous-mêmes*) (1:113) plunges the world of a child into incessant motion. Every new event, internal or external, throws it off balance, making it move in an unpredictable direction to an unforeseeable new state. This is the principle on which the strategy of "progressive education" is founded.

The other consequence of the unpredictability of the ongoing differentiations is that its "progression" can take an infinite number of roads. The sequence of concrete steps taken on the road of cognition is unique for every child; each is as good as any other. Yet, for each individual child, its particular road is "most important"; we see events happening to us as "true [*veritable*] events" (1:11). This thought finds a parallel in what Saussure calls the "immutability" of sign systems: for all the fortuitousness of the interconnections between signifieds and signifiers to be found in any particular language, for a speaker of that language they present themselves as a unique and inexorable reality.

To appreciate these fundamental features of the world of infants—its uncontrollable "mutability" and inexorable "immutability," to use Saussure's terms—one has to abandon all preconceptions concerning child psychology and development and look at things from the perspective of the child "himself" (*lui-même*) (1:19–20). The opening of Saussure's *Course*, in which he strives to formulate the subject of linguistic studies, shows an almost ineffable resemblance to the way Necker de Saussure addresses what she sees as the principal task of child psychology in the opening pages of her book. The common mistake of works on education so far, Necker de Saussure argues, has been that they proceeded from the point of view of the educator. If observed from an outside perspective, child development can be seen as a succession of universal stages that follow each other in a prescribed order. Yet from the perspective of the child *lui-même*, his movement from one universal checkpoint to another reveals itself as a unique chain of steps that are neither sequential nor teleological. Once one adopts this approach, what one sees in a small child is, first and foremost, the unstoppable "progressive" movement of his spirit.

While Necker de Saussure applied her principle of "dual consciousness" specifically to the world of small children, she was aware of its universal validity as the fundamental condition of the human spirit. To be sure, the very nature of "progressive education" makes it a continual lifetime process: "Everything in human life is education" (1:12). As this process evolves, the spirit retains its mutability, albeit, as Necker de Saussure always emphasized, to a reduced degree, in the face of learned orderly patterns of thought and accumulated knowledge of the world. Here is where the gender difference comes to the foreground, since, according to Necker de Saussure, women are more able to retain spontaneity. In any event, preserving, at least to a degree, the "dual" nature of the spirit, which enables it to continue its free-flowing evolution, is crucial for every person. Necker de Saussure's adherence to the principle of "duality" showed itself in her admonition to her (by now grown-up) children "to grasp the meaning" of the Gospel "without ever stripping it from its form. Penetrate into its spirit, while returning unceasingly to its letter" (2:408–409).[9] "Separated from its envelope, the spirit evaporates or becomes altered," she concludes. The metaphor of the meaning "evaporating" when stripped of its "envelope" vividly recalls an image Saussure used to elucidate the interdependence of the form and the meaning of a sign, which he compared with a balloon filled with hydrogen (*ELG*, 115/78).

It seems that the similarities and coincidences between Necker de Saussure's insights into the world of infants and Saussure's revolutionary concept of the arbitrary duality of linguistic signs are simply too numerous and too weighty to be accidental. What separated Saussure from the conventionalist approach of *les philosophes* and Whitney—namely, the emphasis on the arbitrariness and, as its principal consequence, volatility of linguistic conventions—was precisely the point his theory shared with the idea of "progressive education." In a remarkable coincidence of terminology, Saussure and his great-aunt called the phenomenon of idiosyncratic duality in language and in (children's) thought "pure convention" and "pure intelligence," respectively.

Necker de Saussure's "infant" and Saussure's "speaker" can be seen as transmutations of the same fundamental principle—that of cognition as a chain of differentiating steps whose progression is devoid of any guiding principle but differentiation itself. What Saussure discovered was that this phenomenon of ultimate negativity—and by the same token, ultimate freedom—was not limited to a prereflective age, as *L'éducation progressive* had claimed, but was the universal principle of signification by means of signs.

## Progressive Education as a Romantic Concept

The main theme of Necker de Saussure's book, suggested by its title, had little to do with "progressiveness" in the conventional sense. Rather, it referred to "progressivity," a philosophical concept that constituted one of the cornerstones of early Romantic metaphysics.[10] The notion of "progressive education" could be viewed as an extension of early Romantic epistemology into the domain of child development, particularly at its earliest stages. The "progressive" approach, in this Romantic sense, rejected the Enlightenment idea of a priori given predispositions, be they transcendental categories of cognition or universal parameters of child development.

The early Romantic response to Kant put at the core of cognition the free movement of the spirit catalyzed by its dialogical interaction with the world, a movement that neither follows any prescribed pattern nor evolves in a predetermined direction. Necker de Saussure's book carried this principle into the domain of child development. She calls "Stoic" the Enlightenment's ideal of submitting one's self, through reasoning and experience, to the universal dictates of reason, in contradistinction to the Romantic principle of the uniqueness of every individual soul, which she calls "Christian" (1:60). The book takes as the fundamental premise of child psychology and education the ceaseless spontaneous movement of the child's inner world. In this sense, a newborn child shows some of the fundamental features of the early-Romantic cognizing subject, which in fact make it possible to take a close look at those features at the crucial moment of their emergence. According to Necker de Saussure, one can never understand the human soul without acknowledging its mobile nature (1:43);[11] "the character of the spirit is constantly modified," it finds itself "in incessant activity" (1:13). From the moment of his birth, the human being lives in a torrent of ever-changing states of the spirit, whose commotion is "impetuous, blind" (1:103). (These expressions sound very close to how Saussure later conveyed the sense of the unstoppable commotion of language in his notes.)

An educator may have goals that are perfectly reasonable by themselves, but he must be aware that his input falls on the mobile spiritual terrain of a child, whose constant ferment defies any prefigured pattern. There is, and indeed should be, an "accidental" element in education (1:13). It is the fundamental freedom of the human being—rather than deviation from the "natural" ideal—that makes perfection unattainable and our desire for it unquenchable. The road to perfection suggests an ultimate goal toward which we strive again and again, while again and again it "slips away" (*s'élève*) from our efforts (1:57); "to desire more than one can obtain is our destiny" (1:45). Yet without freedom, "if our will were chained," the very striving for perfection would be impossible (1:83).

An important aspect of early Romantic critique of Kantian pure reason consisted in pointing to its distinctly "masculine" character. Friedrich Schlegel personified the rationalist predilection for abstract universal patterns and the isolated, nondialogical nature of the rationalist subject as features of the stereotypical "male" character, which, according to Schlegel, need to be counterbalanced by such stereotypically "female" features as a heightened aesthetic sensitivity and a predisposition for dialogical interaction.[12] Schlegel argued that Kant's over-rationalizing approach was rooted in his lack of any deep understanding of art and his treatment of women as a "deviation" (*Abart*).[13] In a similar vein, he suggested that the Christian idea of God could not be whole unless it were expanded to include a feminine component (the Virgin Mary).[14]

Necker de Saussure's idea of the "education of women" was grounded in this attitude.[15] The early Romantic dialogical duality of the masculine and feminine elements as the embodiment of the dualism of reason and "genius" (i.e., aesthetic and religious sensibility) acquires an additional dimension in Necker de Saussure's work by bringing the world of small children into the picture. In Necker de Saussure's vision, the symbolic figures of a woman and a child stand together in opposition to the relative uniformity and predictability of the "masculine" element, which is more inclined to conform to universal cognitive and behavioral patterns. This makes women and children the first and foremost carriers of the principle of the "progressive," in the Romantic sense of the term. While men of mature age tend to a higher extent to adhere to a uniform mold, the book argues, women never cease evolving (1:60). It is because "women listen when they are spoken to" that their thought, as a consequence, knows "little rest" (1:15). The essentially dialogical nature of the consciousness of the woman and the child allows them to wrest themselves free of the presets of pure reason, with its "Stoic" acceptance of its own limitations for the sake of coherence and universality, and to reach for the mobile, "progressive" Romantic world.

By projecting the central idea of early Romanticism—the incessant motion of the cognizing spirit, whose efforts, due to the representational character of the process, are doomed to remain ever fragmentary and inconclusive—on the world of an infant, whose cognizing efforts are inseparable from acquiring and engaging signs of language, Necker de Saussure's work posited itself as a crucial link, or transition point, between early Romantic semiotics of cognition and Saussure's semiotics of language.

What underlay this intellectual succession was the vision of a "progressive" free-flowing succession of fragmented acts of oppositive signification, arbitrarily related to each other. According to Schlegel and Novalis, this was the only way Kantian pure reason could reckon with that peculiar endowment of humanity—its free will or, to put it in Necker de Saussure's words, its ability to be interested in "alien objects"—to act for action's sake. Like Necker de Saussure's toddler, Saussure's *la langue* could find its cognitive home neither in rationalism nor in empiricism, because adhering to either would mean giving up its most fundamental feature—its unconditional freedom.

Although Necker de Saussure began her close observation of her children's behavior and characters in the 1790s and came up with the principal ideas of her book during the next decade, it took her another twenty years to overcome her perpetual uncertainties and procrastination and bring her work to completion. She struggled with her notes, more than once putting the project aside for years, despite the support and encouragement her friends gave to her project (de Staël suggested that it be entitled, "The Education of the Heart by Life Experience" (*L'éducation du coeur par la vie*); Schlegel exhorted her to move on with it, praising her "intellectual vigor" and "subtlety of observation").[16] The situation bears a curious "family resemblance" to the encouraging efforts of Saussure's friends and disciples concerned with the public fate of his lectures and private notes. When Necker de Saussure spoke—in a transparent allusion to herself—of those burdened with "seeing a thousand faces in every object, which deprives them of "the energetic impulse that would follow some single motive out of many" (2:87), it sounds as if she were addressing her great-nephew directly. Still, she succeeded in pulling her work together despite the debilitating depressions from which she suffered.[17] But her remarkable book, which was in essence a major intellectual document of early Romanticism, appeared in a later historical epoch. Although some theses and observations in *L'éducation progressive* proved to be influential in its immediate field, its philosophical background was lost on its readers. That may be one of the reasons why the book's impact on Saussure's ideas has remained unnoticed in Saussure studies.

Despite the book's great success, its author, late in her life, having experienced many disappointments in her relationship with her own children,[18] expressed doubts about her educational ideas, which she had developed and tried to practice in a more dynamic epoch. As she acknowledged in a letter to her daughter, "a great deficiency of the education that I had given and received consisted in its constant demand for new impressions, distraction, diversity, and a strong fear of boredom. The ideas of developing oneself, of activating one's faculties, of giving one's soul constant nourishment—those were the ideas I was preoccupied with."[19] Whether these words of regret, addressed to a daughter who had turned outright hostile to her, truly reflected her later convictions, is hard to say. In any event, in her book Necker de Saussure did not waver from the idea of progressivity that stemmed from her years of immersion in the spirit of the early Romantic era.

## THE SPEAKER OF *LA LANGUE* AND THE EARLY ROMANTIC SUBJECT: SAUSSURE AND NOVALIS

### Cognition as Semiotic Process: The Interdependence of the "Defined" and the "Defining"

A century prior to Saussure's mid-1890s notes, in which he put at the foundation of theoretical linguistics the incongruous yet indissoluble duality of the sign—whose "spirit" and "matter," on the one hand, are totally independent from each other, yet, on the other, and precisely because of the lack of any external common ground, incapable of existing except in a mutual correlation—Novalis, in an extensive series of fragmentary notes now known as *Fichte-Studien* (1795–96), addressed the epistemological dilemma exemplified by the sign in a strikingly similar fashion. The *Fichte-Studien* offered a powerful critique of the subject-centered epistemological strategy, whose tenor showed intrinsic links to Saussure's critique of the monolithic vision of language.

Novalis's study was triggered by Fichte's repsonse to Kant, which, by carrying out the principle of consciousness-oriented cognition to the utmost, exposed the limitation of that approach. Fichte countered Kant's thesis of the categorically conditioned nature of cognition by asserting the absolute, unconditional character of the subject's awareness of his own "I." Fichte's famous formula "Ich = Ich; Ich bin Ich" made the absoluteness of the subject's identity with himself as the firm ground upon which all cognitive appropriation of the world by the subject can be built.[20]

Novalis's principle objection pointed to the inescapably representational character of all the appropriations of the world by consciousness, including its awareness of itself. According to Novalis, the Fichtean absolute "I," defined in terms of self-equivalence ("Ich bin Ich"), would simply remain inaccessible to itself. Nothing can be perceived from inside without being externalized as an object of perception; to perceive himself, to become aware of his own existence, the subject has to gain an outside perspective from which he can contemplate his own being.

By assuming an external perspective, "I" becomes a representation of itself, a "thing" perceivable from a particular point of view. Paraphrasing Fichte's thesis that the existence of "I" is "unconditional" (*unbedingt*), Novalis declares, with a tinge of irony: "Wir suchen überall das Unbedingte, und finden immer nur Dinge" (We seek the unconditional everywhere, and always find merely things) (*BS*, no. 1). To translate Novalis's aphorism into the terms of Saussurean semiology, it could be said that we are always seeking meaning and are always left with signs. Prior to Saussure's *Course de linguistique générale*, perhaps no other author of modern times showed such an appreciation of the key importance of the fact that the substance of cognition can be reached only through semiotic externalization.

The crucial point that connects Saussure's "general linguistics" with Jena epistemology lies in the essentially representational nature of both the cognizing and the linguistic consciousness. According to Novalis, cognition exists only in and through external projections, as does language as a semiotic phenomenon. It is the semiotic duality of the sign—the fact that it exists only as a reified externalization of itself—that sets it apart from all other phenomena, both material and spiritual. This is what makes language so intractable as the subject of linguistics. Both Novalis and Saussure were able to appreciate the fatal epistemological consequences of the symbiosis of the signifier and signified: namely, that all their duality can offer is an indirect and partial comprehension, made from a contingent point of view and bound to be challenged by the infinite plurality of alternative acts of comprehension made from other points of view.

Novalis was as explicit as Saussure in asserting the inseparability of meaning from its external representation: "We know something only insofar as we express it" (*VF*, no. 267); "Something becomes comprehensible only through representation" (*AB*, 246, no. 49). The signifier breaks the intractable wholeness of the signified phenomenon (its *Beharrlichkeit*) by exposing its heterogeneous constitution (*heterogene Bestandtheilen*) (*FS*, no. 464). By doing so, it becomes a "differential" of the idea. In a statement presaging Saussure's semiotics of differences, Novalis proclaims: "Phenomenal appearances are differentials of ideas" (Novalis 1901:93). By "carving out" a phenomenon, through its representation, from the continuum of the world (the *Weltall*), a sign makes it contingent on its stance vis-à-vis other signs: "An object emerges out of a counterpart, a counterpart out of the object, so that the identity of the object for itself must be determined contrastively. Coexistence and co-determination are one and the same" (*FS*, no. 284).

As if anticipating Saussurean terminology, Novalis avoided the traditional terms *form* and *meaning*, which presented the two poles of the sign as separate. Instead, both authors adopted terms whose close etymological kinship highlighted the inseparable bond between the sign's "spiritual" and "bodily" aspects. The close parallel between Novalis's German terms, *das Bestimmende* ("defining, distinguishing") and *das Bestimmte* ("defined, distinguished") (*FS*, no. 1), and their Saussurean French counterparts, *signifiant* and *signifié*, reflected how similarly they understood the double nature of the sign. The way Novalis emphasizes the interdependence of the "defined" and the "defining" sounds almost like a quotation from Saussure's *Course*: "The subject matter is defined not otherwise than by its defining, its counterpart defines not otherwise than by its defined" (*FS*, no. 291).

Cognition through externalization is a process whose results are of necessity fragmentary and partial. It is impossible to access the world directly; all that can be accessed is an infinite variety of partial visions created by various representations. The fragmented character of signification causes it to evolve "parabolically," by leaps from one instance of cognition to another (*TF*, no. 349). The process essentially lacks any consistent pattern—it is an "inner matter" of the sign, not to be subjugated to or directed by any outward principle.

Novalis's famous *Monologue* is an emphatic declaration of the total freedom of language, grounded in the immanency of the double structure of the sign:

> It is a ridiculous delusion, which causes one to marvel, to think that when one is speaking, one does so for the sake of things. Nobody is aware of the proper nature of language, namely, that it is concerned with nothing but itself.... If only one could make people understand that language is like a mathematical formula. Both constitute a world of their own—they play with nothing but themselves, express nothing but their own wonderful nature, and it is precisely because of this that they are so expressive.... They become a part of nature solely as a result of their freedom, and it is solely through their free movement that the universal soul expresses itself, making them a gentle scale and foundation of things. (Novalis 1981:672)

Novalis's free-flowing discourse (itself a vivid representation of what he strives to convey) could easily be interpreted as mere "Romantic" effusions about the wonders of glossolalia-like irrationalism. Yet seen in the context of Novalis's critique of contemporary theories of the sign and cognition, the

*Monologue* highlights points of crucial importance about the most fundamental nature of language, which foreshadow Saussure's philosophy of language. That seeing language as a tool through which one reaches the phenomena of the world is "a ridiculous delusion" (here, Novalis's *lächerlicher Irrtum* anticipates Saussure's favorite *ridicule*); that it is in fact a free interplay, responsible to and expressing nothing but itself; and that it is precisely this total freedom of language that connects it to nature, making it a "gentle scale and foundation" of things rather than a label attached to them—these points of the *Monologue* contain, in embryonic form, the quintessence of Saussure's teaching about language: its immanent "emptiness" resulting in its unbounded freedom.

## Asymmetry of the Sign: "Linearity" as a Philosophical Concept

One of the points in Saussure's *Course* that provoked much controversy even at the heights of its influence concerned the notion of "linearity." Saussure presented the "linearity of the signifier" as one of the two fundamental (a priori) properties of the sign, on a par with the principle of arbitrariness. Once again, he resorts to a grave admonition to potential addressees who might fail to recognize this "obvious" issue, whose consequences, meanwhile, are "incalculable," without further elaborating on what he actually means by this (*CLG*, 103/70). And once again, as in the case of arbitrariness, this typically Saussurean emphatic yet elliptical assertion gives rise to all kinds of critique based on numerous examples, indeed quite "obvious," that seem to contradict his thesis.

When examined against the empirical data of language, the thesis that linearity is universal seems to run up against a number of instances in which the relations between linguistic units supersede a linear order. Even on a purely phonetic level, the Saussurean pronouncement "c'est une ligne" (*CLG*, 103/70) seems to be an oversimplification. As Jakobson convincingly argued, relying on this principle in accessing the flow of sounds in speech would create a vicious circle: one considers speech to be a succession of sounds because one segments speech into successive sounds (Jakobson and Waugh 1987:22). The phonic texture of speech at large could easily refute the idea of its linearity: in continuous speech, the intonational curve, word stresses, and changes of speech tempo evolve according to rhythms of their own, which overlap with each other and frustrate the linearity of the sound progression (Harris 1987:70). When all the sound dimensions of speech are taken into account, its phonic texture appears to be, at the very least, "multi-linear."[21]

Even more obviously, the linear progression is often broken at the syntactic level, where structural relations between words often supersede their linear order in a phrase. Lucien Tesnière (1959), one of the founders of structural syntax, suggested a distinction between what he called the "structural" and the "linear" syntactic order (*l'ordre structurale* versus *l'ordre linéaire*)— a concept clearly aimed at amending Saussure's thesis. Generative "syntactic rules" departed even further from the idea of a sentence as a sequence of words, overriding not only the linear but even the structural order of "surface" syntactic structures.

Finally, elements of the rhetorical, or "poetic," fabric of a text feature manifold patterns of repetitions and parallelisms that defy the linearity on the textual level (Jakobson 1987). Jakobson (1960) famously defined the "poetic" aspect of language as that in which "the axis of selection" (i.e., paradigmatic copresence) is superimposed upon "the axis of combination." According to Jakobson, nonlinear associative relations between various points in a text rearrange it in multiple ways, complicating, or even frustrating, its linear progression. Moreover, the discovery of Saussure's anagram studies revealed his own awareness of the nonlinear aspect of discourse (Holdcroft 1991:58–60).[22]

Both Saussurean fundamental principles—linearity and arbitrariness—received a very similar treatment in the critical literature. In both cases what Saussure declared to be a transcendental property of language was understood—due in no small part to his elliptical presentation of the issues—as a statement about a certain empirical feature directly observable in linguistic data. Once placed in the empirical domain, however, the concept runs up against copious evidence that contradicts it—evidence so obvious that it seems strange that Saussure could overlook it.[23] The question should be asked, however: when Saussure referred to linearity as to one of the two fundamental properties of the sign, did he really mean by that the rather trivial—and not entirely correct—fact that when we produce speech it emerges piece by piece in a "linear" temporal succession? Here as elsewhere, Saussure's thought should be examined in the context of his general philosophical postulations about language—which he expressed at length and rather eloquently—rather than on the grounds of the cursory definitions and impromptu examples with which he often approached more specific issues in his lectures.

In assessing the issue, one should take heed of the fact that Saussure discussed linearity as a property specifically belonging to the signifier—in contradistinction to arbitrariness that characterized the bipolarity of the sign as a whole.[24] In a letter to Gaston Paris (December 30, 1890) Saussure elaborated on this distinction, stating that linearity, which represents the point of view of "phonetics," is "primordially incompatible" with the point of view of "morphology"; the former has to do with successivity, while the latter has to do with (nonsuccessive) "sense, valeur."[25]

Once again, "phonetics" and "morphology" seem rather poorly chosen terms, capable of obfuscating even further the "primordial" nature of the issue. Here is a point at which Saussure's putative link to Novalis can offer a way out of all the confusion. Thanks to his concentration on the metaphysical rather than specifically linguistic aspects of the sign, Novalis comes to the rescue of Saussure's concept by giving it an unequivocal philosophical dimension that Saussure himself could not or would not articulate.

For Novalis, the indissoluble symbiosis of *das Bestimmende* and *das Bestimmte* is as important as their *asymmetry*. The signified belongs to the spiritual realm. It is not a material "object," which means that it does not occupy a particular physical space. The semantic space allotted to a signified when it is "captured" in a signifier is not its own; to remember Saussure's metaphor, the signified "fills" the signifier the way hydrogen fills a balloon—without the signifier, it would not have any distinct semantic space at all. Contrary to this, *das Bestimmende* belongs to the world of physical objects. It is a "thing"—a thing of a peculiar kind, to be sure, since it comes into existence solely by being connected to something it "defines"; still, with or without this connection, it remains a piece of matter. Like any matter, it is *fragmentary*: it is a piece, a particle that exists alongside many other particles of various sizes and shapes. Spiritual phenomena are not fragmentary: one cannot say that a portion of meaning captured in a sign is a "particle" of spiritual matter. The etherlike spiritual domain knows neither finitude nor any shape of its own. The spiritual realm is ultimately whole, although its ultimate unity is doomed to remain nameless (*AB*, 290, no. 285). It appears to us apportioned into signs, yet any phenomenon of meaning thus apportioned can dissolve into or fuse with any other at any moment. The world of signifiers, on the other hand, is a world of fragments. It is not whole: it exists only as a conglomeration of fragmentary entities; no matter how many signifiers are at hand, they never cease to be fragments. They never "fill up" the whole space of signifying possibilities because, by their very nature as "pieces," they can never attain wholeness.

The credit for recognizing the metaphysical dimensions of Saussure's linearity, which go beyond syntagmatic successivity, belongs to Roy Harris. According to Harris, Saussure's linearity means that the signifier "occupies a certain temporal space (*une étendue*)" (Harris 1987:71); what linearity means in this more abstract sense is that "all human activities in the external world take place in time" (76). Indeed, linearity belongs to the "external world," as opposed to the internal spiritual world of semiotic values. What Harris's explication does not highlight, however, is the constitutional fragmentariness of semiotic activity, brought about by its attachment to the material world with its spatial/temporal dimensions.

The fragmentariness of signifiers constitutes a "primordial" contrast with the world of signified values, which always, under whatever configuration, constitutes a hermetically closed system. It creates a fundamental paradox in *la langue*: on the one hand, it is hermetic, always perfectly self-sufficient, but, on the other, it is perpetually fragmentary and, as a result, ever in a struggle with and under tension over whatever its current state is. Being a "thing" (*das Ding*)—a piece of the matter with which both Novalis's subject and Saussure's speaker try to capture the "unconditional" (*das Unbedingte*)—a signifier always turns out to be a fragment among a multitude of other fragments, in a field that could expand through all eternity without ceasing to be an agglomeration of piecemeal entities. It makes the drive for changes in the realm of signs (what Saussure calls "mutability" and Novalis describes with metaphors of "hunger" or erotic desire) unquenchable and unceasing.

In the spiritual domain, everything can potentially be connected with everything else. There is nothing to prevent thought from running from one idea to any other, from conflating them, transforming them one into another, modifying them into infinite variations in which they brush up against an infinite number of other ideas. Yet the oppositive character of the sign system makes it locked, or "immutable," in mutual oppositions in which the "values" exist literally by clinging to each other. Under these conditions, there seems to be no room to set the system in motion, to unlock its crystalline nodal junctions. Here, however, is where "linearity" comes into the picture. The noncompartmentalizable, ethereal, volatile nature of meaning evolves alongside its apportioning and reapportioning into enclosed semiotic entities. By exposing the inherent fragmentariness of every sign, linearity undermines the seemingly impervious intrasystemic balances on which the whole system rests.

Viewing the system in all its hermetic splendor, one may feel that nothing can be done to sign A because it is correlated with sign B, while nothing can be done to B because of its correlation with A. That would indeed be the case if the signs were devoid of "linearity." However, the nature of signifiers as "things" whose number and configurations are absolutely fortuitous means that the manner in which they divide meaning into signifieds is always provisional and inconclusive. Two signs defined by the mutual difference "A-is-not-B" and "B-is-not-A" never present an airtight opposition. A "breach" will always remain between the two signifiers, leaving room for the signs' proliferation or elastic extension. The semiotic space expands as if ever striving to fill the gap between existing signs; in Novalis's words, "and thus philosophy grows into infinity, outward and inward, while it strives to fill the infinite space between its elementary components" (*LF*, no. 18).

## Form and Substance Revisited

In his notes, Saussure repeatedly speaks about the impossibility of reaching beyond the network of purely oppositive and negative differentiations in which the perpetually elusive essence of language presents itself: "One will never ever penetrate the purely negative, purely *differential* essence of every element of language to which we precipitously accord reality"—albeit, Saussure "has to admit," perhaps we need to adhere to the usage of conventional "fictions" as labels, without which those very differences would be impossible even to point out (*ELG*, 64–65). Saussure's writing moves along with this elusiveness of language, never reaching beyond fragmentary adumbrations of his ideas. In this it recalls the *Athenaeum* strategy of fragmentary writing as the only way to convey the constant motion of the spirit as its cognizing condition. The "truth" about the matter never allows itself to be addressed directly; it is lurking, as it were, in the cracks between fragmentary representations, each manifestly inconclusive because of the very fact of its representational character: "We speak neither of axioms, nor of principles, nor of theses. These are, simply put and in the purely etymological sense, aphorisms, or delimitations . . . yet the ones [indicating] limits between which the truth can always be found, whatever the point of departure" (*ELG*, 123).

It was in 1906, more than a decade after his sketchy linguistic notes and just before he began his lectures, that Saussure made an attempt at reckoning with the "substance" of the problem in his notes on the Rig Veda. There, he spoke about the "ardent preoccupations directed at (making) the object of cognition unequivocally absolute" that drove the thought of the Indian Brahmans. Yet such an object is "absolutely *indifferent* insofar as it is absolute"; no one can declare that he has "grasped" the absolute substance (*qu'on l'a saisie*), since there is "nothing to cognize" in it (Saussure 1993a:218–219). The ideal condition for reaching the absolute would be dreamless sleep;

in this case the subject could be said to have reached an ideal harmony between the world and his *propre moi* precisely by becoming totally oblivious of both (221, 223).

Quite characteristically, Saussure does not fail to plunge into an angry outburst against this unreasonable longing: "It is paradoxical in the highest degree, though, or childish if you prefer, this picture of so ardent a preoccupation directed toward an object that is doubtless absolute but also, insofar as it is absolute, absolutely indifferent. We, adherents of the spirit of the Occident, understand the dilemma: cognize, or, if it is inaccessible, don't try to cognize. None of this is understood in India."[26] For a moment the "Western" spirit emerges in all the rationalist glory of the Kantian critique of cognition, scoffing at "Oriental" irrationality. And yet—"néanmoins, toutes notres distinctions, toute notre terminologie, tout nos façons de parler sont moulées sur cette supposition involontaire d'une substance" (nevertheless, all our distinctions, all our terminology, our whole manner of speaking are molded by that involuntary supposition of a substance).[27]

As it turns out, the principle of the indifference of the substantial absolute does not make "ardent preoccupation" with it futile. The only way to "reach the supreme substance" is to channel it into a plurality of "forms" that are "conditional, diverse, and multiple." Which one of these relative "forms" one chooses is of no importance in itself. Their relation to each other is not hierarchical: they are a company of "neighbors," each related to its absolute "base" in one way or another (Saussure 1993a:220). Whatever choice one makes among those possibilities, it is necessarily an *arbitrary* choice (198). One should abandon attempts to unite all these pluralities into a single rationally founded doctrine: "rien de plus découragement que de chercher une formule rationnelle" (194). The substantial object can be grasped from all the alternative possible systems of its differential representation, with no need to settle on any one of them (196).

We can now see the implications of Saussure's thesis that language is a form and not a substance, that its nature is "oppositive and not positive, absolute," and that there is nothing in language but differences. It would be a profound mistake to take these assertions of the *Course* as professions of an unperturbed relativism (or, otherwise, as a perversion of Saussure's thought perpetrated by the publishers). The connection with early Romantic philosophy of language reveals what stands behind these terse formulations. By endowing it with freedom, the representational nature of language defies any universal order. You can "grasp" language as a whole only by giving up its representational utility—e.g., by assuming a deathlike state of dreamless sleep in which, ironically, you would not be aware of having grasped it. (Novalis presented a grimmer version of the same thought, with which he became increasingly captivated in the last years of his life, namely, that death is the only state in which one can hope to attain the absolute, while Necker de Sassure posited the absolute of nondifferentiation at the opposite pole of the life spectrum—in her vision of a newborn as "the direct creation of God"). As long as one is awake, or alive, one can "grasp" only tangible forms (Novalis's *Dinge*). But, whenever one grasps at a palpable entity, all one ends up with is its relation to another entity. Saussure's thesis, like that of his early Romantic predecessors, is anti-utopian in tenor. In this it stands in marked contrast to the totalizing visions of twentieth-century "Saussurean" linguistics.

# Diachrony and History | FIVE

## TOWARD IMMUTABILITY: CONSTRUCTING THE PAST

### Reconstruction or Construction? The Saussurean Revolution in Comparative Linguistics

The only book Saussure published in his lifetime appeared in 1878 in Leipzig under the title *Mémoire sur le système primitif des voyelles dans les langues indo-européennes*.[1] The book received instant, albeit somewhat controversial recognition. While hailed in the Francophone world as an achievement of revolutionary proportions that in one stroke ended the supremacy of the "Germans," Saussure's *Mémoire* largely displeased his teachers.[2] Karl Brugmann, Saussure's principal mentor—whose two-volume compendium of Indo-European comparative phonetics and morphology (followed by three volumes of comparative syntax by Berthold Delbrück) would eventually become the definitive accomplishment of nineteenth-century comparative linguistics—though praising the author's knowledge, criticized his approach as "speculative," something that went against the grain of the staunch positivism of the Leipzig school.[3]

By the last quarter of the nineteenth century, Indo-European comparative linguistics could claim enormous achievements in describing patterns of similarities and differences between related languages and formulating the ensuing laws of their historical change. Applying those laws in reverse would supposedly allow one to arrive at the state of related languages *avant la lettre,* i.e., at their unrecorded prehistoric past form, all the way back to the proto-language of their common origin. The Leipzig school particularly distinguished itself by the uncompromising strictness of its methods of historical reconstruction—a scientific severity that earned its adepts the nickname of *Junggrammatiker* (by analogy with the "young Turks"). According to the Leipzig doctrine, for a "phonetic law" (i.e., a pattern of phonetic change) to be worthy of the name, it had to be formulated as a universal law that brooked no exceptions, similar to the laws of nature.[4]

Nineteenth-century historical linguistics rejected with scorn all the speculations about the "origin of language" with which the previous century had been so preoccupied. Yet it retained the latter's faith in the existence of some initial point, at least as far as a given family was concerned, from which all the languages in that family had sprung, as from a single stem. This monolithic projection of the protolanguage in turn created an illusion that reconstructing the *Ursprache* in full, as the *ur*-people spoke it, was a task within the reach of a few generations of scholars; linguists liked to compare this process to the reconstruction of prehistoric biological species from scattered fossils. Adolphe Pictet's panoramic depiction of the material and spiritual culture of the "Indo-European people"—an effort Saussure later called, diplomatically, the "best of its kind"—fully reflected this mindset. Saussure was less kindly disposed toward August Schleicher's Indo-European "compendium" (1866)—overall, a significant advance upon Bopp's—which gained notoriety for the "Indo-European fable" "The Sheep and the Horses" ("Avis akvâsas ka"), whose reconstruction—complete with vocabulary, grammar, metrics, and *ur*-plot—Schleicher placed at the beginning of the book as concrete evidence of how close science had ostensibly come to the full reconstruction of a language spoken by the "Indo-Germanic" people ten to twelve millennia ago.

By the 1870s the spectacular successes achieved by comparative studies mostly applied to the reconstruction of IE consonants. The task of reconstructing proto-IE vowels and tracing their subsequent development in various languages proved more challenging. The principal difficulty was posed by the so-called Indo-European ablaut or vowel alternations in different forms of the same stem. Such alternations could be either qualitative (involving different vowels) or quantitative (involving different vowel lengths): Eng. *bear / bore / birth,* Rus. *ber-u* "I take" / *br-at'* "to take" / *so-*

*bir-at'* "to pick" / *s-bor* "collection, gathering," Germ. *Geburt* "birth" / *gebären* "to be born" / *gebar* "born" / *geboren* "have been born", etc. In order to explain the manifold overlaps between the ablaut patterns in different IE languages, one needed to project into the past an ever-increasing number of distinctions that could account for later splits. By the time Saussure addressed the problem, the tentatively reconstructed system of Indo-European vowels had grown to eleven or twelve phonemes: long and short [*a*], [*o*], [*e*], [*i*], and [*u*], plus either a single reduced vowel (*schwa indogermanicum*) or two distinct versions thereof. And yet a convincing common denominator for ensuing vowel alternations remained elusive.

Saussure's book overturned the conventional approach to the problem. Instead of starting with vowel alternations in particular languages, trying to reach back from the observable data to a protostate, he took the *Ursprache* itself as the deductively postulated starting point, a system that followed its own intrinsic logic (Béguelin 2003:152). Instead of *reconstructing* the protolanguage by trying to piece together its "fossils," Saussure *constructed* it by a leap of visionary intuition, then projecting the construct onto the diverse available data. While the inductive reconstruction of the protolanguage, in its effort to accommodate all observed divergences, experienced an implacable growth in the complexity of the picture, the Saussurean deductive construction resulted in dramatic structural simplification. (It is worth mentioning as a curious footnote that, for all the difference in knowledge and sophistication, the reduction Saussure thus achieved was not dissimilar to what he had aspired to, with extreme naïveté, in his adolescent treatise on the possibility of "reducing" the entire vocabulary of all languages to a few abstract root schemes.)[5]

Saussure's deduction took as its starting point the generally accepted postulate according to which vowel alternations had emerged as a result of positional changes effected in a stem vowel by the sounds that preceded or followed it. Yet no observable positional conditions could hitherto be found to explain the varied qualitative and quantitative modifications of the principle vowels. Saussure resolved the issue by putting forth the hypothesis that the original sound system of the proto-language must have featured a sound entity (or two different entities) that had disappeared so early as not to leave any trace in any of the known Indo-European languages, old and new. The original presence of those entities, however, could be deduced from the impact they had left on adjacent vowels—an impact that manifested itself in the ablaut. Since the postulated sounds were nowhere to be seen empirically, little could be said of their actual phonetic character—

their phonetic "substance," to use Saussure's later terminology. One could not even determine whether they were vowels or consonants. To emphasize the purely systemic (nonsubstantial) character of his findings, Saussure called the deduced entities "sonic coefficients."

The postulation of sonic coefficients instantly made a complex set of protovowels superfluous. According to Saussure, the protolanguage must have had just one original vowel—an indifferent vocalic element necessary to fill out the syllable. The whole system of vowels and their alternations developed out of interactions between that core protovowel and the preceding or following sonic coefficients, whose impact remained after they disappeared, leaving a seemingly inscrutable maze of alternations in their wake. Depending on which of the two coefficients stood next to it, the protovowel turned out either nonrounded (later to be split into an [a] and an [e]) or rounded (later evolved into an [o]). If a coefficient preceded a vowel, the vowel remained short; if it followed a vowel, its loss resulted in the vowel's compensatory lengthening. The vowels long and short [i] and [u] emerged at the next step of positional changes, after the sonants [l], [r], [n], and [m] lost their original ability to function as carriers of a syllable, developing into the combinations [ir], [ur], [in], [un], etc. as a result.

Like some other works of art, science, and philosophy of the late nineteenth and early twentieth century, Saussure's reconstruction undercut the most fundamental premises of positivist thinking. Its underlying logic was akin to that of Freud and Einstein, Schoenberg and Malevich. With a single leap, its transcendent vision penetrated the experiential surface of things, instantly reshaping it according to a new order.

Although Saussure's admirers and detractors alike acknowledged his supreme command of the data and the power of his logical inference, during his lifetime his work remained more an intellectual tour de force than a substantial step in the steady progress of Indo-European studies. When Antoine Meillet published his *Introduction to the Comparative Grammar of Indo-European Languages* (1903), perhaps the best comprehensive account of the subject ever written, he dedicated it to the twenty-fifth anniversary of the publication of his teacher's *Mémoire*. Yet in his account of the original set of vowels, Meillet largely followed the eleven-vowel model of the Leipzig school. Throughout his life, Saussure was dismayed by the fact that his only book—despite its acknowledged brilliance—failed to affect the mainstream of comparative studies in any tangible way.

In a poignant twist of events, the situation changed dramatically almost immediately after Saussure's death. In 1915 the Czech archeologist

Bedřich Hrozný succeeded in deciphering the cuneiform writing of Hittite, a language from Southern Anatolia that proved to be the oldest of all the known members of the Indo-European family. It didn't take long for linguists to spot in the stems of Hittite words the prominent presence of two sounds, each marked by a distinct written character, that consistently corresponded to "zero" in all other IE languages. The distinguished Polish Indo-Europeanist Jerzy Kuryłowicz was the first to suggest, in the late 1920s, that those two unique Hittite sounds were in fact the extinct "sonic coefficients" whose original existence Saussure had predicted half a century earlier. The positions the sounds occupied vis-à-vis vowels corresponded almost precisely to the pattern according to which Saussure had explained the subsequent vowel alternations: when they followed a vowel, the vowel would become long, while if they preceded a vowel, the vowel remained short. Now the approximate phonetic quality of the hitherto unknown sounds could be determined, chiefly from their appearances in proper names in bilingual Hittite-Accadian documents. As it turned out, they were guttural consonants, or "laryngeals," the name by which they have been universally known since the 1920s.[6] Later, the data from Hittite was augmented by sporadic evidence from a few closely related languages, which eventually allowed the establishment of a whole hitherto unknown "Anatolian" branch of the Indo-European family. The comprehensive Anatolian data suggested the expansion of the laryngeal set to three items, a development that in fact better accounted for the ternary vowel split *a—e—o* out of the original generic vocalic element.

Ironically, what had begun as a typically modernist visionary breakthrough became solid empirical knowledge, the cornerstone of twentieth-century Indo-European studies. Needless to say, new problems soon arose, leading to various hypotheses about the original state of the system of the laryngeals that could account for certain irregularities in their impact on vowels. These later developments, however, are irrelevant to our discussion of the intellectual premises that stood behind Saussure's reconstruction.

First, and quite obviously, Saussure approached Indo-European vowels not as a set of separate entities but as a *system* whose members are defined by their mutual relations. Conventional comparative studies focused on the reconstruction of separate entities by means of comparative analysis, without worrying about the overall shape or plausibility of the whole assemblage of individual reconstructions. Saussure, on the contrary, is interested not in the proto-entities as such but in their systemic relations. The ultimate manifestation of this approach can be seen in the deduction of the sonic coefficients on purely inferential grounds, without any attempt to flesh them out as phonetic units.

Second, by constructing a certain systemic state of the past, the Saussurean approach in fact abandoned history. The reconstruction emerges as a hermetic state resting on a balance of mutual relations between sounds, whose description presupposes no continual movement in time. All that can happen to this oppositional system is its wholesale transformation into a new systemic state. By shifting attention to systemic balances between elements and away from the movement of those elements in time, Saussure's early work implicitly took the approach that would later be explicitly formulated in the *Course*.

The least obvious yet perhaps most important methodological consequence that could be drawn from the *Mémoire* was that Saussure's reconstruction negated the idea of the Indo-European *Ursprache* as an actual original language from which the various Indo-European languages evolved. By exempting the constructed picture from continuity in time, Saussure undermined faith in the *Ursprache* as a palpable reality of the past. In later Saussurean terms his construction was concerned with the "form" of a prehistoric language and not with its "substance" as an actual linguistic phenomenon. That the title of his book omitted the usual reference to the "Indo-European language," declaring its subject to be instead "the primal system of Indo-European vowels," was not an oversight. Saussure was not interested in the hypothetical language ostensibly spoken by "Indo-European people," whoever they may have been, some millennia ago.

The substance of the *Ursprache* literally disappears under the conditions of Saussure's construction. What remained was the bare systemic necessity: an indifferent vocalic base and the differentiating vocalic coefficients. Saussure's "primal system of vowels" emerges as an a priori postulation stripped of any substantial features. It would be futile to ask when and where a language thus constructed may have existed, who its speakers were, whether any *ur*-dialects of it existed, and so forth—in short, to pose the questions that preoccupied comparatists throughout the nineteenth century. Saussure's book played a pivotal role in the development of a more cautious and abstract attitude in comparative studies, an attitude that has become prevalent in the twentieth century, when hunting for the *Ursprache* and its speakers gave way to the sober realization that all that could ever be achieved was to place the relations between kindred languages into a coherent model.

## Two Faces of Immutability: Synchrony and Diachrony

The picture offered by the *Mémoire* in fact reflected what Saussure would later call the principle of immutability. It was a picture of an unperturbed stability, grounded in the balance of intrasystemic oppositions. A systemic model of this kind could be constructed for any point on the temporal axis: for any modern language or any interim stage in language history.

The guiding principle implicit in the *Mémoire* received a resolute codification in Saussure's lectures (particularly in the third course) and, eventually, in the posthumous book. It was formulated there as a strict division between "synchrony" and "diachrony." Synchrony envisioned language as an immutable state, as it is perceived by speakers when they use it, while diachrony was supposed to register the succession of such states that emerges as a language moves from one point in time to another. The *Course* left no doubt that the priority, even preponderance in this opposition, should be given to synchrony, since it reflected the way language is perceived by speakers, while diachrony views language as if from the outside. This shift of priorities revolutionized a discipline that for over a century had been entirely preoccupied with issues of history, while treating nonhistorical descriptions of language as a textbook triviality.[7] The subsequent development of twentieth-century linguistics, in which atemporal model building took decisive precedence over historical studies, derives, to a large extent, from this thesis in the *Course*. Consequently, the *Course* has received the lion's share of either praise or blame for the fact that, in sharp contrast to the staunch historicism of the nineteenth century, in modern linguistics it is historical studies of language that find themselves in a marginal and theoretically subservient position.

Yet as far as the *Course* itself is concerned, its division of linguistics along the axes of synchrony and diachrony did more than merely marginalize history. It would be more precise to say that the opposition between synchrony and diachrony did not involve the history of language at all. Because of the systemic character of synchrony, it could not evolve incrementally. In a system built on mutual balances, Saussure repeatedly emphasized, every single instance of change yields a new state of the system as a whole (*ELG*, 267/191; see also *CLG*, 122/85). As a result, the movement of a language along the axis of diachrony could be perceived only as a series of shifts from one distinct systemic state to another. Thus defined, diachrony appears to be totally derivative from synchrony, amounting in fact to nothing more than a succession of synchronic states. The opposition between "synchronic linguistics" and "diachronic linguistics" turns out to be no opposition at all. Both approach language from the same perspective—that of immutability.

Saussure's famous comparison of language to a chess game is symptomatic in this regard. Saussure was obviously fond of this metaphor: it appears more than once in the *Course*, as well as in his notes, to illustrate the principle of arbitrariness and the ensuing immutability that lays the foundation for the synchronic approach to language. Every single move on the chess board, Saussure points out, creates a qualitatively new position; it is not just the position of one figure on the board that has been changed but the state of the game as a whole. The progress of the game can be described as a succession of synchronic positions, each emerging after a single move. Moreover, when players appraise a given position, how it was achieved is irrelevant. Each shift of the balance on the board, effected by a single move, emerges as an absolute actuality for the given "synchronic" moment, only to be pushed into oblivion by the next move, which produces yet another synchronic actuality.

This seemingly elucidating comparison, cited innumerable times thereafter, has become a veritable emblem of the mind-set predominant in modern linguistics. Yet, upon closer examination, its heuristic value turns out to be extremely problematic. True, the values of chess pieces, like those of linguistic signs, are arbitrary; it would be "absurd," Saussure remarks with characteristic scorn, to suppose that the chess queen, knight, or king exist as phenomena in their own right, outside the game (*ELG*, 67/43). But these are "on the record" values, firmly established as codified rules of the game. Arbitrary as they are, once established, the parameters of the game function as distinct entities, each characterized by stable features of its own; the way the knight moves depends neither on the way other figures do nor on its position on the board.

It is not difficult to see how profoundly different the situation on the chess board is from that of language, whose fundamental feature, Saussure passionately asserted again and again, is that its conventionality is an empty, or "pure," convention, "truly disengaged from all concrete facts" (*ELG*, 76/43). By the same token, arbitrariness makes language vulnerable to any challenge, even pure accident, precisely because its current state can find no support either in logical order or in worldly experience: "A language is radically powerless to defend itself against the factors that every moment displace the rapport between the signified and signifier. This is one of the consequences of the arbitrariness of the sign" (*CLG*, 110/76). To access the systemic condition of language as a pure form, one needs to perceive it synchronically; yet synchrony turns out to be unsustainable, precisely because of the character of language as pure form.

The "synchrony" of a position in a chess game is a "solid" phenomenon. Once it is achieved, it can be recorded, contemplated in isolation, and compared with other, equally stable, positions. This is what in fact happens during a chess game, whereby the players are at liberty to assess the current position before moving to a new one. A chess game is *sequential*, not historical. But with language, as with any truly historical phenomenon, the fundamental condition of its existence in time is fluidity. The evolution of such a phenomenon proceeds as an elemental flow wherein, first, it is impossible to say how many "moves" occur simultaneously and, second, there is no respite between the "moves" that would make it possible to perceive their causes and effects. History, including the history of language, can be narrated as a sequence of episodes. But its apportioning into discrete episodes amounts to nothing more than an arbitrary convention of description that does not reflect the movement as such. If one needed a metaphor for language drawn from the domain of games, a more fitting one could be soccer, because of the game's fluidity: no matter how many snapshots of synchronic moments in the game one took, one could never capture the unceasing and manifold movement of players in the field.

In a note Saussure described "one Russian original named Boguslavsky" who took a photo of himself every month, in exactly the same posture, over the course of twenty years, eventually amassing 480 snapshots. Whereas the differences between any two successive photos were virtually imperceptible, the overall development was significant; yet it was "the same Boguslavsky" in all 480 photos (*ELG*, 156/104). This example illustrates Saussure's point about the speaker's inability to register the movement of language while he is continually using it. Turning the history of "the same Boguslavsky" into a series of snapshots that can be contemplated and compared with each other, while allowing the results of evolution to register, leaves out the element of Bergsonian "duration," i.e., the uninterrupted continuity of the evolutionary process.

In the first half of the twentieth century, structural linguistics, inspired to a large extent by the dazzling success of the *Mémoire*'s reconstruction, but even more by its own reading of the *Course* as a manifesto of systemic determinism, embraced the pseudoduality of synchrony and diachrony by redefining historical linguistics as "structural diachrony."[8] Post-Saussurean structural diachrony simply declared that diachrony *is* history. From this perspective, language development could be viewed as a series of intrasystemic shifts driven primarily by pressures and contradictions within the system rather than by "extralinguistic" accidents of usage.[9] Structural diachrony achieved spectacular success in discovering new patterns of change in various languages and making previously discovered ones more effective by placing them within a comprehensive framework of the system as a whole.[10]

Presenting *la langue* as either a synchronic state or a diachronic chain of states turned it into a "solid" object—a system that could be observed and described as a self-sufficient and stable entity. While seemingly accepting Sassure's central thesis about the intrasystemic and oppositive nature of language, Saussurean linguistics turned that very thesis into a substance of a new kind—the substance of the systemic construct, as solid and self-sufficient as ever.

## TOWARD MUTABILITY: DURATION

### The Phantom of Historical Laws

It can be said without exaggeration that the vision of language in continual motion in time and space stood at the core of Saussure's intuition about language during the last two decades of his life. In his notes the throbbing dynamism and unfettered freedom of language development came to the fore with such force that they threatened to render the systemic construct barren.

The shift from the impeccably "immutable" construction in the *Mémoire* to the passionate exploration of the dynamic side of language may have been triggered by Saussure's trip to Lithuania in 1889. The trip bore all the signs of a major scholarly success: Saussure's field studies resulted in the formulation of another spectacular phonetic "law," which now bears his name: a rule of stress recession, contingent on the tonal (ascending versus descending) character of stress, in Baltic languages that has become the cornerstone of twentieth-century Balto-Slavic accentology. Yet Saussure was not blinded by the pattern he discovered, for all its apparent explanatory power. It was Meillet's enthusiastic reaction to Saussure's paper on the subject (Saussure 1922a [1894]) that triggered the latter's famous letter of January 1894, in which, starting from the precariousness of his argument about Lithuanian accentuation, Saussure went on to question the fundamental premises of linguistics.

Saussure's notes of that time show him overwhelmed in the face of methodological problems whose complexity he has now come to appreciate in full. A crucial dimension of this complexity lay in the relentless and untamed character of language change. In a pointed rebuke to the Leipzig school's emphasis on historical "laws," Saussure notes that a language is "composed of *facts* and not *laws*" (*ELG*, 149/98; Saussure's emphasis). The movement of language in time is open to all kinds of "accidents," i.e., unpredictable, haphazard moves that defy any coherent evolutionary pattern.

Saussure was not alone at this time in his critique of nineteenth-century comparative grammar, with its belief in the absolute validity of the patterns of change it discovered and its own ensuing reconstructions. A vocal challenge to the convictions of the previous epoch, epitomized in works of the Neogrammarians and their followers, was raised by Hugo Schuchardt (1885). Schuhardt emphasized the pivotal importance of interlingual "crossings," which interfere with orderly patterns of change, confusing the whole picture. Saussure expressed a similar view when he remarked that diverse languages can acquire a common feature that was not inherited (*CLG*, 315/228).[11]

What distinguished Saussure's critique was its philosophical and methodological bent. For him, the matter goes beyond the empirical fallacy of certain claims. At stake is the essential nature of language and, consequently, the fundamental character of the methods of inquiry by which language can be approached.

The inadequacy of evolutionary law is not merely a result of the multiplicity of the factors that may affect language's development. Stable laws are impossible, as a matter of principle, because of the uninterrupted duration of an evolution that never stops to allow itself to be captured in an orderly picture. The similarity between Saussure's idea of the "grand duration" (as he called it) underlying the process of the transmission of symbols, and Bergson's *durée*, which became extremely popular just as Saussure was taking his notes, is remarkable.[12]

The vision of history that emerged from Saussure's notes does not resemble in the least the "diachronic" movement of figures on a chess board from one position to the next: "There exists no example of an absolute immobility. What is absolute is the principle of the movement of language in time" (*ELG*, 311/218); a sign is "never the same twice" (203/140); language is a phenomenon of "absolute continuity: an interruption is inconceivable" (179/121); its flow is indeed never interrupted, "not even for 24 hours" (202/140).[13]

The same principle of uninterrupted continuity applies to the way language spreads and diversifies through space. As Saussure mentioned in his notes, he first came upon the question in his inaugural lecture in Geneva in 1891, in which he depicted linguistic space as a plethora of diverse overlapping features rather than an assemblage of compact dialects (*ELG*, 171/114–115).[14] It is in this sense that the notes call the spread of the "linguistic mass" through space "fatal" (318/224–225). Diversification in space is just as protean as change across time (313/220).

The history of language, Saussure asserts, is "blind";[15] "isolated" instances of change occur with every act of language use, without speakers' being aware of it (*ELG*, 231/163). Language goes through a succession of changes as if climbing a ladder, each rung of which disappears as it steps onto the next one (*ELG*, 190/130). Language is a constellation of accidents, not an "organic" unity: "All that *seems organic* in a language is *in reality contingent* and completely *accidental*" (149/98; Saussure's emphasis); Schleicher did a "violence" to language when he considered it an organism (*CLG*, 317/229). With a defiant paradoxalism reminiscent of Schlegel's aphorisms, Saussure declared: "The life of language is made up of . . . mishaps" ("La vie de la langue est faite de méprises") (*ELG*, 185/127).

Such a state of things has catastrophic consequences for historical reconstruction, whose ultimate limits Saussure outlines with merciless clarity. The progress of language is not totally devoid of logically explainable regularities, but all such regularities have only a local value—they are "semi-analyses," as Saussure puts it, that can be undone by any "accident." Even if a certain feature seems to work consistently, that very consistency is no more than an accident (*CLG*, 313/227).[16] Language "is a robe whose fabric is covered with patches of its own fabric," Saussure tells his students (*CLG*, 235/170).

A rule of change is no more than a codification of one such patch of regularity. It is a tentative "formula" framed by an observer to capture an arbitrarily chosen instance in a continual process—the one to which this formula is applicable. To believe in its ontological value is to suffer from an illusion (Saussure 1993a:223). If, for instance, one speaks of "ablaut," this is nothing but a figure of speech; meanwhile, people "prescribe" this phantom of their own descriptive vocabulary as if they were in possession of "all the truths" (*ELG*, 234/165).

This last reference to ablaut sounds particularly poignant. It refers to Saussure's own reconstruction of the origins of the Indo-European ablaut, which brought him early fame. Saussure the Indo-European linguist continued to feel anxious and frustrated at the lack of recognition his early work received; he died just two years before his "speculative" hypothesis achieved a dazzling vindication. Yet Saussure the philosopher of language characterizes his achievement as being no more than an ingenious "figure of speech" that gave an orderly "formula" to what was, in the end, nothing but a stream of coincidences.

The most obvious victim of this critique is diachrony or, rather, its claim to represent the history of language. The existential condition of language is total continuity: "*Tout* dans la langue *est histoire*" (*ELG*, 149/98).

However, in a more far-reaching consequence, a full recognition of the principle of continual motion profoundly undermines synchrony as well. If "the stream of language flows without interruption," what breathing space does it allow for any synchronous state to emerge from that "stream"? The different answers Saussure gives to this question at various times betray his frustration with the issue. At one point he mentions a "generation" of speakers for whom language remains stable, while the next generation finds itself at a different synchronic plateau. At another point he concedes that language could not be sustained even "for twenty-four hours"; at yet another he proclaims that a synchronic state "is never anything but momentary" (*CLG*, 126/88). As the logical end of this relentless shrinking of the time span allotted to synchrony stands Saussure's acknowledgment that it cannot have any time span at all: in the "ocean of differences, of characterizations, of features" that is language, "not for a single moment" does anything surface that could be taken as a solid state. Synchrony is not self-sufficient; it should in fact be called "idiosynchrony" (*ELG*, 104/69).

## Accidents and Coincidences: The Transmission of Collective Memory

Perhaps as a consequence of his debilitating findings, by the 1900s Saussure seemed to have lost interest in linguistic studies. During the last fifteen years of Saussure's life, the share linguistics occupied in his private studies was meager. By the time of his lecture courses, his intellectual interests lay elsewhere.

One of the targets of Saussure's attention in the 1900s was Germanic legends. His interest in the subject dated back to his early years in Leipzig and Berlin; at that time, disappointed by the reception of the *Mémoire*, he had even thought of abandoning linguistics altogether, making Germanic epic studies his principal occupation (De Mauro 1967a:296). This subject continued to interest him later in Geneva, where Saussure occasionally taught it alongside his core courses in Sanskrit and Indo-European linguistics.

Saussure's involvement with the subject had a "familial" aspect. As mentioned earlier, the roots of the Saussure family were in Lotharingy, from which they immigrated to Geneva during the religious wars of the sixteenth century. The political turmoil that caused the migration of Saussure's ancestors "rhymed" (to use a Saussurean term) with events in the sixth century—another time of political and religious troubles in what was then the kingdom of Burgundy—that forced one strain of its population to move to the Helvetic area. The Germanic language of those earliest migrants—in Saussure's guess, a close relation to Gothic—left traces in a number of toponyms in Suisse Romande and Savoy. In a lecture presented in September 1904 at the Société d'histoire et d'archéologie de Genève, "Les Burgondes et la langue burgonde en pays romain" (Saussure 1922b), Saussure argued that certain toponyms of the Vaudois area contained clues to historical events and figures of the kingdom of Burgundy that—in a transformed shape—had also left their traces in the Nibelung legends.[17] Having started from microtoponyms of his immediate surroundings, Saussure's etymological inquiries led him to a daring hypothesis about Burgundy as a pan-Germanic playground of legendary motifs that made the kingdom and its fate the prototypical scene of the Nibelung epos. In view of its historical prototype, the legend of the Nibelung, Saussure asserted, could be called the "Légende Bourgogne" (Saussure 2003a:381).

The lecture reflected the extensive private studies of the subject in which Saussure was involved through the greater part of the 1900s. His two principal focuses were the history of the Nibelung epos and the Tristan legend in its relation to the Theseus myth. Most importantly, Saussure's notes on the subject contained far-reaching theoretical ideas about the way in which memories of the past are transmitted through time and space. These ideas take up Saussure's earlier interest in the dynamics of the history of language and continue them on a larger scale.

The discipline to which Saussure's inquiry belonged, known as comparative mythology, became popular in the second half of the nineteenth century. Inspired by comparative grammar, it strove, by observing numerous parallels in mythological narratives from various nations and epochs, to reconstruct the prototypical "master plot" or plots in the same way that comparative studies of Indo-European languages were aimed at reconstructing their common linguistic forerunner. By sorting out the similarities and differences between diverse versions of a narrative, one hoped to restore not only its original state but the historical past out of which it had sprung into life.

At face value, Saussure's methods of comparing epic narratives looked similar to those employed by Max Müller (1881) or Alexander Veselovsky (1896), to name just a few. He observes parallels, identifies migrations of common narrative details, and examines the emerging patterns against known historical events. Having traced numerous motifs in the Nibelung epos pointing to events in the kingdom of Burgundy, at one point he exclaims in excitement: "All the life of the little kingdom of Burgundy circa 435, whose very existence is otherwise barely acknowledged save two mentions in chronicles, is here right before our eyes, and moreover in an incomparable profusion of details!" (Saussure 2003a:362). Yet the theoretical conclusions Saussure drew from his study not only challenged the common beliefs of the discipline but could be seen as a radical reformulation of the methodological premises of historical inquiry in general.

For Saussure, the innumerable reappearances of common or related motifs in various guises and different combinations testified not to an original state from which they had presumably branched out but, on the contrary, to the random character of their wanderings through time and space. To depict this process as a coherent history of a narrative, from its putative original form to distinct later versions, would mean, in his opinion, to give oneself over to a self-serving illusion. Situations, motifs, or splinters thereof diverge and converge, split and reassemble in transient associations, producing constellations whose infinite variety defies either a common denominator or any coherent path of development. Even as one registers and collects the spots of commonality, one has "zero ability to judge their comparative value" (Saussure 2003a:427).

Saussure does subscribe to the idea that at the beginning of a legend there usually stood a historical event or events, some of which were registered in contemporary chronicles. But he refuses to take such an event as the *ur*-story to which a legend can be traced back. Between an event and its representation in memory as reflected in a legend, an unaccountable gap always remains. This happens because, from the very first moment, the perception of the event proceeds as *differentiation*. Differentiation is an inalienable aspect of perception; one simply cannot perceive something except as a "difference (and difference of another difference)" (Saussure 2003b:334).

The legend departs from the events that inspired it through a continuum of differences whose nature and direction can be neither logically explained nor predicted; "the sum of modifications is not calculable" (Saussure 2003a:368). Diverse historical facts (or, rather, their presence, already differential, in memories) are arranged in a certain fashion in a legend; but that there was a definitive, consciously shaped story at the beginning—"that I will never believe." From the very moment a story based on some remembered events emerges, there are "a hundred forces at play to thwart (*empechêr*) what is perceived in the popular memory as an account of facts that conforms to reality" (374). The plot of a legend lacks, and has always lacked, any coherent substantial content; the story has been patched together: the "absence of unity of composition in epic narrative" is constitutional (375–76). "The base of all marvelous stories . . . is a suite of episodes, accountable to neither any general moral tendency (*moralité*) nor even to any coherence outside the sequence of actions in the story itself" (421).

There is no guarantee that the legend, as it evolves through unceasing moves of differentiation, will not absorb some extraneous detail, however alien to or insignificant in an earlier scheme of events. The possibility of such accidents defies any hierarchy of motifs with regard to their greater or lesser significance for a legend's "core": "it is a mistake to believe that it would be possible to any degree to learn which of its features were essential by comparing different versions of a story" (Saussure 2003a:368). The story of Orion inspired someone to see a certain constellation as a representation of that mythological figure; here it was, Orion the hunter, with his belt and his bow, outlined by a certain group of stars that received the name of the "constellation of Orion." It was also noticed that a nearby group of stars recalled the shape of a dog, so it was called the Dog (Canis Major). The proximity of the two constellations had nothing to do with the story of Orion as such; however, the association that arose from their positions in the sky inspired the motif of "Orion's dog," which was then co-opted into some versions of the Orion legend (382).

Any motif in a legend—be it the name of a character or place, a certain situation or a component thereof, of whatever significance—can become affixed to or substituted for something else. Suppose, Saussure remarks, referring to various legendary accounts of the early medieval kingdom of Burgundy, there is a "king X" who has three sons, Gunther, Gêernôt, and Gîselher, as well as a cousin Hagen; in another version, Hagen displaces Gîselher as one of the sons; in yet another, he is given the story allotted elsewhere to Gunther (Saussure 2003a:289). (It may be that Saussure chose this example because of his awareness of a further transformation of this motif in Wagner's *Götterdämmerung*, wherein Hagen appears as the half-brother of Gunther). In another typical figure of transformation, names are interchanged due to a paronomastic connection between them (Saussure 2003a:400).[18] Occasionally, a whole story is "invaded" by another legend;

according to Saussure, this was the way the Theseus myth became incorporated in the legend of Tristan (2003a:392).

At one point, Saussure makes the comment that attributing a consistent narrative to the history of a legend is "the remarkable error of those who occupy themselves with signs" ("c'est là l'erreur remarquable de ceux qui s'occupent des signes"; 387). This is itself a "remarkable" statement, coming from the author who proclaimed, with such intellectual force, that language is nothing but a system of signs. What Saussure apparently meant here was the "nomenclaturist" notion of the sign whose meaning is stably attached to its form. In a considerable departure from his usual terminology, on this occasion Saussure uses the term *symbol* as the counterpart to this false idea of the sign: "The identity of a symbol can never be fixed even for a moment insofar as it remains a symbol, that is to say, is plunged into the social mass that determines its value at every moment.... No symbol exists except by being launched into circulation" (367). A story floats in the volatile human "mass" like a bottle flung into the sea.

Once again, as earlier in his notes on language, Saussure arrives at the idea of historical reconstructions as "formulas"—at best, conventions of scholarship; at worst, self-serving illusions. An "epic arrangement," i.e., the original *ur*-plot that a modern observer seeks to (re)construct as the origin of a legend, "is nothing but a phantom obtained by combining two or three ideas.... One should tell oneself that it is nothing but a formula, which we attach to an assemblage [of motifs] achieved for a moment" (387).

In the end, Saussure argues, there is nothing but the process of transmission. The process evolves through the incessant accidental convergences and divergences of the scattered fragments retained by memory. According to Saussure, this is the only way that collective memories can be transmitted through the vicissitudes of time and space by iterative collective efforts. Instead of seeking a rational resolution to these accidental formations, one has to accept history as a pool of free-flowing details that have been repeatedly patched together in different ways in the effort to maintain the continuity of recollection somehow or other. The "final object" of a historical reconstruction should be not a "solid" product but a flow of evolving "coincidences": "We cannot work under any other principle but that of coincidences," Saussure asserts (294). He concedes that the principle of coincidences may look irrational; but in the end this is the predicament of cognition in general. All anyone, whether astronomer, historian, or student of myths, can do is to examine coincidences, taking them for "no less and no more than they are." Scholars have to be aware that those coincidences, patterns, and echoes are "not their means but their ultimate object" ("ce n'est pa là leur moyen, c'est leur objet final"; 294).

## A WORLD IN TRANSITION: SAUSSURE AND FRIEDRICH SCHLEGEL

An anecdotal story tells how, upon being introduced to Fichte, the young Schlegel launched into an enthusiastic monologue about the possibility of projecting Fichte's metaphysics onto a historical axis; to which Fichte replied that he would rather count beans than muse about history.[19] According to Schlegel, Fichte's atemporal, a priori postulated self claims "the infallible power to open and close heaven and hell with his key," a position of supreme isolation that leaves him unperturbed by the historical relativity of cognition (*PhL*, 2, no. 5). Schlegel and Novalis responded by "Romanticizing" or "potentializing" this vision of the world, which meant setting it into historical motion. As Schegel put it, "nature is not something grown up but growing" (*PhL*, 152, no. 344). Grand metaphysical systems resting on a priori postulates are unable to meet the challenge of the historically dynamic nature of the universe.

In its vision of history as a continual flow knowing neither beginning nor end, the small Jena circle of the second half of the 1790s occupied a precarious position between two major teleologically oriented epochs in the history of thought: the eighteenth-century Enlightenment, with its ideal of the "natural" original state, and the nineteenth and early twentieth century, with its utopian vision of universal synthesis in the future. As if responding to both temptations, Schlegel declares: "Alle Historie nur interimistisch" (The whole of history is intermediary; *PhL*, 257, no. 765); like epic, history begins in medias res (*AF*, no. 84). Both future and past, Schlegel asserts, exist only as fragmentary sketches. It is essentially the same task to reconstruct the past out of the fragmentary glimpses that remain in memory as it is to construct the future out of the hints or "sketches" of it that can be detected in the present. In a remarkable instance of his witty paradoxalism, Schlegel proclaims that the historian could be called a "retrospective prophet."[20]

We have seen how far Saussure went, particularly in his later years, in understanding the process of historical development as a stream of coincidences. One might be tempted to call the radicalism of Saussure's position "unprecedented," if not for the presence of a very clear precedent in Schlegel. An unwavering allegiance to the idea of the chaotic, accidental, volatile mode in which signifieds and signifiers "seek" each other along the historical path was a veritable trademark of Schlegel's thought.

Schlegel sees history as a continuum of coincidences existing only in a perpetually transient state. He emphasizes the chaotic character of this process; the seeming lawlessness of history is the result of the motion of heterogeneous spheres that collide and interfere with each other (AF, no. 227). That does not make the process meaningless; on the contrary, all meaningful moments happen spontaneously, as lucky coincidences. All the notable achievements of the spirit, Schlegel proclaims, are "happy accidents of wit" (witzige Einfälle; AF, no. 220). They are like lucky turns of phrase in a spontaneous conversation—witticisms that emerge "like the unexpected reunion of two friendly thoughts after a long separation" (AF, no. 37). This is what epistemology must aspire to become, Schlegel argues: instead of striving for a universal explanation, it should present cognition as "forces that are ever separating and mixing" (AF, no. 412). He does not hesitate to apply the same principle to science: the most important scientific discoveries are "*bons mots* of a kind";[21] nothing could be more pitiful than a physicist without wit (PhL, 154, no. 378).

Saussure, of course, would never have said that science was a matter of making puns. The anxious mood in which Saussure conceded his findings—that ultimately any scholarly model emerges and evolves in exactly the same way as a legend, that is, as a "formula" clothing a set of coincidences—is far from Schlegel's exuberant paradoxalism. But the substance of Saussure's position was essentially the same, and to put it forth—even if only in sketchy private notes—against all the positivist and rationalist convictions of his time required as much vision and intellectual courage as had been shown by the circle of the *Athenaeum* a century earlier. In both cases this vision stemmed from a profound understanding of the nature of signs and their transmission, leading to the remarkable intuition about the deeply rooted kinship between science (or epistemology in general) and the spontaneous flow of language. For Schlegel, "nature is mythological through and through" and not merely physical (PhL, 156, no. 392); physics' "ultimate goal" is mythology: without its roots in astrology, physics would have been just a banality (PhL, no. 378). Once again, one is reminded of Saussure's intuition that all a scientist really does is look at coincidences and try to find a "formula" for them—a vision that indeed portrays science as astrology (or mythology) in disguise.

We can now see both the similarities and the differences between Schlegel and Saussure. They come strikingly close to each other in their vision of history as a free-flowing process of incessant divergences and reconstitutions. Holding to that vision, they remained isolated in the sea of assertions of historical determinism and aspirations toward a "paleontological" reconstruction of the past that predominated throughout the nineteenth century. What distinguished Saussure from his early Romantic predecessors was his willingness to go the full distance both in the fearless exploration of the untamed accidental forces of historical transmission and in his uncompromisingly logical construction of a hermetic model of a prehistoric past.

## A TENTATIVE COMPROMISE: LINGUISTICS AS A "NATURAL" AND A "HISTORICAL" SCIENCE

After everything Saussure had said in the notes about the untamed volatility of the linguistic and cultural collective memory, he quietly put the issue aside in his lectures, giving way to a static approach that refused to see in language development anything but a succession of chesslike structural "positions." The authenticity of this thesis in the book is not to be doubted: as students' notes of the third lecture course show, it was there that, while taking note of the "all-powerful" character of the "factor of history" (Saussure 1993b:95), Saussure asserted the possibility of considering language "outside" it (101). To this end, he introduced the term *synchrony*, explaining its meaning by comparing it to a schematic rendering of a three-dimensional body on a piece of paper or a screen (123). Whatever the merits of this, yet another Saussurean "comparison," he proceeded as if it offered a sufficient "reason" for exempting language from *le facteur historique*.

One can spot occasional remarks in the *Course* showing that Saussure neither forgot nor disavowed what he had said about the "historical factor" in his notes on language and the Nibelung epos. Here, however, such remarks pass by without consequence, like a slip of the tongue, so to say, leaving the established coordinates of synchrony-diachrony unchallenged. This is what happens, for instance, in a section of the book in which Saussure discusses writing. With his characteristic antipathy toward all deliberately constructed semiotic phenomena, Saussure argues that, as a matter of principle, writing cannot match language proper, adding casually: "d'abord, la langue évolue sans cesse" (*CLG*, 48/27)—as if forgetting for a moment that the language he strives to construct in his lectures does not "evolve unceasingly" at all.[22] On yet another point, Saussure admonishes his listeners:

"The stream of language flows without interruption" ("La fleuve de la langue coule sans interruption") (*CLG*, 193/139).

As to his notes, here, while writing passionately about the perpetual wanderings of language in the "sea" of arbitrary changes, Saussure did not abandon the issue of the "state" altogether. In fact, he explicitly acknowledges the two opposite modes in which language exists and under which it can be viewed, which he calls the "motus" and the "status" (*ELG*, 223/156). As the notes make clear, Saussure had no illusion about the static nature of diachrony, i.e., its belonging to the modal pole of the "status"; to this effect, Saussure concludes, diachrony should be distinguished from a "historical point of view" (*ELG*, 21–22/6).

The distinction between the motus and the status, emphasized in the notes, was in line with contemporary trends in philosophy of science and cognition. One of the central theses of neo-Kantian epistemology was the division of all sciences into "natural" and "historical." According to Rickert, this division reflected a difference in approach rather than in subject matter: every subject could be studied either from the "natural" or the "historical" perspective. A "historical" science positions every phenomenon along the axis of change, while a "natural" science, even when it addresses changes, would describe them as a succession of phenomenal states. Since the historical approach is inseparable from process, it cannot present its object systematically. What it deals with is individual and unique (Rickert 1902:chapter 4). As if echoing Rickert, Saussure notes: "The veritable truth (*la vérité vraie*) is that even those sciences that deal with objects would profit from marking more definitively the difference between the two axes along which things exist" (*ELG*, 332/237).

Saussure's notes testify to his steady effort to distinguish between language as a "natural" object and a "historical" one (or in his own terms, between language as "static" and "motional"), a move that would in effect "cut" linguistics into two sciences (*ELG*, 331/236). The possibility of such a distinction rests on the assumption that language changes spontaneously, but speakers' perception of language does not. An innovation emerges spontaneously and incrementally through intercourse in speech, until it is "smothered" (*étouffée*) by a restructuring move in *la langue* (*ELG*, 294/207), emerging as what speakers perceive as a new state. The continual motion of history proceeds without speakers being aware of it; once a change enters speakers' consciousness, it presents itself synchronically. This is why Saussure sometimes refers in his notes to "the conscious state" as the antipode of the "historical state" (*ELG*, 117/80).

Excluding the reality of continual development from consideration and focusing on the "conscious state" and, as a result, substituting "diachrony" for history proper reflected a deliberate heuristic strategy, made in view of Saussure's conviction that language, unlike the typical objects of the natural and social sciences, is lacking any substantial core and, as a consequence, cannot be addressed in an integral way. Due to the dual nature of the linguistic sign, language can mix any phenomena whatsoever in any fashion whatsoever. To speak of any linguistic matter as a primary object upon which its study could rest is simple gibberish (*simple charabia*). Would you expect a student of optics to take the combination of blue and red in heraldry as the "object" of his study, to be probed for the presence of physical laws?—asks Saussure in the wake of the apparently remarkable success of his studies of Lithuanian accentuation (Saussure 2003b:337). The unresolvable heterogeneity of language has catastrophic consequences for its description, making every thesis about it seem to have been "planted in a swamp" (*ELG*, 95/64).

Saussure sought a remedy by proposing various "divisions" in the science of language that would try to capture the protean subject in a multiplicity of snapshots taken from different angles. In a typical outburst of anger, he declared "profoundly false" all hopes of achieving a "radiant synthesis" in the picture of language; instead, it must be divided into "little" theses (*en paragraphes minuscules*) (*ELG*, 95/64). His defiance as seething as his sarcasm, Saussure proclaims: "I have no fear whatsoever of resorting to diagrams that may look ridiculous, or even insult the intelligence of a reader. The point of those elementary cases of semiology is not to apply intelligence but to fight against the extraordinary [*le formidable*]" (*ELG*, 131/87). The obviously flawed presentation of language through the "diagram" of synchrony-diachrony—a resolution shutting off what Saussure declared on innumerable occasions to be the most crucial attribute of language, namely, its ungovernable mobility—was precisely that: an acknowledgment of the inevitable fact that, to be able to confront "the extraordinary," one must pay a price.

Yet the necessity of succumbing to this solution left Saussure perpetually dissatisfied. The relentless motion of history remained in the back of his mind, even as he strove to emphasize the primacy of the "status." To construct language as a synchrony, or a diachronic chain of synchronies, was to turn it into a substantial object accessible to empirical observation. This substitution, perhaps unavoidable, went against the grain of Saussure's insight about the metaphysical nature of language, which is nothing but "difference (and difference of another difference) . . . without anything in between or any default state [*sans aucune intermittence ni défaut*]," a situation that makes language a phenomenon that "does not exist in itself even analytically" (Saussure 2003b:334). In its metaphysical essence, language eludes description, just as it eludes any other purpose whatsoever.

The drama of this ever-unresolved contradiction erupts in full force in the concluding chapter of the *Course*. Throughout the *Course* Saussure remains careful to keep to the orderly picture he has carefully built up: that of a synchronic system of language that moves through time by restructuring itself into discrete systemic states. Even if occasionally—particularly when he spoke about the "mutability" of the sign—Saussure could not avoid making some statements that, if carried to their logical conclusions, would subvert his rationalist construct, he refrained from drawing such conclusions. The physical discontinuity of a lecture course, "arbitrarily" divided up by the class schedule, allowed this tension to remain implicit. Yet, as his dismay over the outcome of his courses attests, it never left Saussure's mind.

The declared subject of the concluding chapter was innocuous: "Families of languages and linguistic types." For Saussure, however, this issue was potentially explosive: his conviction that there are no limits whatsoever to the variety of structural profiles of languages, and to the possibilities for their transformation, went against the grain both of high Romantic (Humboldtean) organicism, which tied the structure of a language to the collective "national spirit" of those who speak it, and of the proliferation of artificial international languages, prompted by the modernist drive toward rationalist universalization. Incensed by his ubiquitous opponents, Saussure, in his oppositive manner, passionately proclaims the absence of any outward law that could be imposed on language—of any law whatsoever but that of its absolute, unfettered freedom. Suddenly, the whole edifice of synchronic-diachronic duality Saussure has been building throughout the course with such care seems to collapse. As it turns out, "all that time has made, it can unmake or transform" (*CLG*, 317/229); "there are no immutable features; permanence is the effect of an accident" (316/229).

The spectacular discovery in the *Mémoire*, and its later theoretical codification in the concept of diachrony in the *Course*, can be viewed as an act of "Stoic" acceptance (to use the word with which Saussure's great-aunt described the submission of the "progressive" spirit to the pattern of reason) of the inherent limitations of any construction one might devise in order to reach the object of one's study. This achievement carried with it a promise that linguistics at large could join the family of modern (modernist) sciences—a promise that was brilliantly realized over the course of the following half-century.

What this development left in shadow was Saussure's "dual" intellectual profile—a volatile and self-negating combination of tormenting doubts and the desperate longing for their resolution, of the ability to hold one's doubt at bay, once a choice "whence to begin" had been made, while never abandoning the feeling of ultimate defeat inherent in the very act of making such a choice.

Saussure began his exploration of the epistemological foundations of language with the discovery that, unlike the natural sciences, linguistics does not possess a substantial object. For him, this was a catastrophic discovery; the science of language seemed banished from the assembly of modern sciences, which proved capable of properly defining their respective objects because they had the luxury of taking the existence of the objects themselves for granted. In his notes from the 1890s, Saussure revealed his despair at the way language resisted all attempts at rational construction, a predicament that left the science of signs out in the cold. Yet, ten years later, he recognized that what he had discovered about language and linguistics was actually the common predicament of all cognition. With this assessment, he detached himself from modernist illusions and came closer to early Romantic metaphysics, with its idea of cognition as the eternal "hunt" for meaning without any definitive destination. Saussure's observation that all either an astronomer or a historian of language and myth can ever do is to register coincidences, "rhymes" remarkably well with Schlegel's aphorism that all the most fortunate discoveries are *bons mots* of a sort.

Yet amidst the stoic equanimity and outbursts of angry negations one can sense a glimmer of hope in Saussure's writings from the 1900s—a hope that showed he still had not abandoned his quest for a positive solution to the dilemma—an "ardent preoccupation" with it, as he himself called the philosophical attitude of the Rig Veda. Ten years passed between his notes on language, in which he articulated the intractably volatile nature of the evolution of signs for the first time, and his epic studies. In the latter, the whirlwind of chaotic movement and accidental collusions by which the transmission of sign values proceeds, and the inanity of all the formulas one strives to impose on it, are described even more emphatically. And yet one can sense a positive content looming behind the overwhelming negativity of "grand duration," as Saussure once called the process. This positive aspect is "grand duration" itself.

The immanent character of signs makes them the only source of their development. New constellations of symbolic values arise out of nothing but other constellations. Yet, precisely because of that, scattered instances of signification find support in each other, insofar as they happen to overlap by chance or somehow resound together. Saussure calls these accidental resonances a "rhymed account" (*une chronique rimée*). Having come into contact by chance, pieces of different stories that originally had nothing to do one with another emerge as "rhymed," which facilitates their migration between stories and their adaptation to a new narrative environment. For instance, the incorporation of "Orion's dog" into the Orion legend, prompted by the proximity of two constellations in the sky, was facilitated by the fact that the motif of a dog "rhymed" with the original image of Orion as a hunter.

This gives the process a consistency of its own—grounded not in logical coherence but in opportune rapprochements between the elements as they float in the stream of duration. "What constitutes the nobility of the legend, as well as of language, is that both are condemned to serve nothing but the elements at their disposal.... They are being reunited, continually yielding a new sense" (Saussure 2003a:421). Tradition proceeds as "continual nourishment which thoughts digest, order, direct, but cannot pass over" (421).

Somewhat mysteriously, the more diverse the process of transmission, the larger its spatial and temporal scale, the denser the network of echoing coincidences grows. Paradoxically, when the transmission of symbolic values is affected by an especially enormous "mass" of diverse forces, it may show a higher degree of consistency, because of the enhanced density of the process. In his notes on Indian mythology (circa 1906) Saussure expresses his fascination with the enormous size of the human mass and the extraordinarily long time span involved in the collective maintenance of the Rig Veda.[23] In both respects, India dwarfs the European world; in particular, it makes one aware of how puny and short-lived the history of Classical Greece was (Saussure 1993a:213–214). And yet what makes the tradition of the Rig Veda so remarkable is the astonishingly high degree of integrity in which it has been maintained through enormous expanses of space and time. (Curiously, the roots of this remark could be traced to Pictet's book on the Romantic concept of beauty, in which he drew a sharp opposition between the "proto-Romantic" Rig Veda and the "proto-classical" Homeric epics—an opposition that implied the supremacy of the open-ended diversity of the former over the "classical" compactness of the latter.)

One must look for clues, then, in full awareness of the relativity of one's findings: "So, one has to stick to one kind of doctrine, as if in spite of oneself, and while possessing perhaps a thousand ways of exposing one's own doubts."[24] And yet there is hope against hope that a glimpse of a lost time can be regained. After all the dazzling successes, disappointments, and struggles Saussure had experienced over his decades of Indo-European studies, he could say, with a whiff of defiance, that he was absolutely certain of at least one thing: that if he, Ferdinand de Saussure, had somehow found himself among proto-Indo-European people, many thousands of years ago, and had said to them: *esmi* —"I am"—they would have understood him (Saussure 1993a:195).

# Language in Discourse | PART 3

## The Anagram | SIX

In the course of his scholarly career, Saussure worked in three widely diverse areas, each of which came to be the focus of his interests at different periods: the epistemology of language, with the exploration of the transcendental properties of the sign at its intellectual core; the history of language and other semiotic systems (legends), including theoretical problems of historical evolution and its reconstruction; and finally, the semiotic nature of sound repetitions, particularly in poetic discourse, a phenomenon known since the 1970s as Saussure's theory of the "anagram." While the relationship between the first two aspects of Saussure's work is obvious, the arrival of the last subject, late in his life, may look fortuitous. The studies of the anagram, whether they are embraced with enthusiasm or referred to with some degree of embarrassment in later critical literature, seem to stand on "the other side" of the Saussurean world—a nocturnal side, one could say, with its larger-than-life revelations and dangerous proximity to the realm of the ineffable and oneiric. Saussure's private, almost secretive preoccupation with the subject, however short-lived, exposed his susceptibility to the more extravagant aspects of the intellectual atmosphere of the turn of the twentieth century. The overheated emotional modality that underlay this line of his studies stood in contrast not only with quiet rationality projected by Saussure's public academic persona but also with the tormenting doubts and debilitating uncertainties typical of the private aspect of his intellectual life.

Saussure's involvement with the anagram comprised a short span of time, sharply framed by an abrupt start in 1906 and an equally abrupt withdrawal in 1909. During this period Saussure gave himself up to the subject with feverish intensity. It is curious to note that those were precisely the years of his lecture courses in general linguistics, an occupation that seems totally disengaged from his private intellectual pursuits of the time.

Godel's 1957 publication of excerpts from Saussure's notes barely touches on the delicate subject of the anagram. Some light was shed on the subject a few years later when Benveniste published Saussure's letters to Antoine Meillet, including the long letter of September 1907 in which Saussure explicated his new concept in considerable detail. (As we now know, his first confidant was Bally, with whom he raised the subject in the summer of 1906; Bally's reaction, however, was utterly unsympathetic). Saussure's studies of the anagram didn't come into full public view until 1971—by which time the structuralist intellectual epoch, prompted by the publication of the *Course*, was already receding into the past—thanks to Starobinski's account, which included extensive excerpts from Saussure's notes on the subject.[1] As for Saussure's manuscripts themselves, they have not yet come out in a comprehensive publication to this day. While studies of the anagram mushroomed soon after the material came to light,[2] this part of Saussure's heritage still remains available for the most part only in the form of excerpts interspersed with the publishers' comments.[3]

Saussure's first brush with the subject apparently came during his stay in Rome in the winter semester of 1906. We remember that when Saussure took a leave from his teaching in Paris in the early 1890s he used the free time for a trip to Lithuania, which proved to be instrumental in shaping his views on the heterogeneity of the historical development of languages. Fifteen years later, Saussure once again took a leave from his duties to travel. This time, however, it was supposed to be a pleasure trip for Saussure and his wife, the only lengthy excursion abroad Saussure made during his Geneva years. And yet this respite from his rather monotonous academic routine resulted once more in a dramatic turn in Saussure's intellectual interests, with far-reaching consequences.

In a letter to Meillet from Rome in January, Saussure mentioned—perhaps responding to worries about his health—that he was keeping himself busy at the moment with a matter of no particular consequence: just amusing himself by reading archaic inscriptions during strolls in the

Roman Forum, with the sole purpose of proving to himself that he had not yet lost the taste for occasionally racking his brains (*casser la tête*) over a linguistic puzzle. The damaged state of the inscriptions, together with their elliptical writing style, made reading them a rather challenging task. Saussure reported having already established a working rule, according to which wherever an inscription featured the letter *i*, it usually implied a combination *i*+*x*, wherein the *x* stood for any omitted character, whether a vowel or a consonant, either preceding or following that *i*.[4] One can see a curious parallel between this formula and Saussure's reconstruction of the Indo-European vowel system more than a quarter of a century earlier, whose key "working rule" rested on the hypothesis that any vowel in a protostem should have been originally either preceded or followed by another sound of an indeterminate value. What Saussure was trying to reconstruct this time was not a protolanguage but prototexts—in particular, the proper names that constituted the core of the inscriptions. Having assumed the presence of a coherent message hidden behind the sketchy representation, one then proceeds to retrieve it with the help of "working rules" formulated, if not completely ad hoc, at least, in a way that allows for an adjustment in each particular case. It was this analytical method— which admittedly paved the way for as many abuses as insights—first pursued as a vacation pastime, that would soon emerge in Saussure's notes as a general strategy of textual analysis whose implementation promised a major breakthrough in understanding the fundamental nature of writing, if not of speech in general.

By the time Saussure resolved to speak out, a few months later—only to his closest friends and colleagues—about the peculiar phenomenon he had stumbled upon, he had already covered scores of notebooks with his analyses. He showed his usual terminological hesitancy in selecting a name for the new phenomenon, using a variety of terms for it, sometimes distinguished as subdivision of the general concept, sometimes thrown in casually as synonyms. The term *anagram* has become the standard name in later critical literature chiefly because of the prominence given to it in Starobinski's publication.[5] Saussure's starting point was Homer; studies of Virgil and Latin Saturnian poetry (a poetic tradition closely related to tomb inscriptions) followed in close succession.[6] About the same time, Saussure discovered that the entire Rig Veda was "literally wall-papered" (*littéralement tapisée*) with anagrams.[7] Further steps extended the analysis to Germanic epics;[8] to some examples of French poetry, from Villon to modern times; and finally, to nonartistic prose.[9] As the circle of texts he studied got wider and wider, the ubiquitous presence of anagrams became absolutely compelling. In Saussure's words, he "tried in vain, by expanding the scope of the studies in all possible directions, to stumble across a single blank passage" (i.e., one not containing an anagram).[10]

The principal mechanism of the anagram as formulated by Saussure was the following.[11] At a certain point in a poetic text, persistent repetitions of certain sound combinations occur in a rather conspicuous way. These repetitions are not purely euphonic; rather, they can be construed as latent representations of a theme word—most often, a name—of key importance for this particular passage. On the phenomenal level, the key word is represented only indirectly; all one sees in the text are rudimentary sound combinations whose recurrences show some degree of regularity (they need not be precise, though, allowing for rather wide variations). Each recurring sound fragment as such has no meaning; yet if put together in a certain way, they add up to a word, and, moreover, one that could be understood as the key word of the message carried out by this particular text or textual passage. The effect is as if the signifier of a crucial sign had been broken into splinters and scattered all over the text to be reconstituted—consciously or unconsciously—by the reader. One could say that recurring sound combinations in a text are connected to a key signified of that text not directly and explicitly, as signifiers in a language are, but implicitly and potentially. Such ad hoc semiotic connections are latent signs that are not "given" to the speakers by the language itself but have to be "found" each time anew for a given occasion in the text for which, and only for which, they are relevant. They are transient semiotic phenomena created in the speech act itself.

As far as classical poetry was concerned, the theme word implied in an anagram typically featured the name of a hero or deity, a relevant location, or (in inscriptions) the name of the donor;[12] occasionally, an anagram might also contain the name of a "literary deity," so to speak, that is, of the author's literary precursor—the last case being typical particularly for Latin poets, who often employed anagrammatic references to their Greek forerunners. The theme word could be mentioned directly in the text as well, alongside its anagrammatic representation. In many cases, however—Saussure called them "cryptograms"—the theme word figured in the text only "cryptically," via the anagram, without being directly mentioned. In the latter case, the effect of the anagram was particularly striking: the key word literally lurked beneath the text's surface, making its presence felt only through overtly meaningless sound repetitions whose presence might be conspicuous but

143 | THE ANAGRAM

lacked any order. It was this situation that prompted Starobinski to call his pioneering book on the subject *Words Under Words*.

Saussure's analysis of a line from book 11 of *The Odyssey* can serve as a typical example of both the anagram itself and of the analytical methods with which it could be retrieved from the surface of a text. In the line in question, Odysseus is asking Agamemnon, whose shade he has found in Hades, about the cause of his death: was it because Poseidon "aroused the breath of painful hostile winds" against him? The line is repeated twice in quick succession, as Agamemnon replies that no, it was not Poseidon, etc. Agamemnon's name is mentioned several times in the passage, but not in this particular line, which Saussure cited as ᾿Άασεν ᾿αργαλέων ᾿ανέμον ᾿αμέγαρτον ᾿αϋτμή (*áasen argaléôn anémôn amégartôn aütmê*). The line contains—in an arbitrary order—the sound clusters *a-ga-am-me-em-en-on*, which collectively point to the name *Agamemnon*. It is not particularly important but nonetheless psychologically curious that Saussure apparently misquoted Homer, perhaps citing the line from memory. The initial verb in Homer is not *áasen* "[he] has exhaled, breathed out" but ᾿όρσον (*órson*) "[he] has incited, aroused." The difference both in sound and meaning is small, but, in Saussure's version, the supposed anagram comes out somewhat more strongly. A possible explanation of the psychological mechanism of this substitution could be that Saussure's memory, prompted by his perception of the anagram, offered him a synonym that fit the anagrammatic pattern better than the word actually used in the text. Ironically, this mechanism was essentially the same as the one Saussure's theory claimed was directing the unconscious choice of words by the poet as he composed an anagrammatic line.

Another interesting example is Saussure's analysis of an emotional plea to Venus, the instigator of all life, in the opening passage of Lucretius's *De rerum natura*. The name of Venus is, of course, invoked there explicitly. Yet Saussure also observed persistent repetitions of sound clusters that alluded anagrammatically to Aphrodite, i.e., Venus's Greek antecedent. For instance, in the sentence that stretches over lines 10 to 13, the following sound combinations appear, most of them more than once: *a-te-di-af-raf-it-pr-ord*. Put in a certain order, they add up to an almost precise rendition of the Greek goddess' name—not without minor deviations, though, such as *ord* for *rod*, or *pr* in lieu of *fr*. To justify the latter anomaly, Saussure suggested that Lucretius must have been well-versed in the late classical Greek pronunciation of *f* as the affricate *pf*, which could justify the anagrammatic substitution of *p* for *fr* (pronounced as *pfr*) (Starobinski 1979 [1971]:59). In the previous passage (lines 5–9), another less-than-obvious reference appears in the word *flores*, supposedly presenting *fro* as a fraction of the goddess' name. For the representation to be precise, the word in question would have to be *froles* rather than *flores*; Saussure justifies this implied substitution by the fact that it often happens in speech practice. Sometimes, Saussure confesses, one needs to repeat a line several times before the convoluted transmutations of its sound motifs conjure up the cryptic name in one's mind (60).

The liberty with which Saussure bends any claimed operational rule as soon as it runs into a counterexample has struck many observers. Callus (2002:179) argues that Saussure's analytical procedures "degenerate into desperate and capricious speculation"; their initial strictness is compromised to such a degree that "suspicions of fortuitousness and meaninglessness become relevant." Mejía (2005:44) calls Saussure's anagram studies "the greatest disaster (*échec*) of his career as a researcher." In a dubious compliment, Vilela (1998/99:265) asserts that the study of the anagram attested to Saussure's "poetic" side, as opposed to Saussure the scientist. Saussure himself made attempts to alleviate this impression of analytical frivolity. On one occasion, for instance, he spoke of "hypograms" as a "licentious" deviation whereby the sounds of a theme word are represented in a particularly irregular fashion; excluding the "hypograms" would mean that "not everything is permitted" in anagrammatic permutations (Starobinski 1979 [1971]:29).

Yet, in the end, those irregularities proved to be irremediable, because they were inherent to the phenomenon. The patterns of recurrence out of which an anagram emerges are infinite in variety. In this sense, they could be called arbitrary. No a priori rules could be formulated to describe how a scattered collective of sound clusters might aggregate into an implied theme word on one or another occasion—nothing beyond a general principle according to which one finds a number of sound repetitions on one end of a semiotic pole, for which a relevant theme word can be construed on the other. No analysis of this phenomenon could possibly be anything but fortuitous and improvisatory.

When Saussure shared his findings with Bally—not without trepidation[13]—the latter's reaction, which did not reach us directly but could be inferred from Saussure's subsequent response, was downright negative. We should keep in mind Bally's principal scholarly interest was in the stylistic and aesthetic dimensions of language—an area from which Saussure had hitherto stayed aloof—which made him particularly sensitive to matters involved in the issue of the anagram. Not only was Bally doubtful about Saussure's analytical methodology, but he complained that the vision of poetry as a playground of sound manipulations did a disservice to poetry itself.

In Bally's words, the overall picture that emerges from the anagrammatic analyses makes Homer look like a "strange, frivolous and futile character."[14]

Saussure responded with a remarkable confession that his studies indeed made him experience an "aesthetic cooling" (*froissement esthétique*), verging on losing all affection, toward the "old bard" (Saussure 1994a:117). As to the studies themselves, he readily admitted his own "moments of doubt" in view of their rather extraordinary consequences, only to reiterate his ultimate conviction that the phenomenon he had discovered was real. His later letters to Meillet on the subject showed the same characteristically Saussurean mixture of timid uncertainties and emphatic, at times almost arrogant, assertions. Responding to Meillet's "little mountain" (*un monticule*) of notes pointing out the procedural liberties in Saussure's analyses, he wrote that all the "obscurities" in Virgil or Lucretius—by which he meant instances where his own analytical principles could not be sustained without ad hoc adjustments—would not "sway" him from believing "with the most absolute certainty in the world" ("je crois absolument certaine pour tout le monde") that the phenomenon he had discovered extended beyond isolated examples.[15]

As to Meillet's general assessment of his venerable teacher's idea, it sounds diplomatically ambiguous. Meillet acknowledged that after he himself took a look at some texts they turned out to be permeated with anagrams. For instance, a line in Horace's ode 2 from book 4: "Nititur *pin*nis, vitreo *da*tu*rus* Nomina ponto" (Soaring skyward, doomed to give His name to a sea)—contains combinations *pin, da, rus*, which add up nicely to the name of the poet to whom the ode is dedicated. But why should one limit oneself to the classical languages, Meillet adds: let us open any book at random, say, Chateaubriand's *Mémoires d'outre-tombe* (a curious choice, given the atmosphere of a spiritualist séance lurking behind the whole affair). He did, and, lo and behold, in a passage referring to Chateaubriand's companion Lucile, she is described by a chain of epithets that anagrammatically evoke her name: "Tout *lu*i était sou*ci*, chagrin, b*l*essure." Next comes Baudelaire's turn: in one of his lines the key word *hysterics* appears both directly and anagrammatically: "Je sent*is* ma gorge *s*errée par la main *terri*ble de l'hystérie."[16] These offerings could be read as both a reassurance and an implicit doubt. They resounded with Saussure's own fears about the "superabundance" of his discovery.[17] As examples proliferated, it became increasingly clear that one could find an anagram virtually everywhere—in any text in any language, of any genre, epoch, and literary tradition.

It is quite obvious that, given the rudimentary character of the sound combinations into which the theme word is claimed to be anagrammatically decomposed (they mostly amount to just two sounds, sometimes even a single sound), one could expect any number of words to be potentially reassembled from the same nearly elementary sound material.[18] Saussure was too much of a scholar not to be aware of this problem. His claim to veracity was that the theme word could not merely be composed out of sounds represented in a piece, but that its meaning was of key relevance to that piece. The anagrammatic sound constellations that appeared in a text were not random; they would emerge in a topically relevant passage and fade away as the narrative shifted to another topic.[19] In producing an anagrammatic effect, the sound and the meaning reinforce each other. One can sense the underlying presence of Saussure's fundamental idea about the indissoluble interconnection between the signifier and the signified in this reasoning: the sound repetitions point to an anagram only insofar as they can be connected to a key word, while the latter reveals its presence only insofar as it is represented through sound repetitions. In a letter to Meillet, Saussure described the anagram as "phonic play" (*jeu phonique*) in which a sacral name becomes "indissolubly involved" (Saussure 1964:114). Saussure compared the double nature of the anagram with the "famous principle of the leitmotif of Wagner": in both cases, all the various reiterations of motifs are identified only insofar as they are tied to an idea (Saussure 1994a:118).

Nevertheless, worrisome questions remained, first and foremost among them—why would poets play these games in the first place; why would they all choose to involve themselves in a kind of semiotic tinkering that Bally found, not without reason, "frivolous and futile"? Saussure clearly sounds defensive when he asserts that "preoccupations apparently as childish (*puerile*) as that of the anagram obsessed Sebastian Bach," which did not preclude him from writing "extremely expressive music"; a disparaging attitude toward such symbolic games betrays the rationalism of modern art (Starobinski 1979 [1971]:128).

To justify the ubiquitous presence of anagrams in poetic texts, Saussure initially suggested that the phenomenon was of religious, or rather magical, origin, and that it might originally have served as a magic evocation of divine names.[20] As the supernatural function of such incantatory texts was gradually supplanted by their aesthetic perception as "poetry," Saussure argued, the anagram shifted from a magical device into a literary one; it became a matter of literary tradition that subsequent generations of poets acquired and maintained, either consciously or not, through imitation. In a clear reference to his general view of history, Saussure noted that even if there had been a sacral or magic function in the beginning, there was "no mysticism" in the subsequent development of the phenomenon: whatever its origin, it proceeded through (arbitrary) transmutations of the tradition (Starobinski 1979 [1971]:42–45).[21] For example, while Homer may have borrowed anagrams in his epics from earlier religious practices, later poets (particularly Latin) acquired them by imitating Homer, and poets of still later times by imitating classical poetry at large.[22] The only trouble with this argument was that, much as he tried, Saussure could not find convincing evidence from any ancient tradition pointing to the original sacral function of anagrams. Explaining "the embarrassing silence" about the issue in ancient documents by suggesting that secrets of the mystical tradition would have been "meticulously kept" (Starobinski 1979 [1971]:94) was a rather lame excuse. Furthermore, the proliferation of disparate examples, particularly from modern literature, including prose, watered down any claim of even purely literary continuity.

It was Bally's criticism that helped Saussure find another argument—one born of the general conditions of speech production rather than magic or literary practices. It is well known, Saussure remarked, that euphonic richness is a widespread, indeed universal feature of poetry. To object to the idea of the anagram is not to deny the existence of poetic euphony; rather, it is to deny the presence of a meaning behind euphonic repetitions. Would you be more satisfied, he asked Bally, if it turned out that all that poets do when they employ euphony is pure sound play, a vacuous "waltz of syllables"? Perhaps, Saussure mused, when a poem is being conceived, the poet begins not with an articulated meaning, not even with key words; perhaps the most rudimentary step in a poem's composition involves the spontaneous emergence in the poet's mind of fragmentary sound clusters, whose shapes vaguely allude to a nascent poetic idea without yet articulating it. An anagram then constitutes a prototext out of which the text of a poem is born. An anagrammatic effect emerges in a poem not because the poet deliberately sought words that would contain certain sound combinations; on the contrary, it was those primary sound combinations at the core of the poetic idea that "sought" words in the poet's memory fitting the nascent poem's prearticulated design (Starobinski 1979 [1971]:96).[23] The sound texture of the poem and its meaning emerge interactively. The original awareness of the ability of sound clusters to attract a potential meaning might have come from ancient rites of mystical glossolalia or else from the heightened awareness of sounds' combinatory potentials in the Indian poetic tradition resulting from the meticulous phonetic descriptions of Indian grammarians. But whatever their origin, these latent phonosemantic synapses lay stored in a poet's mind as the primeval linguistic material—semiotic rudiments *avant le signe*, so to speak—whose coalescence into an articulated meaning proceeded in discourse by means of the anagram.

Whether or not one is convinced by Saussure's anagrammatic analyses, his general argument reiterates the two properties unique to language: the principle of duality, according to which the material and spiritual elements of a sign have no value of their own, but become a semiotic phenomenon by virtue of their mutual relation; and the principle of arbitrariness that defies any general pattern according to which such relations could be structured and any predictable direction in which they could evolve.[24]

In this respect the anagram can be seen as a particular facet of Saussure's exploration of the metaphysics of the sign. The phenomenon of the anagram presents itself as yet another kind of interdependence of a signifier and a signified—one that is not preestablished in language but emerges in the process of speech. What surfaces in a poetic text is, on the one hand, a texture of sound repetitions that by themselves do not signify anything beyond euphony and, on the other, a theme word whose presence in the text remains mute. It is only when these two polarities meet (or, as Novalis would have said, "embrace") each other in the anagram that their implicit and disparate presence comes into focus as a key element of the poem's message. The connection between the two poles of the anagram is arbitrary: it exists solely by virtue of being established in this particular way for this particular instance in the text. Nothing in the character of repeated sound combinations itself suggests the name they represent; as a matter of principle, an infinite variety of words could be construed from those combinations. By the same token, looking at the general content of a poem, regardless of its sound texture, one can imagine many words that could serve as its thematic emblem. It is only by projecting our awareness of the highlighted sound material onto our awareness of the poem's topical content that we grasp their connection in the shape of an anagram. Such moments of semiotic crystallization of the latent textual material emerge as an "imbroglio des formes semi-concordantes," not bound by any strict rule.[25] The manifest lack of rigor in Saussure's analyses reflects the fundamental nature of the phenomenon. Whatever "working rules" one might form in the process, one should be prepared to bend them at any moment in response to an arbitrary turn in an anagram's configuration. In the end, no general formula could be found that would cover every single instance of the anagram—nothing beyond simply registering its presence.

The difference between linguistic signs and the anagram is that while the former belong to speakers' prerequisite knowledge of *la langue* that exists—at least theoretically—prior to and independent of their speech activity, the latter is entirely a matter of speech itself. The arbitrariness of the anagram is an arbitrariness of the second degree, so to speak. No command of the arbitrary structure of *la langue* could help one to create or perceive anagrammatic signs. They must be constructed each time anew as a transient connection between an improvised signifier and an ad hoc signified— a connection valid only in a particular instance in a particular text.

Linguistics of Speech | **SEVEN**

*An Unrealizable Promise?*

## FROM LANGUAGE TO SPEECH: BRIDGING THE METAPHYSICAL GAP

To understand what motivated Saussure in this sudden and somewhat dubious pursuit, one needs to appreciate the depth of his uncertainly about the key issue on which the whole edifice of theoretical linguistics was supposed to rest: namely, the idea of *la langue* as a plethora of oppositive differentiations whose arbitrary hermeticism makes it "immutable." The negative nature of *la langue* as pure form means that no single entity can ever change on its own because it simply does not exist by itself. Yet language changes all the time, and no one was as keenly aware of that as Saussure. For him, language change was not merely an empirical fact that could be set aside while one focused on the transempirical oppositive system. Interminable development is constitutional for language; it is its mode of existence, as inextricable from the principle of arbitrariness as immutability.

Saussure's uneasiness with this issue is evident in the *Course*. In one of the early sections, when he introduces the notions of synchrony and diachrony, he speaks with quiet assertiveness of language evolution as something secondary and derivative: merely a succession of synchronic states. Yet later in the *Course*, when Saussure concentrates on an exploration of the metaphysical consequences of arbitrariness and, in particular, their impact on the character of language change, the notion of the synchronic state turns out to be rather precarious: it amounts to no more than a point on the developmental continuum that "is never anything but momentary" (*CLG*, 126/88).

But if a synchronic state of language—unlike that of a chess game—cannot be sustained even for a moment, how can it serve as the base from which all speech activity emanates? If *la langue* is perpetually volatile, how can it dictate speech behavior to speakers in the imperative way described in the *Course*? In other words, how is speech possible? Neither the *Course* nor Saussure's notes offer an answer to this problem, and the quiet omission from his lectures of the issue of *la parole*, after it is declared in the beginning to be dependent on, yet distinct from, *la langue*—an omission that caused his editors no small amount of bewilderment—is telling.[1]

For Bally the problem was as important as it seemed clear. He addressed it with his influential concept of "actualization" (Bally 1932), which he himself viewed as a logical consequence of the foundational categories of language laid out by Saussure. According to Bally, *la langue* constitutes a "virtual" knowledge of language, abstracted from the concrete circumstances of its use. It is when language is used in speech that its "virtual" signs receive actualization by being projected on the concrete stylistic, social, and psychological circumstances of a given speech situation. By virtue of their actualization, the signs acquire a positive value they do not possess as phenomena of language. The inner knowledge of oppositive values that constitutes language remains constant (until the system as a whole is changed, by way of Saussurean diachrony), while its actualization occurs each time anew, under conditions of speech that are never repeated. This makes a new "actual" meaning possible without undermining the stability of the "virtual" system. From Bally's perspective, after Saussure had established the purely oppositive nature of *la langue*, the move to its positive actualization in speech was just the next logical step; that Saussure never made it seemed an accidental and, from Bally's personal perspective, lamentable omission.[2]

If speech is viewed as an "actualization" of language, the matter indeed appears straightforward, so evident perhaps as not to require much special attention. Subsequent linguistic tradition mostly held that the reason for Saussure's failure to make good on his promise to outline a distinct *linguistique de la parole* was simply that he did not much care about the phenomenon, having invested all his intellectual effort in defining the categories of *linguistique de la langue*.[3] Such an interpretation is contradicted by repeated assertions in Saussure's notes that language can be perceived as language only when it leaves the structural "dock" and is plunged into the open sea of usages; its most fundamental categories, immutability and mutability, can be perceived only under this condition.

It could be, however, that Saussure remained silent on the issue of how an inner knowledge of language becomes an externalized act of speech not because he considered the problem unimportant or self-evident but, on the contrary, because it posed a fundamental theoretical challenge. The relationship between language and speech loses the seeming self-explanatory lucidity with which it appeared to Bally if one takes into account the full consequences of Saussure's exploration of the nature of signs. For language as Saussure envisioned it, an entity whose arbitrariness makes it both absolutely immutable and absolutely unsustainable at the same time, the transcendent leap into speech eludes logical explanation.

Every time a speaker is involved in an act of speech he poses as a "speaker," that is, claims to possess a knowledge of the language that enables this act. The very arbitrariness of this knowledge makes it absolute: one must take the language as it is. At the same time, however, the fact that our speaker proceeds in implementing his language not for its own sake but for external purposes reveals its inadequacy, precisely because of its arbitrary constitution, for any such concrete purpose. Whenever the task of "expressing something" is pursued, it has to be pursued by pressing into service some arbitrary semiotic configuration offered by the language, and the fit is never perfect. The existing arbitrary relationship between a signifier and a signified always leaves the speaker with a "yearning" (to use Novalis's vocabulary) to express something that lies beyond the given values, which leads to interminable ad hoc efforts to patch them up. The stretching of the meaning of a word or grammatical construction by analogy, or the new intonational inflection of a phrase challenging phonetic routine, emerge for the purpose of filling that gap, yet in fact they create new situations just as arbitrary as preceding ones and as liable to be challenged in due time, once again in a fortuitous, and thus fatally flawed, fashion. To be sure, not all these little dramas of speech have far-reaching consequences; many fall into oblivion the moment after they emerge. As Saussure remarked in the *Course*, "nothing enters language without being tried in speech," while many features that emerge in speech are "not adopted" by language (*CLG*, 231/167). But there is no way to know which of innumerable speech modifications will vanish without a trace and which will not. Speakers are as all-powerful in inflicting changes on language as they are helpless in controlling their consequences.

If this is true, however, where is that inner knowledge of language that enables speakers to speak? If language is liable to be affected by every act of its use, it is unclear how a shared common knowledge can possibly be the basis for an exchange between speakers.

Bally's theory of actualization envisioned units of language securely returning to their respective matrices after venturing into the open space of speech.[4] Yet if "actualized" signs could return intact to their place in the system, that would mean that they could be separated from the system to face the needs of the moment. To entertain such a possibility would be, indeed, to equate language with a chess game, its figures always maintaining the same values no matter how many new combinations they participate in. The fatal flaw of this interpretation is that it fortuitously makes language into a "fact" whose parameters are as firmly set (and, by virtue of this, as sturdily substantial) as the rules of chess or a production manual. The volatility of language would be lost, and, together with it, the very foundation of the whole system. If, on the other hand, one were to admit that each act of speech constitutes a "point of no return"—that there is no way to hold on to this gaseous phenomenon as it diffuses in all directions in speech usages—how could speakers achieve that "command" of a language without which speech is manifestly impossible?

If we contemplate the Saussurean speaker in all the glory of his inner knowledge of *la langue*, he appears locked in that knowledge—immutable and, as a result, mute. What the speaker of Saussurean *langue* seems to be lacking is precisely the ability to speak; his knowledge of language is doomed to remain "tacit knowledge" in the literal sense of the word. The moment he starts speaking, his immanent knowledge dissolves into concrete instances to whose challenges language never responds without an adaptation, however slight. Because speakers are accommodating language material to new speech tasks unconsciously, they remain convinced that what they are doing is simply putting language to multiple usages. Yet the moment one begins putting language to use, it is stirred into a commotion that undermines the values that were supposed to be "used." Had the speakers relied solely on their systemic knowledge of language, the volatility of this knowledge would have left them incapacitated, speech-wise.

A full view of the metaphysical properties of Saussurean *la langue* shows speech to be a *metaphysical impossibility*. Speech is an empirical phenomenon, while language is not. Constructing *la langue* as a negative system of oppositive values exempts it from the substantial empirical reality to which speech belongs. To be able to speak, one has to break away from *la langue* into the realm of distinct palpable entities and substantial values; yet, to be able to speak, one also has to accept language unconditionally in its immanent state.

It was this distressing state of affairs concerning *la linguistique de la langue* that might explain the feverish intensity and almost desperate arrogance with which Saussure embarked on his studies of the anagram while at the same time teaching his overtly serene if potentially explosive lecture courses. The answer to the problem of the metaphysical incompatibility of language and speech could come from speech itself, or so Saussure hoped, at least for a while. The promise of a solution emerged from the universal principle of discourse organization that he found—rightly or wrongly—in the anagram.

Discovering the anagrammatic texture of poetic discourse presented an opening for, or at least an initial step toward, *la linguistique de la parole*[5]— built along the same fundamental semiological principles of arbitrariness and durational mutability as, yet distinct from, in a certain sense even diametrically opposed to, the linguistics of *la langue*. It offered (at least tentatively) the promise of resolving the dilemma of speaking a language—that is, of making a positive realization of a constitutionally negative phenomenon—for which no answer could be found within the domain of language "in itself."

The anagram emerged as a phenomenon of speech that retained the most fundamental feature of language—the interconnection between signifier and signified that was inseparable and arbitrary at the same time. The principle of freedom, which makes the inner composition of language responsible solely to its own immanent structure, is maintained in the way the anagrams evolve in speech in a free flow of coincident assemblages. Yet the effect of arbitrariness in language is the opposite of its effect in speech. Within *la langue* the values of signs are constructed through oppositive differentiation; in the anagram, speech shows the ability to construct semiotic values through integration.

Thanks to the ability of particles of language to become spontaneously attracted to each other in an anagram, the disintegrating volatility of language is offset by the integrative forces of speech. The discovery of the ubiquitous presence of anagrams in discourse creates a vision of speech as a stream of free-floating fragments, arbitrarily splintered from the stationary network of signs by the force of associative attraction and ready to congregate into a new whole under the specific demands of the moment. Perhaps this was what Saussure meant when he remarked at one point in his notes, rather cryptically, that discourse provides, "in however rudimentary a fashion and in ways we do not understand," a link between the two polar sides of a sign (Starobinski 1979 [1971]:4). When free-floating particles of signifiers and signifieds come together at a certain moment in a text, superseding preestablished patterns of language, their improvised assemblages yield a positive speech product—an anagrammatic discourse. It lasts as long as it is needed, dissolving as speech progresses to give way to opportune assemblages in response to a new speech situation and its semiotic needs.[6]

Some scholars have pointed out that the associative nature of the anagram offsets "linearity," which Saussure proclaimed to be one of the a priori properties of the sign.[7] We should remember, however, that Saussure's linearity meant more than the mere successiveness of speech. At stake was the contradiction between the signified as a spiritual phenomenon, with no space of its own, and the material and therefore linear (i.e., spatially bound) signifier. The arrival of the anagram resolves, or at least alleviates, the intrinsically contradictory nature of the sign by undermining the spatial integrity of the signifier. Under the conditions of an anagram, what a signified faces is not a "linear" counterpart but a dispersed plurality of shapes that could be reconstituted on the spur of the moment.

In the anagram the issue of arbitrariness is shifted from the knowledge of language—which is immutable and, as such, untranslatable into speech—to the process of speech itself. With the addition of the anagram, the system of language attains mobility without any need for the kind of interminable restructuring that would make the whole system untenable. The network of linguistic signs, locked in its "emptiness" as it is, proves capable of emanating free-floating latent particles of signifiers and signifieds, ready to form new semiotic interconnections in an improvisational mode from one speech act to another.

Speech does not emanate directly from language as its performative implementation or "actualization." What the freedom of language arbitrariness yields "if left to itself" is a negative phenomenon of distinctions that makes language as a pure form essentially mute. The moment speech takes off from the ground of language, it abandons that ground, making a transcendent leap into a different metaphysical space—from the immanent and oppositive to the situational and substantial. Yet despite this fundamental metaphysical gap, speakers prove to be capable of acting in a meaningful way by setting the intractable system into commotion: splintering it into fortuitous particles, and seeking and finding momentary attractions between those particles, to serve transient speech situations.

## "LINGUISTICS OF SPEECH" AND "ROMANTIC POETRY"

### Differentiation and Integration: Two Sides of the Semiotic Process

It has been argued in this book that Saussure's treatment of the metaphysical nature of language shows a close kinship with the philosophy of language and cognition of the early Romantics, particularly Novalis. It comes as no surprise, then, that in their treatment of discourse Novalis and Saussure also show significant points of coincidence, whether as a result of direct influence or—more probably—due to the similarity of their fundamental premises concerning the sign, from which the theory of discourse ensued. There is a close affinity between Novalis's subject, striving to break away from the muteness of his inner self by building externalized representations, and Saussure's speaker, trying to break out of his essentially mute immanent knowledge of language into the worldly act of speech.

Every act of speech sets language adrift in the outside world, its order impinged upon by transient circumstances. Somehow the process does not end in total chaos. The bodies of semiotic representation—signs—show a propensity for proliferating by mutual differentiation. But precisely because they present themselves as graspable, distinct bodies, like all bodies, they have the potential to resemble each other. The empirical world is fragmented by virtue of being represented in signs. Yet arbitrarily apportioned semiotic entities retain the potential to be interconnected by revealing analogies that reach across the network of oppositions. Behind the divisions between disparate phenomena lurk resemblances or analogies that flout all established boundaries and differentiations. As a network of pure oppositions, language strives to apportion and to compartmentalize. Yet free-flowing associations superimpose themselves over this network of differences; they hover over the system of pure oppositions, superseding its negative values by positive (substantial) resemblances.

It is the process of differentiation itself that opens the way to the integration of differentiated signs by association. The denser the network of oppositions, the more crowded the repertory of differentiated semiotic bodies, the better the chances of them "touching" or "brushing" against each other through an analogy: "The more diverse the individuation of a phenomenon, the more diverse are the ways it comes into contact with other individual phenomena" (*AB*, no. 113). The growing network of differentiating oppositions becomes entangled in the growing network of integrative analogies. The way both networks evolve is essentially free: it is as impossible to prescribe the emergence of new distinctions as to predict what resemblances will be recognized and used in the process of associative integration. The two free-flowing networks evolve by interaction, with new distinctions leading to fresh associations, which in turn evoke a need for further differentiations: "What was divided—must be bound; what was bound—[must be] divided" (*FS*, no. 303). Each sign strives simultaneously along two axes: "centrifugally"—to be distinguished from as many phenomena as possible, and "centripetally"—to reveal its resemblance to and association with as many phenomena as possible (*VF*, no. 274).

However, the forces of differentiation and integration belong to different planes of the semiotic process. Differentiation is the principle according to which the system of signs is structured and perpetually reinvents itself; in other words, differentiation belongs to what Saussure calls *la langue*. In contradistinction to this, integration is essentially a phenomenon of discourse. It is when signs are used that they reveal resemblances and analogical attractions.

The communicative defeat inherent in any act of using language—because no state of the semiotic system can be adequate to the open-ended possibilities of its usage—is offset by the semiotic gain when the message, although never fully adequate, shows an ability to reintegrate itself in an unpredictable way by setting its components into free analogical interplay. This gain emerges as a "mystery"—something above and beyond anything the language as such could offer. While the perpetual restructuring of semiotic differences is the result of the subject's insatiable semiotic "hunger"—i.e., his perpetual dissatisfaction with what can be expressed by means of language as a pure form—the effect of integration emerges as if by itself, as a revelation that transcends the subject's struggle with given semiotic values.

Novalis explicates the way semiotic integration proceeds by using the metaphors of sleep and drowsiness. Sleep "neutralizes" the will of the self, "unties the bands that hold the system together" (*AB*, no. 381). The grip of the oppositional grid, through which all phenomena are established vis-à-vis each other, is loosened, allowing all perceptions to drift, a process in which they freely superimpose themselves over and merge with each other. In its waking state the soul "devours" the phenomena of the world, assimilating them as semiotic entities; the dream state signifies spiritual "digestion," a process in which semiotically distinct phenomena dissolve in consciousness by willfully reconfiguring themselves (*AB*, no. 211).

An important clue to the process is contained in the term *vélleité* or *Vellëitaet* (i.e., a state on the border between sleeping and waking) that surfaces in yet another series of Novalis's fragments. The state of *vélleité* allows the subject to lose his diurnal oppositive grip on phenomena while not completely losing the ability to register impressions; it is a state in which the integrational constellations phenomena achieve in their nocturnal free floating can be glimpsed by consciousness in a transient revelatory moment.

Saussure was struck by the metaphor in the Rig Veda describing the only state in which the subject could grasp absolute substance as dreamless sleep—a state in which the subject remains fully oblivious of both the world and himself. Novalis's subject finds himself just a notch away from, or rather on the precarious brink of, that absolute nirvana. The twilight state of *vélleité* allows some vague hints at the ultimate unity to descend on the subject before he falls into oblivion, leaving an imprint on his almost (but not quite) receded consciousness. Here, at this crucial moment, lies the "germ" (*der Keim*—one of Novalis's favorite words) of diurnal cognitive activity.[8] It is this almost imperceptible—and never fully graspable—imprint that invisibly directs the seemingly chaotic and arbitrary semiotic pursuit, giving it a premonition or promise of coherence.

In the wake of Nietzsche's critique of rationalism and Freud's exploration of the unconscious, references to "oneiric" trances and their revelatory and therapeutic powers became extremely popular within certain trends in philosophy and avant-garde art, notably French surrealism and existentialism. In his *Manifeste de surréalisme* (1924), André Bréton extolled dreaming as the state of universal acceptance in which "the nagging question of possibility" doesn't arise;[9] consequently, dream and madness are declared the principal operational modes for an artist. Georges Bataille seconded this by asserting the principle of "non-achievement," which is conducive to discovering "the coincidence of intellectual plenitude and ecstasy."[10] After the Second World War, Jean Baudrillard transformed this principle into a broader paradigm of negativity: "Death, illusion, absence, the negative, evil, the accursed are everywhere, running beneath the surface of all exchanges" (Baudrillard 2001:7).

Nothing could be easier than to carve Novalis into the Baudrillardian figure of a "precursor" of twentieth-century modernist or postmodernist (as one prefers) trends and ideas. His preoccupation with eros, dreaming, and death seems highly suggestive in this regard. Some of Novalis's "interpretations of dreams" (notably the famous "blue flower" dream in *Heinrich von Ofterdingen*) look, at times, as if he simply cannot have been unaware of Freud.

It is important, therefore, to reiterate the differences that set Novalis apart from the late-nineteenth- and twentieth-century enthusiasm for the oneiric. What makes Novalis unique in this flamboyant company is the utmost intensity with which he pursued both extremes in the cognitive enterprise—active and receptive, rational and transrational—without succumbing to the comfort of either a total rationality or a wholesale irrationality. Fascinated by Calderon's proposition that "life is a dream," Novalis does not forget to add a characteristic qualification: "Our life is a dream insofar as it is a thought" (*FNS*, 63). Neither rational distinctions nor the plunge into somnambulistic fluidity have the last word; the moment when they meet in a perfect synthesis never comes.

### The Anagram as a "Potentializing" Discourse

To express the complementary relationship between the differentiation and integration of signs, Novalis introduced a mathematical formula derived from Newton's calculus: $1 : \infty \times \infty = 1$ (*FNS*, 55). The absolute unity of 1 undergoes infinite divisions and infinite reconstitutions simultaneously, whereas its original wholeness stands as the mathematical limit of the process. Novalis calls this ambivalent process *Potenzierung* (*AB*, no. 295). Bringing the whole world into the "potentialized" state—i.e., making it strive at the same time toward maximal differentiation and maximal integration—by means of creative discourse was the principal mission of Romantic poetry.

The principle of potentialization means that integrative resemblances thrive under cognitive conditions whose "unsystematic," piecemeal character is manifest. The more fragmented, fraught with elliptical leaps, or—to use the key Romantic term—"progressive" the discourse, the more intense the network of analogies that grows spontaneously as it evolves.

The essentially "potentializing," or suggestive character of Romantic discourse, as it was conceived by Schlegel and Novalis, was exemplified in the enormous agglomeration of fragments produced by these two authors in the second half of the 1790s.[11] In this mass of fragments, associative connections, based on different common features, spread from each point in the text in all directions to many other points. Various expressions are related to each other by contiguity. The meaning of a certain expression is partially elucidated by references to it at other points in the text. This fragmentary discourse shies away from "direct" meaning, delivering its message by means of metonymical deflection instead.[12]

Even in its broadest interpretation, the Saussurean concept of the anagram remained considerably narrower in scope than the early Romantics' vision of the "potentializing" forces of discourse. In his studies of the phenomenon, Saussure limited himself to just one aspect of the integrating analogies potentially at play in a text. It was an aspect that attracted his interest throughout his academic career: namely, recurring sound combinations (a subject, we may add, that also loomed large in the ancient grammars of Sanskrit). This limitation undermined the semiotic weight of the integrating forces, making their ubiquitousness in texts inexplicable and even suspicious.

Eventually, Saussure himself either lost faith in his discovery or lost hope of convincing others. The issue of the anagram never surfaced in his courses. It remained on the sidelines as something extraneous to the content of Saussure's lectures and, subsequently, to the book, leaving the problem of *linguistique de la parole* cloaked in silence. The question of how the speaker manages to turn his possession of *la langue* into speech was simply thwarted by omission. The anagram was doomed to remain a rather extravagant episode that, from the later perspective created by the tremendous response to the *Course*, may seem incongruous with Saussure's overall intellectual persona and scholarly activity.

Yet the scope of Saussure's anagrammatic studies, and the excitement and anxiety he invested in the process, attest to the significance of the theoretical breakthrough this discovery initially promised. The anagram emerged as a phenomenon beyond belief, defying rational explanation, something that simply "could not be" and yet was. Its transrational unexpectedness, in particular, made it a counterweight to the rationally constructed negative metaphysical properties of language. With the anagram one sees the principle of arbitrariness shifting from its a priori nature onto the terrain of tangible phenomenal presence, showing how the pure form that is language could become a phenomenon of the world.

Rhetorically and temperamentally, Saussure stood worlds apart from the *Athenaeum* thinkers. Especially the florid metaphorical language in which Novalis and Schlegel deliberately clad their metaphysical pursuit was alien to Saussure's style of thinking and writing. Yet if we consider that both were fundamentally concerned with the semiotic nature of language, whose oppositional negativity makes its substantial content ever evasive, we will find "family resemblances" between Saussure and the early Romantics. Both rejected rationalist categorization and idealist organicism as two poles that proved to be equally inapt in the face of the peculiar duality of language as an instrument of semiotic representation. Both realized that they were dealing with a phenomenon in a state of perpetual ferment. Saussure would never have expressed this relentless commotion of signs in terms of erotic desire or hunger. But his longing to grasp language in its essence, and his despair upon experiencing its perpetual elusiveness, is palpable in his fragmentary notes. Saussure's notes themselves present a compelling example of what the Jena Romantics called "potentializing" discourse. Much as he, in his capacity as a scholar and thinker of the neo-Kantian generation, yearned to construct language as a string of postulates, he proved unable to do so, except in sketchy notes and transient classroom presentations, due to the insurmountable barriers that stood in the way, which he could not bring himself to ignore.

Yet another thread that connected Saussure to the early Romantics is his willingness, however tentative and hesitant, to enter the world of the unconscious and the oneiric in search of something beyond reasonable expectation or explanation—something of a "mystical" nature, capable of grasping the phenomenon he was pursuing as no rational method ever could. It was this world that he came in touch with in his studies of the anagram.

## THE MYSTERY

One of the metaphors that Novalis, a man of science, employed to elucidate his idea of integrating semiotic forces was electrical magnetism. According to Novalis, when the subject falls into a state of passive receptiveness, he becomes a "perfect conductor" (*AB*, no. 88). In particular, Novalis shared his contemporaries' keen interest in the idea of animal magnetism, a rather fanciful outgrowth of studies of electrical conductivity and magnetism. The principal claim of the theory of animal magnetism (introduced by Anton Mesmer in the 1770s, and further developed toward the end of the century by the Scottish physicist and doctor John Brown, with whose work and healing practices Novalis was particularly impressed) was that all bodies in the universe, animate and inanimate alike, are attracted to each other by means of the magnetic impulses they emit.[13] The "invisible fluid" (or, alternately, "invisible fire") of electromagnetic impulses flows through bodies, connecting the whole universe.[14] (At one point, Novalis referred to this universal cosmic flow as "*menstruum universale*" [*BS*, no. 57].) During Mesmer's healing séances, patients were plunged into a trance that was supposed to heighten their receptiveness to magnetic impulses; this allowed an experienced therapist to detect extremely subtle electric signals in certain parts of patients' bodies and to restore the free flow of current, the blockage of which was presumably the cause of the patients' nervous and physical malaise.

In Novalis's day, the scientific validity of these discoveries (especially Mesmer's) was hotly disputed but not yet definitively rejected; it was only in the first quarter of the nineteenth century that the notion of animal magnetism was put to rest as a scientific concept. By that time, however, the idea of subsensual magnetic signals from the universe, which one could perceive by plunging oneself into a somnambulistic trance, had acquired a life of its own. It persisted through the following two centuries, no matter what science had to say about it. The idea attracted the poets and philosophers of high Romanticism from Schelling to Hugo;[15] it thrived as a means of healing mental afflictions, particularly hysteria, in Victorian England.[16] From this perspective, Novalis's fascination with Brown can be compared with the reliance of so many modern philosophers and literary critics on Freud, whose intellectual heritage has gradually shifted from the domain of experimental science to the humanities and the realm of popular beliefs, exactly as had happened with "mesmerism" in the course of the previous century.

The trend persisted well into Saussure's time and beyond. Perhaps its apex came in the 1890s and 1900s when spiritualist séances became a veritable mania, commensurable in intensity with Mesmer's and Brown's healing séances a century earlier. During that time a curious episode occurred in Saussure's life that brought him into unexpectedly close touch with the world of the trans-sensual and oneiric.

We can now return to the curious confession Saussure made to Bally about the *froidissement* he felt toward Homer after he discovered the pervasiveness of the anagrammatic texture in his epics. An echo of the same sentiment can be found in Saussure's notes of 1906 on Brahman philosophy; at one point, amidst his copious and passionate writing about the Rig Veda, Saussure makes the sudden confession that he has little expertise (*très peu versé*) in Sanskrit literature, which he knows solely as a linguist; he has always felt "profoundly bored" with it and was never tempted to leave his state of ignorance (Saussure 1993a:223). The passage stands in stark contrast with the free-flowing monologues about Indian cultural tradition, mythological thinking, and metaphysics that surround it.

To understand these sudden professions of *froidissement* or *profonde ennui*, we should recall the mode of passive, self-effacing contemplation that, according to Novalis, is conducive to the transcendent integration of differentiated phenomena. The distinction between Saussure's "coolness" and "boredom" and Novalis's enchanted reverie is more temperamental than substantial: both attest to the same state of spiritual somnolence, each in his own way. This intuitive, revelatory aspect is palpably present in Saussure's explanation of the psychological mechanism of the anagram: the anagram emerges not because the poet deliberately selects fitting words, but because those words are triggered in his memory by the subliminal theme of the nascent poem, which manifests itself at a prerational stage as a vague confluence of certain sound combinations. It is this nondeliberate, vague, irrational character of the process that makes it vibrant with meaning, whereas producing sound play for its own sake could well turn out to be, to use Bally's words, a "frivolous and futile" game.

Saussure's involvement in the transrational processes of spontaneous integration, of which the anagram was a tangible example, exposed his susceptibility to the mystical aspect of language. Behind Saussure's frustration, one can sense his yearning for something that could offset the relentless forces of arbitrariness, which to all appearances should make language unsustainable yet somehow do not. It was this predisposition of mind that brought him in touch with the world of spiritualist séances.

In the mid-1890s, Saussure befriended the psychologist and philosopher Théodore Flournoy, who soon became his colleague as professor of psychology in Geneva. Flournoy's interest in spiritualism was motivated by his scholarly research. He sought clues to the unconscious state of mind by observing the behavior of a medium in her (it was always her) trance state. In a way, his ideas corresponded to Freud's discovery of the unconscious in the same years as well as to the works of William James (with whom Flournoy maintained an extensive correspondence).

Flournoy was well aware of mediums' usual limitations, the most pertinent of which were their typically very poor educational level and a pedestrian disposition of mind, which drastically limited the paths along which their visions tended to travel. Eventually, however, he had the good fortune to find a true star for the role. She was a woman in her early thirties named Élise-Catherine Müller; eventually, she rejected her original name and began calling herself Hélène Smith, the name under which she has become known in scholarly and popular literature. Although not systematically educated, she apparently possessed scattered bits of knowledge about a lot of things and had considerable creative capabilities and aspirations.

In the course of her several years of collaboration with Flournoy,[17] Hélène assumed several different personalities in succession, all ostensibly reflecting her previous incarnations. One of them was that of an inhabitant of the planet Mars. During her trances Hélène spoke and wrote in the Martian language, using an exotic Martian writing (which Flournoy assiduously deciphered); she also made drawings of Martian landscapes and scenes of Martian life, in exotic colors—orange skies, trees with blue leaves, etc.—recalling more than anything the palette of Symbolist poetry. Another incarnation, into which she ventured but with which she apparently did not go very far, was that of Marie Antoinette. But the most elaborate and intriguing of Hélène's other selves was Princess Simandini, the daughter of an Arabian sheik, who became the eleventh wife of the Indian Prince Sivrouka Nayaka around the year 1400 and was eventually burned at his cremation in accordance with local custom. During her lapses into Simandini's self, Hélène conveyed numerous stories of her lavish but at times stormy life with the volatile prince in the fortress Tchandraguiri, which he built for them in northwestern India in 1401. It is Hélène's identity as Princess Simandini that brought her into connection with Saussure.

Flournoy (whose relationship with Hélène eventually soured) wrote a book about his experience with her under the title *Des Indes à la planète Mars* (1900). The book became a best seller, appearing in a number of languages, including several English editions. It owed its success to the skill with which Flournoy kept a balance between his genuine excitement as he followed Hélène's reveries and sought explanations for her often enigmatic pronouncements, on the one hand, and his detached observations, at times tinged with irony, on the other. In particular, Hélène's Martian language, although totally exotic in appearance, turned out to be, as Flournoy eventually discerned, simply "French in disguise." Its words were nothing but French words with arbitrary sounds inserted in place of the original ones, while their meanings remained identical with those of their French counterparts; the Martian syntax was purely French. Hélène disguised her French as Martian the way children sometimes create a private "secret" language by mangling common words.

In her creation of the Martian language, Hélène inadvertently followed the strategy that Saussure criticized most pointedly in his theory of the sign: she treated words as mere labels whereby a new signifier can simply be attached to a ready-made signified. Not surprisingly, he was rather skeptical, occasionally even sarcastic, toward attempts to make her Martian language a subject of serious linguistic investigation. The case of the Indian princess, however, was more complicated, and rather intriguing. The language Princess Simandini spoke turned out to be not entirely whimsical; it contained, amidst a lot of rambling, some expressions that could be distinctly identified as belonging to a kind of mangled Sanskrit. For instance, at one point she exclaimed, as a kind of solemn salutation: *atiêyâ ganapatinâmâ!* The first word is unintelligible; if it was not Hélène's own invention, it had to be a vocabulary unit hitherto unknown to students of Sanskrit. But the second word was easily identifiable as a composite of Ganapati, the name of a known deity, and *nama,* "name." The whole expression could be hypothetically interpreted as "Greetings [?] to thee who bears the name of Ganapati!" On another occasion, in a state of high agitation, the princess uttered a string of expressions that contained a few distinct Sanskrit words; the most coherent among them was *mama priya Sivrouka,* ostensibly meaning "my beloved Sivrouka." As Saussure eventually pointed out in his meticulous analysis of the event, the expression *mama priya,* although well-known in Sanskrit, is always used independently as a form of address; he was not aware of its usage as a qualifier attached to a name. But this grammatical imperfection might have been expected from a speaker whose native tongue was supposed to be Arabic. That Hélène could produce some scattered yet discernible resemblance to Sanskrit, a language of which she could not have possessed any shred of knowledge in her everyday life, seemed genuinely striking. It could not fail to attract the interest of Saussure in his capacity as the foremost expert in the subject.[18]

At some point during 1898, Saussure's involvement in the séances with Hélène apparently grew quite intense. At least once, the princess recognized him as her beloved husband. Flournoy describes a scene wherein the princess produced passionate exclamations and singing, all directed at her husband, whom she perceived as sitting next to her; it was actually none other than "Professeur de Saussure," who was sitting close to Hélène on the floor in a concentrated effort to distinguish words in the rushing torrent of her speech.

The fruits of this collaboration were extensive analyses of Hélène's Sanskrit produced by Saussure,[19] which Flournoy cited at length in his book. His contention was that Hélène assembled her speech partly as pure fiction, partly out of scraps of languages other than French she might have a rudimentary knowledge of, such as German and English, and finally out of whatever scattered knowledge she might have had of Hindu mythology and history. Thus the enigmatic *atieya,* which supposedly meant "I greet you," might have been inspired by English "I" [*ai*] and "you" or "ya," with a purely fictional "tie" in between. The strikingly genuine *Ganapatinama* might have emerged from the authentic name of a deity she may have heard about, and the addition *nama* as "name" could have come out of English *name* or German *Name*. The idea of using it as a solemn address might have come from the German expression *in Gottes Namen*, which could also provide a phonic protopattern for *Ganapatinama* as a whole. Hélène's tendency to replace various vowels in prototypical words with an *a* might have been purely intuitive, *a* being a vowel often associated with solemnity; but it happened to coincide with one of the most conspicuous features of Sanskrit phonetics, in which *a* was indeed by far the most frequent vowel—thus lending to Hélène's glossolalia its overall Sanskrit-like appearance.[20]

As we can see, Saussure did not buy the idea of previous incarnations and primordial memories. But in addressing the phenomenon of Hélène's discourse, which apparently transcended rational explanation, he turned to analytical procedures that clearly overstepped the bounds of any orderly linguistic analysis. What Saussure envisioned as a kind of subliminal "protospeech" that might have been surfacing in Hélène's speaking consisted of disjointed scraps of memory—half-distorted foreign words and expressions, some mythological names, a general idea of how a solemn or passionate speech should sound—that were ostensibly adrift in Hélène's mind, coalescing almost randomly into a discourse that might suggest, at least in the form of scattered hints, something that had a relevant meaning.

He would not have been Saussure if, having offered a daring hypothesis, he did not then retreat from it, only to put a question mark on his retraction afterward. In 1901, Victor Henri, the French linguist and Saussure's former colleague in Paris, published the book *Le langage martien*, in which he claimed that Hélène's Martian language was related to Hungarian. In a letter to Flournoy of May 14, 1901, Saussure confirmed that her "Martian language" seemed to have certain restrictions on vowel combinations within words (a somewhat loose version of vowel harmony) characteristic of Hungarian and other Finno-Ugric languages; however, he expressed skepticism about Henri's principal thesis because of the scarcity of related words he was able to cite (in fact, Henri found just one word in Martian that seemed to be related to Hungarian). Later, in another letter to Flournoy of May 16, 1906, Saussure remarked that perhaps he had encouraged Henri to produce those "hilarities" (*folichonneries*) by his own "élucubrations" of the phrase *a-tyê-yâ*, which were of the same character of a "conjecture quasi divagante" as Henri's hypothesis. (The word *élucubrations* is an interesting neologism, whose compositional recipe is not far from those Saussure had ascribed to Hélène's mangled Sanskrit expressions: it replaces *élucidation*, derived from Lat. *lux, lucis* "light, shine," with an analogously built derivation from Lat.

*lucubrum* "faint light, a tiny light spot in the darkness.") Saussure's skepticism about Henri's findings may have been genuine, but his tone of mocking (self-)deprecation might also have been prompted partly by his knowledge of Flournoy's utter skepticism about the "Martian" language.[21]

As mentioned, Flournoy did his work with mediums in connection with his studies of the unconscious. In particular, he embraced the writings of F. W. H. Myers, whose theory he called the most perfect expression of the unconscious. (Myers was in turn connected to Freud, which eventually led Flournoy to acknowledge the significance of Freud as well.) An interesting feature of Myers's theory was that it was partially based on his studies of poetic texts. In his book *Human Personality and Its Survival of Bodily Death* (1903) he wrote that when one observes the supreme achievements of the human spirit, such as Aeschylus's *Agamemnon*, "it is hard to resist the obscure impression that some form of intelligence other than supraliminal reason or conscious selection has been at work. The result less resembles the perfection of rational choice among known data than the imperfect presentation of some scheme based on perceptions which we cannot entirely follow."[22]

As Lepschy (1974:192) points out in this connection, "collaboration with Flournoy in analyzing texts produced by Hélène apparently put Saussure in direct contact, in a most suggestive manner, with the theory and practice of the unconscious." The suggestive character of the experience may have been enhanced by its implicit connection to poetic texts, in particular, to classical poetry. In a way, Hélène's pronouncements, delivered in an emotionally charged, occasionally fiery tone and florid to the point of obscurity, represented "poetic" discourse of a kind, whose unconscious associative underpinnings Saussure attempted to disentangle in his analyses.

This curious episode took place eight years before Saussure came upon the idea of the anagram. We can see in it the seeds (or, as Novalis would call it, the germ) of how Saussure later tried to explain how the latent—prerational and preverbal—state of the poet's mind could be conducive to the emergence of a poetic text. He found a possible explanation of the phenomenon of Hélène's speech by viewing it as representing Sanskrit latently or, to use the term he would coin a few years later, anagrammatically. This was not a conscious and deliberate manifestation of knowledge of the *langue* of Sanskrit, which Hélène obviously did not have, but neither was it entirely incoherent. It reflected the transconscious, almost miraculous integrative power by which fragmentary scraps of semiotic material stored in memory can reconstitute themselves and reassemble, as if by their own power, in discourse.

Saussure's involvement with the anagram was as short-lived as his prior involvement with Flournoy's experiments. For a while he withstood criticism and the half-hearted acceptance of his idea with a defiance in which one could easily discern undertones of his own nagging doubts. In a letter to Meillet of October 9, 1908, he wrote that, on the one hand, his studies of "hypograms" carried him to conclusions "de plus en plus abracadabrantes," but on the other, they were becoming more and more precise; to this, he added: "You'll take me for someone completely deprived of good sense, someone not far from being taken by an idée fixe."[23] Saussure's tormenting ambiguity about his work also showed itself in an episode with Léopold Gautier, one of the most dedicated members of the small circle that constituted the audience of his linguistics courses. When Saussure shared his findings with Gautier,[24] the latter was at first bewildered by their sweeping character; in a letter to his son on December 4, 1907, he spoke of his fears that Saussure might fall "victim to an illusion, a discovery or pseudo-discovery that is very inventive, too inventive!" Later, however, Gautier was so taken with the idea that he embarrassed his teacher, who then urged some "restraint."[25]

In the spring of 1909, Saussure wrote a letter to Giovanni Pascal, a noted proponent of the tradition (which had never died in Romance lands) of writing poetry in Latin. Having discovered anagrams in Pascal's Latin verses, Saussure was eager to learn whether they were the fruit of the latter's consciously following the classical tradition or arose in his poetry spontaneously, without his awareness. After asking Pascal, in the initial letter in March, for permission to ask him some questions about the matter, on April 6 Saussure sent him a few samples of his analysis of Pascal's verses. Pascal's reply is unknown; most probably, he never answered the second letter.[26] As Arrivé points out, whatever Pascal might have said would not have undermined the case: even if he had claimed that this was all an "accident"—"is not the accidental the name for the unconscious in Saussure?" (Arrivé 2007:181).[27] Even if Pascal did not reply at all, this could be interpreted, given Saussure's frame of mind concerning the subject, as his reluctance to betray a mystical ancient tradition (180).

Be that as it may, soon after this abortive attempt to obtain outside verification, Saussure abruptly abandoned his last project once and for all. It was nearly at this time that he felt the first symptoms of the illness of which he would die four years later. A conversation between Saussure and one of his close friends, Jean-Elie David, recorded about that time, is colored with a mood of almost morbid resignation (not unlike Novalis's late notes):

"Here are the studies which I began on numerous subjects. For some of them I drafted hundreds of pages. I have abandoned them.—[David: And why didn't you finish them?]—Because the further one digs, the more one encounters obscurity and uncertainty. One would never penetrate the final mystery of language. All this labor is in vain."[28]

# Conclusion

## *Freedom and Mystery—*
## *the Peripathetic Nature of Language*

### MADE IN LEIPZIG

The most active phase of Saussure's scholarly and teaching career (at least outwardly speaking) comprised approximately a decade and a half between the late 1870s and mid-1890s. It was a time dominated by "positivism" in philosophy, the natural sciences, and social studies. In 1844 Auguste Comte had proclaimed the end of the "metaphysical" era of abstract philosophical speculation and the beginning of the "scientific" era of concrete or "positive" knowledge and exploration. To Comte also belonged the credit for introducing the principles of empirical science into the sphere of social studies; this new perception of the social element as something that can and should be studied with essentially the same methods and criteria of demonstrability as natural phenomena became one of the pillars of the positivist ideology. Following Comte's basic principles, Herbert Spencer presented a compendium of modern sciences in the framework of positivist methodological postulates in his monumental *System of Synthetic Philosophy* (1862–1897), whose ten volumes presented the foundations of biology, psychology, sociology, and ethics. Appearing in the wake of Darwin's *The Origin of Species*, Spencer's compendium particularly emphasized the principle of causality in development, an emphasis that triggered or reinforced a shift toward the historical approach in many disciplines, notably in linguistics. Like Comte, Spencer was inspired by the goal of wresting the study of "human" phenomena—fields such as sociology and psychology—from the speculative humanities and forging them into full-fledged sciences.

This positivist tide was rising high in linguistics, too, in the last third of the nineteenth century. One can see the impact of Comte's and Spencer's emphasis on sociology in Whitney's view of language as a social convention. As has often been pointed out, Whitney's idea of conventionality inspired Saussure, who saw in it a remedy for the despised idea of language as an "organism." But unlike Saussure's later concept of arbitrariness, Whitney's idea of conventionality was a "positive" concept: a social contract regulating speakers' linguistic behavior. Whitney's protobehaviorist approach tended toward Bloomfield's (1926) "postulates for the science of language" more than toward Saussure's "general linguistics."[1]

However, it was the Leipzig Neogrammarians whose works embodied the spirit of "positive" science in linguistics in the most radical and uncompromising way. The Leipzig "Young Turks'" strict adherence to a causal explanation of the historical past of languages, coupled with a rejection of anything that lay beyond empirical observation, exemplified the very core of positivist ideology. The school's central theoretical claim, that laws of phonetic change must work like laws of physics, "without exception," reflected the positivist aspirations of the social sciences.

So why, after a year of study at the University of Geneva, did Saussure decide to move to Leipzig? He obviously felt uneasy in Leipzig, since he strove, under various pretenses, to minimize his physical presence in the program. Saussure's sensational first book was written during his stay on leave in Berlin, in an almost surreptitious way that baffled his Leipzig teachers, while the work he officially submitted as his dissertation turned out to be (excepting some embryonic thoughts whose meaning would come to light much later) a rather pedestrian, if solid, manifestation of generic "positive" scholarship. With very few exceptions, his subsequent relationships with his former teachers remained cool at best. As for the school's doctrine and the concrete results it yielded, Saussure's favorite epithets, whenever he spoke about it in his notes, were *obtus* and *stupide*. His efforts to formulate the premises of language and linguistics always implied, as their negative antipode, the unreflective empiricism of Leipzig scholarship.

Perhaps the answer to the puzzle of why Saussure moved to Leipzig—besides the obvious, namely, that its program indeed stood at the forefront of linguistic studies at the time—lies in what Saussure was leaving behind with this decision. Remember that at the age of fifteen, after two years of intense studies with Adolphe Pictet, Saussure produced a treatise in which he offered a universal key to the protoroots of all words in all languages. After his first effort fell apart, Saussure abandoned linguistics altogether for a few years—in fact, until Leipzig; he never touched on any linguistic subject in his year at Geneva. Perhaps there was more at stake in this abrupt withdrawal than wounded adolescent pride.

A clue to what this early episode meant for Saussure's inner development may lie in the word with which he referred to it in his memoirs in 1903: *enfantillage*. In his notes, Saussure employs the epithets *enfantine* or *puerile* with the same generosity as *stupide*, yet typically he applies them to a separate category of things. What Saussure usually considers *enfantine* is the aspiration to capture language in a single all-encompassing picture. The mature Saussure's approach, on the contrary, lay in trying to divide the cognition of language into mutually exclusive facets, an effort accompanied by constant reminders (to himself as well as to others) that there exists a plethora of alternative perspectives on language, yielding different snapshots that are equally valid yet mutually incompatible.

Saussure's own *enfantillage* was indeed a childishly naive example of the "grand narrative" about language he later strenuously opposed. The truth was that, for all the difference in the level of scholarly competence, the work of his early mentor represented the same mindset. It is not difficult to see how Pictet's sweeping reconstruction of the life of the "Indo-European people" inspired the adolescent Saussure to a no less awesome reconstructive venture. In his later judgment of Pictet's book—beginning with his review of its second edition a year after Pictet's death and followed by quite a few remarks in his notes and lectures—Saussure always sounds as if he is reluctant to say anything negative about his old teacher but unable to say anything substantially positive either, beyond the ambiguous assertion that his work was better than many others of its class. The very idea of an inner link between the structure of a language and the culture and mentality of its speakers never failed to trigger Saussure's vehement refutation, although on such occasions he usually avoided mentioning Pictet, reserving all his sarcasm and fury for *les allemandes*. Saussure's personal sympathies or antipathies aside, he abhorred the holistic vision of language—a product of Schellingian organicism that became a trademark of high Romanticism, German and French alike, in the 1820–1850s.

Saussure's own predisposition toward an essentialist, revelatory solution—a trait that remained palpable behind the immaculate logic of the

*Mémoire* and the impassive epistemological inquiry of the *Course*—made him easy prey to the temptations of late Romantic grandiloquence in his adolescent years, with laughable consequences. One could not imagine a better remedy than the one offered by Leipzig, with its stern scientist ideology, its cult of the concrete, even its human atmosphere of no-nonsense academic camaraderie. It would be futile to muse on how consciously the nineteen-year-old Saussure sought this antidote, but in Leipzig he certainly found it. Later he would assault the oblivious empiricism of his Leipzig mentors with the same fury he used to tear down vestiges of wide-eyed Romantic fascination with the organic "wholeness" of language. But a Leipzig substratum persisted in his thought and, moreover, proved to be indispensable for his formulation of the fundamental categories of linguistic inquiry.

Saussure's construction of *la langue* was, of course, diametrically opposed to the militant empiricism of the 1860–1880s. But his training in the empirical atomism of Leipzig scholarship, with its willingness to concentrate on one tangible task at a time, can be sensed in his modeling efforts. Saussure approaches language with a twofold strategy: as a philosopher, striving to formulate the essential nature of language, and as a linguist, concerned with presenting language as a describable phenomenon. While penetrating into the essence of what language "is" required the utmost generalization that would set aside all its specific features without universal transcendental value (an operation somewhat like the Kantian critique of knowledge and its modernist echoes), approaching language as an object to be described required, on the contrary, a division of labor between the different facets of inquiry approached from different perspectives. While Saussure the philosopher strove toward the ultimate properties of the sign, Saussure the linguist exposed the futility of any efforts to find a general "truth" about language that could serve as a common denominator for its description. On the contrary, the only way to approach language, Saussure argued, was to set up polarized categories and proceed according to the strict division between descriptive domains ensuing from those categorical divisions: language versus speech, synchrony versus diachrony, or both of them together as opposed to "history"; the "phonetic" principle of spontaneous and continual development vs. the "morphology" of the consciously recognized shift from one systemic state to another—and above all, language "in itself" versus its cultural contexts and psychological background. One can see the substratum of Neogrammarian doctrine in the latter aspect of Saussure's thought. Even the choice of "phonetics" and "morphology" for one set of oppositional categories (one in fact rather ill-suited to Saussure's own goals) reflected the division between phonetic changes, ostensibly proceeded according to strict (natural) laws, and morphological changes, directed by analogy (i.e., stemming from conscious perceptions), which constituted the core of the Neogrammarian methodology.

It was the Neogrammarian in Saussure that did not allow him to remain in the domain of pure philosophy of language—in the company of such younger contemporaries as Frege, Cassirer, Wittgenstein, or Bakhtin. He was as interested in the "matter" as in the "principles"; moreover, at least, in the beginning, he had perceived his task of clarifying the foundational principles of language as a means for him and his colleagues to stand on more solid ground when dealing with the concrete data. Thus he was devastated when, in the end, his philosophical inquiries showed him irrefutably that it would never be possible to reach the elusive substance of language. Saussure's Leipzig training made him unable to go along with the sweeping revelations and peremptory logical constructions that mushroomed around him in the era of early modernism.[2] In a sense, Brugmann's complaint about Saussure's reluctance to put a "made in Leipzig" label on his work was not entirely groundless.

## FROM "SCIENCE" TO PHILOSOPHY

In the early 1890s, Saussure took a deep retreat from the buoyant world of Indo-European linguistics in which he had shone so brilliantly both as scholar and teacher. He did so with the same decisiveness he had demonstrated some fifteen years earlier when he cast off the vestiges of late-Romantic megalomania. Suddenly—or so, at least, it seems from the outward evidence of Saussure's letters and notes—the relentless pursuit of explanatory "formulas," without asking where those formulaic patterns fit in a strategic picture of the metaphysical nature of language, appeared futile or, to use his vocabulary, "stupid."

Saussure's awakening to the limitations of a purely "scientific" approach to language was timely; it coincided with the first surge of modernism, with its rejection of positivist empiricism, its highlighting of the difference between matters of nature and matters of spirit, and, finally, its strong emphasis on the essential, a priori features of phenomena hidden beneath their observable surfaces.

The modernist philosophical revolution of the 1890s–1910s rejected positivist complacency about the unequivocal existence of empirical "facts," to be observed and described, and embarked on a critique of the foundational premises of scientific description, building above all on Kant's critique of cognition. Its principal argument was that the object of a study is not given in itself, based on its substantial features; rather, it is always constructed by certain categorical premises postulated at its foundation. The only choice one has is whether to accept certain postulates implicitly, without giving any account of them—as with the positivists and their "facts"— or to construct them consciously through epistemological critique. From this starting point the foundational categories of different disciplines were laid out—beginning with the foundations of mathematics (Frege 1884; Russell 1897); spreading from there to the natural sciences (Avenarius, Ostwald) and to universal oppositions between "sciences of nature" and "sciences of the spirit" (Natorp 1910) or between "descriptive" and "historical" sciences (Rickert 1902); and, finally, leading to a new compendium of the sciences as "symbolic forms" (Cassirer 1923–1929)—an explicit counterpoint to Spencer's positivist compendium.

The awareness that any study is of necessity built on certain postulates led to a sober—if often implicit—acceptance of the fact that every choice of postulated categories imposed its limitations. Ultimately this approach pointed to the universal boundaries of cognition set explicitly by Kant. In this respect the new trend was reductive: by postulating certain features as constitutional for a certain object, it stripped that object of everything that lay outside this constructed approach to it.

It is interesting to note that Saussure's exposure to the new epistemological awareness came, at least in part, in a "Neogrammarian" way—as the result of an encounter with a mass of language data that refused to be sorted out. Curiously enough, the strong commitment of empirical studies to tangible data resulted in a limitation of the scope of that very data. In particular, until the end of the century, historical linguistics dealt almost exclusively with written texts, disregarding the fact (which Saussure later emphasized in his lectures) that writing offers an impoverished and somewhat artificial picture of the language it represents. Saussure's own reconstruction of the Indo-European vowel system had operated within the limited pool of facts of acknowledged relevance; in effect, it was the work of a member of the guild, elaborating, on the same factual basis, on the findings of his predecessors. It was only in the late 1880s that Saussure did field research of his own in Lithuania. The chaotic variety and mobility of the picture of language he found there shook his faith in the work he and his colleagues had been doing and convinced him of the urgent necessity of revising the methods and goals of the whole discipline. This personal experience echoed the rising general disenchantment with the premises and goals of empirical research. Saussure seems to strike down both empirical scientism and the idealist metaphor of language as an organism with one stroke when he speaks about a "ridicule doctrine," according to which linguistics belongs to the natural sciences and linguists work like "botanists": "this is what has been said, and taken seriously" (*ELG*, 116/80).

Saussure's "oppositive and negative" model of language clearly corresponded to the new philosophical trend. While champions of linguistics as a "positive" science saw their principal goal as amassing empirical knowledge about the subject, Saussure's reexamination of the foundations of linguistics was essentially reductive. He strove to strip language of all "outer" vestiges of its existence—the multitude of physical, social, and psychological phenomena with which it is entangled—to reach its inalienable features, which could then be laid out as a priori postulates of linguistic studies. In this quest for the transcendental properties of language, Saussure's critique came particularly close (whether knowingly or not) to Husserl's transcendental reduction.

Saussure's oppositive predisposition of mind, his emphasis on differentiation (in part, an inheritance of his Leipzig schooling) resulted in his highlighting the negative aspects of a reductionist model. Like Husserl in his reductionist critique of consciousness, Saussure finds in the end of the process of transcendental reduction no positive substance that could be acknowledged as given a priori. The only "positive" feature of language that is transcendental (i.e., belongs to language "in itself") turns out to be the absence of any positive substantial features. It is fair to say that Saussure perceived the ultimate state of aporia toward which this postulated model is, of necessity, headed with more devastating sobriety than most of his modernist contemporaries, with whom he shared the fundamental conviction of the postulated character of cognition.

Looking at the psychological underpinnings of the modernist spiritual revolution at large, one could call them essentialist or revelatory. The era of modernist "dawns" showed a great penchant for revelatory insights;[3] it was rife with messianic figures who declared, with great charismatic energy, a radically new order of things—be it theoretical physics, psychology, the social order, or the theory and practice of literature, art, and music. The new vision often looked counterintuitive to conventional "common sense." With a single stroke, it penetrated the empirical surface of the matter to an essential "core" that was invisible to ordinary sight, suddenly reordering things into a picture strikingly different from what straightforward observation had hitherto been able to show.

The essentialist side in Saussure was as characteristic of the turn of the twentieth century as his reductionist epistemological efforts. The revelatory lightning-bolt effect of Saussure's postulates about language was instantly recognizable in the intellectual and emotional environment created by Einsteinian physics or Freudian psychology, Schoenberg's dodecaphony, Khlebnikov's transrational poetic language, or Malevich's suprematism. It was in this vein that Saussure's "teaching" was received by the following generation (itself rich with figures of messianic proportions, such as Hjelmslev, Piaget, and Jakobson). Saussure's posthumous destiny as the founder of structuralism was that of a messiah whose word of revelation redeemed linguistics and semiotic studies as a whole, and did so all the more effectively, for that matter, because his "good news" reached the world only in a rendition—perhaps uncomprehending, perhaps even apocryphal—passed down by his disciples.

## "TO HAVE A SYSTEM AND TO HAVE NONE IS EQUALLY DEADENING FOR THE SPIRIT"

The aphorism at the head of this section belongs to Friedrich Schlegel.[4] It reflected the *Athenaeum*'s critique of cognition, one even more radical than that put forth by the modernist epistemological revolution. The latter, following Kant's critique of pure reason, subverted belief in empirical reality by showing how it is contingent on underlying transcendental categories. The *Athenaeum*'s critique, however, subverted the categories themselves by showing cognition as an essentially unregulated "progressive" process that evolves in a free flow of fragmentary cognitive acts. The principal achievement of the *Athenaeum* consisted of rejecting any universal key to the absolute that could be declared once and for all. In its response to Kant the *Athenaeum* sought the remedy for the limitations of pure reason he exposed not in building a "supercategory" that would supersede the boundaries drawn by Kantian categories (as Fichte did), but in reclaiming the fundamental "impurity" of reason, that is, its mixed and fleeting character.

The key idea behind the *Athenaeum*'s proclamation of "Romantic poetry" was that of merging critical reflection and free-flowing "romantic" creative fantasy. What Kant's first and third critiques strove to distinguish as pure reason, enframed in the transcendental categories, on the one hand,

and the free creative element of "genius," on the other, was transformed by early Romantic metaphysics into a volatile symbiosis in which every vestige of order elaborated by reason becomes dissolved in a running stream of creative imagination, while every visionary leap is undermined in its turn by a reflective "afterthought" (*Nachdenken*). The *Athenaeum*'s reflection on the human experience corresponded to the fundamentally heterogeneous and rhapsodic nature of that experience itself; the "Romantic" quest for the absolute readily embraced the mixed and the imperfect as fundamental conditions of existence. As Schlegel put it, "only in a mixed atmosphere can one breathe normally; inhaling pure oxygen makes one dizzy."

This position allowed the *Athenaeum* to embrace Kantian critique while avoiding its crystallization into a fixed system. The Jena Romantics rebelled against all "systems" of categorical cognition, which Schlegel sarcastically compared with military parades,[5] and Novalis with shoemaking.[6] Commingled with the free flow of "Romantic" creativity, pure spirit loses its purity, but, along with it, its constitutional limitations. Any cognitive state ("system") it produces proves to be limited, doomed to crumble under the pressure of the incessant motion of creative genius; yet that motion itself has neither limits nor any prescribed and predictable way of proceeding.

What destines the whole process to remain forever a fragmentary patchwork is the need for every cognitive act to be externalized through semiotic representation. These semiotic bodies—signs—emerge as fragments; any effort to patch up the relations between the fragmentary bodies, to fill the gap between them, ends merely in a new idiosyncratic agglomeration. There is no way to hold the "mass" of fragmentary phenomena of signification and its spontaneous development within the confines of any general organizing principle.

Yet, for the Jena Romantics, embracing the perpetually "potentialized" state of the semiotic process did not mean giving up on deliberate cognitive efforts. To yield to chaos, giving up any effort to conquer it by reflection, would be as "deadening" as to declare a comprehensive "system" and then force any ensuing cognitive task within its framework (a move that bestows "papal" authority on the champion of the system, as Schlegel once remarked about Fichte).[7] The spirit must perpetually strive for the absolute, "hunting" for meaning, trying to patch up the gaps between existing semiotic entities, while undermining every such effort with a reflective "afterthought" that exposes its fragmentary and transient character.

It is not difficult to see to what extent Saussure's position matches the *Athenaeum*'s epistemological endeavor. In his critique of the empirical approach to language as a phenomenon of "nature," Saussure was in line with the epistemology and philosophy of science of his time. Yet he stopped short of taking the next logical step in this direction, namely, postulating a stable and secure frame for linguistic studies grounded in the a priori properties of language. What Saussure found as a result of his strenuous critical labors was not an underlying logical order but a phenomenon of total freedom that ripped apart any orderly pattern. By arriving at this point of ultimate negativity, Saussure took a step further than his modernist contemporaries: not only did he mount a critique of observable reality from the vantage point of underlying categories but he also subjected those very categories to a critique that revealed them to be unsustainable. This was also what separated Saussure from his followers in the structuralist era, who were happy to use the universal categorical guidelines he had established, such as language versus speech, synchrony versus diachrony, signification as a relative phenomenon versus substantial denotation, to build a new systemic edifice of language and other semiotic systems in the true spirit of modernist science and philosophy. In Saussure's thought, however, language abandons its empirical surface, only to prove incapable of coalescing into a categorized system.

The contradictory world of Saussurean thought—ever striving for an uninterrupted logical inference and ever falling apart into fragments, equally rife with powerful insights and embarrassing false starts, at once feverish and dejected—can be better understood, I believe, when its line of kinship with the spiritual world of the early Romantics is fully appreciated.

## ANXIETY AND STOICISM

Let us now sum up the principal ingredients of Saussure's intellectual world: its drive for differentiations, inherited from the age of empiricism; a reductive epistemological critique that reflected the dominant trend in turn-of-the-century metaphysics and philosophy of science, in which Saussure came particularly close to Husserl's transcendental reduction, Cassirer's philosophy of symbolic forms, and Frege's (1892) distinction between the intrasystemic sense (*Sinn*) and the referential meaning (*Bedeutung*); and, finally, an inspiring yet disconcerting mixture of reflective sobriety and longing for the absolute, of devastating fragmentariness punctuated by moments of miraculous revelatory integration, which constituted a thread connecting Saussure to early Romanticism.

This volatile combination, whose diversity and inner tensions themselves recall the precarious *Athenaeum* moment, constituted a peculiar phenomenon in the intellectual landscape of the late nineteenth and early twentieth centuries, a phenomenon that stood in manifold relations with many events and trends of the time, yet escaped identification with any of them.

The diverse facets of the intellectual world of modernism, from exacting critique of the foundations of cognition to stunning intellectual and aesthetic revelations by charismatic figures, had one feature in common: an assertive attitude toward every object under consideration, whose eventual transfiguration by an upsurge of spiritual energy was all but assured; the eventual triumph of the enterprise was never in doubt. Saussure's cognitive anxiety, which rendered him unable to make his efforts public, set him apart from this aspect of the world of the 1890s–1910s, with which he otherwise showed a close kinship. The anxious, frustrated way in which Saussure pursued the elusive vision of language stood in conspicuous contrast to the assertiveness with which contemporary theories of science and cognition embarked on constructing their subjects. His dejection and perpetual false starts made him unable to claim the mantle of modernist prophet, one who could say of himself in Picasso's words: "Je ne cherche pas, je trouve!"

In this respect Saussure was not quite alone. The triumph of categorizing constructionism caused a sporadic but intellectually powerful reaction. An example of this rebellious undercurrent in the modernist epistemological culture can be found in Walter Benjamin, who began as a neo-Kantian and eventually found a powerful antidote to neo-Kantian complacency in the Jena Romantics. Characteristically, Benjamin did not pursue a full-fledged academic career, inscribing his critique of neo-Kantian critique "on the margins," so to speak (as did Bakhtin sometime later); this position echoed the deliberate marginality of the *Athenaeum* in an intellectual world dominated by the polemic between Kant's followers and the rising tides of idealist philosophy. Saussure, of course, held a regular academic position, yet the silent reticence and self-marginalization of his later years is quite telling.

Judging by appearances, Saussure seems as unlikely a companion for Benjamin or Bakhtin as he would have been for Novalis and Schlegel a century earlier. What reveals his spiritual kinship to the *Athenaeum* brand of Romanticism is his rebellion—uncompromising to the point of self-destructiveness—against any kind of cognitive safe haven, be it postulated categories or adherence to "facts" or simply giving in to the inscrutable volatility of the subject. Saussure discerned the full length to which the principle of the absolute freedom of language, grounded in arbitrariness, could carry the study of language and its development and had the presence of mind to accept the consequences of that principle—or at least proved unable to sweep them aside. Much as he longed for the hermetic refuge of postulated categories, within the shelter of which he would once again feel free to exercise his extraordinary ability for making order out of chaos, he could not be swayed from the principle of arbitrariness—that essence of the linguistic free will—which makes all the revelatory formulas in the world unsustainable or illusory.

His mode of spiritual existence was precarious, a perpetual striving toward a balance he knew could not be reached, yet it was the only antidote to succumbing either to the complacency of an objectified integral system or to the complacency of unchecked subjectivity. There was a heavy psychological price to be paid for the perpetual unresolved tension between fragmenting critique and visionary integration, between the ardent pursuit of a synthesis, on the one hand, and the sober realization of its impossibility, on the other. What I call the "Athenaeum moment" comprised a fleeting but precious span of time—roughly, the second half of the last decade of the eighteenth century. By the end of this period, Novalis was increasingly drawn to a vision of death—that sleep without dreams, to recall Saussure's words—as the welcome terminal station of a restless spiritual journey; he died, without any apparent physical cause except exhaustion, in 1801, at the age of twenty-nine. Schlegel increasingly sought the ultimate solution in religion, in the last published series of his fragments, *Ideen* (1800), proclaiming religion to be the sun whose rays enlighten all earthly tumult. His book on "the language and wisdom of the Indians" (1808), while pivotal in launching the new epoch of comparative studies, reflected Schlegel's new longing for the "organic" continuity of historical development, which he envisioned, predictably, with regard to German as well as Sanskrit and the classical languages.

What makes the case of Saussure truly unique is the length to which he was prepared to go in two opposite directions: toward the reductive construction of an object, on the one hand, and toward its release into unfettered and unceasing commotion, in the true spirit of early Romanticism, on the other. While carefully laying down the categories by which language could be constructed in its present or past state, Saussure did not lose sight of the chaotic fragmentariness in which the subject of his labor dissolves due to the fundamental heterogeneity that makes it unconquerable by "pure reason."

And what made the matter even worse, and harder to endure, was the mystery with which moments of spontaneous integration suddenly appeared amidst the relentless commotion of fragments. As it turns out, language perpetually moves between arbitrary differentiations and tentative and coincidental integrations. The presence of revelatory moments of integration takes away from one the last possible comfort—that of the supposed inevitability of aporia. By keeping tantalizingly alive the promise that things might suddenly come together, those uplifting moments refuse to let one quietly bow to the uncognizable—yet sooner or later they are doomed to undergo the gnawing suspicion that the revelatory glimpses they allowed might be just another illusion, perhaps even a hallucination, a symptom of one's failing intellectual faculties.

The intellectual stoicism with which Saussure endured this rending contradiction, his ability to confront all his doubts and despair in the face of the unachievable absolute, all the while maintaining a perfectly self-possessed composure in doing what could be explicitly done, was truly extraordinary. To be sure, like Novalis and Schlegel, he was able to endure the full force of this tension for only a few years. The "heritage" Saussure apparently believed he was leaving after him was one of dejection and defeat. Yet, as with the *Athenaeum*, this self-defeating volatility, grounded in the unbending freedom of the spirit, was the most precious aspect of what Saussure achieved. And, as in the case of the *Athenaeum*, it takes much time and interpretative labor for the full value of this achievement to be seen.

# Notes

## Introduction

1. Ferdinand de Saussure, *Course de linguistique générale*, published by Charles Bally and Albert Sechehaye, with A. Riedlinger (Paris: Payot: 1916), 2d rev. ed., 1922; subsequent reprintings: 1931, 1949, 1955, 1967. Critical editions: by Rudolf Engler, vol. 1 (Wiesbaden: Harrasowitz, 1967); vol. 2 (supplemental, 1974); by Tullio De Mauro (Paris: Payot, 1972), subsequently: 1985, 1995. English translation: Ferdinand de Saussure, *Course in General Linguistics*, trans. Roy Harris (Chicago: Open Court, 1986).
2. See a survey of the early response to the *Course* in various countries in De Mauro 1967a:334–343. For a comprehensive analysis of Saussure's reception through most of the twentieth century, see Harris 2001.
3. One notable exception was J. R. Firth, who once produced a parodic "structural" classification of twentieth-century linguists as "Saussureans," "anti-Saussureans," "post-Saussureans," and "non-Saussureans," placing himself in the last class. See Harris 2001:189.
4. "Introduction," #1 (Trubetzkoy 1939).
5. On Bloomfield's rather complex reaction to the *Course* (which he reviewed in *Modern Language Journal* in 1923), see Harris 2001, chapter 4.

6. Saussure's influence was palpable in Jakobson and Tynianov's programmatic "Problems in the Study of Language and Literature" (1985 [1928]).
7. *Cahiers Ferdinand de Saussure* (*CFS*) 1–60 (Geneva: Librairie Droz, 1941–2007).
8. Eco 1962. See Eco's later comments (1994:49–50) about his polemics with Lévi-Strauss, who found the idea of the "openness" of a work's meaning unacceptable.
9. Kristeva (1980:23) portrayed proponents of modern linguistics as "men of the seventeenth century" who are "still bathed in the aura of systematics."
10. Saussure's studies of the anagram were greeted by *Tel Quel* as a pursuit that resounded with its interest in the subconscious (Wunderli 2004:184). Derrida spoke of Saussure's contradictions, with their "quasi-oneiric" consistency, as evidence of the "metaphysical desire" of his work; see in Bennington 2004.

   A striking example of putting Saussure in "postmodern" dress can be found in a recent commentary on the anagram (Gandon 2003a:440): "Readers assist in dismemberment of corpses worthy of the Chinese 'death by a thousand cuts.' Afterwards the *disjecta membra* recompose, the corpses glue themselves back together.... Dance of corpses, chaos of the text." In another recent study (Maniglier 2006:42), Saussure is celebrated as a "chasseur de fantômes et poursuiveur de chimères."
11. Starobinski sounds apologetic in his book's conclusion: "Was Saussure mistaken? Did he allow himself to be fascinated by a mirage? Do his anagrams resemble the faces one can read in ink-blots? Perhaps Saussure's only mistake was to have posed the alternatives too sharply between 'chance' and 'conscious deliberation.'" (Starobinski 1979 [1971]:122).
12. A large part of these notes was published, in 2003, in the important "Herne" collection edited by Simon Bouquet (Saussure 2003a).
13. See in Normand 2000:10.
14. Bouquet (1997:ii) speaks of the "most profound and most insidious falsification" of Saussure's thought committed by the editors. See also Hagège 2003:111–124; Bouquet and Engler 2002:11.
15. The expression has become a piece of scholarly folklore to such an extent as to defy any definitive attribution; Gadet (1987:14) suggested that it was introduced by Giulio Lepschy.
16. Hagège (2003:116) points out that by comparing the *Course* with the notes one finds that much of the latter is present in the book, although often implicitly.
17. As Arrivé (2007:9) points out, the epistemological side of Saussure came to the foreground in the 1960s, i.e., after the discovery of manuscript sources.

## 1. The Person

1. Quoted in Gadet 1987:9.
2. Saussure 1960 [1903], published by Robert Godel, who found it among Saussure's papers in 1958.
3. In his obituary Noël Valois attributed Saussure's early years of peregrination to the migratory family spirit. See the appendix 1 to Saussure 1964:127.
4. In German: "glänzende Vermogenverhältnisse zu Leben." See Villani 1990:11.
5. Or even the first: "Despite, or rather because his general fame, it was not Jean-Jacques Rousseau who embodied the spirit of Genevan society, but to a much greater extent the natural scientist H. B. de Saussure." B. de Crue, *Genève et la Société de Lecture*. Cited in Maurer 1938:23.
6. "For a moment, general linguistics appears to me as a system of geometry. It is all about theorems that are to be proven." (From Saussure's conversation with Léopold Gautier, one of the students in his course in general linguistics). See Gautier 2005.
7. See her letter to Pictet published in Bernardinis 1965.
8. Reprinted in Saussure 1922c.
9. Saussure 1978. Although the document was known to have existed (it was mentioned in Bally 1926 [1913], and by Saussure himself in his "Souvenirs"), for a long time it was considered lost. The "Essay" was eventually found among the Saussure papers bought by Harvard in 1960.
10. On the Futurist roots of Jakobson's phonological theory, see Gasparov 1997.
11. "From this moment [1872] . . . I in fact forgot about linguistics, discouraged (*dedouté*) enough by my failed essay" (Saussure 1960 [1903]:17).
12. Ibid., 20.
13. Ibid., 19.
14. Ibid., 15.
15. In a letter to W. Streitberg after Saussure's death, responding to Streitberg's request for personal recollections, Karl Brugmann, one of Saussure's principal mentors at Leipzig, acknowledged that his colleague Hermann Osthoff's "sharp and rough nature" (*derbe und rauhbeinige Wesen*) in particular might have hurt "the young man of gentle constitution" (*den zartbesaiteten Jungling*) (letter of November 11, 1914). He humorously advised Streitberg to seek his sources among colleagues other than Osthoff, those who might speak "saviore mode quam Osthoffius" about the deceased (letter of December 2, 1914); see Villani 1990:29.

16. In De Mauro's words, the fortune of Saussure's book in Germany was "molto contrastata." According to the Danish comparativist Møller (who is credited with introducing the term *laryngeals,* which would later be closely linked to Saussure's discovery), the unfavorable reception of his work in Germany even caused Saussure to abandon comparative grammar for a while in favor of studies of Germanic legends (De Mauro 1967a:297).
17. For Saussure's rapprochement with Baudouin de Courtenay and the Kazan school, see in particular (Sljusareva 1971). See also her comprehensive analysis of Saussure's linguistic theory, which takes fully into account its connections and parallels with East European theoretical thought (Sljusareva 2004).
18. In the above-cited letter of November 28, 1914—written, one should not forget, soon after the eruption of the First World War—Brugmann, noting that he "was not exactly enchanted" by Saussure's conspiratorial ways (*Geheimnistuerei*) concerning his "literary plans," expressed his feelings in no ambiguous terms: "being a Frenchman (I dare say), the *form* was to him ever the main thing. . . . He never perceived things as we Germans perceive them, but rather felt towards us like—a Frenchman" (Villani 1990:30).
19. To which effect Brugmann recalls, not without a smirk, a sumptuous dinner with excellent wine and "phenomenally thick asparagus" to which Saussure treated him and another colleague on the occasion of the completion of his doctoral examination (Villani 1990:31).
20. As he wrote defiantly in the "Souvenirs" (24), he had to mention in his book that the idea of nasal sonants emerged "thanks to works by Brugmann and Osthoff"—"knowing perfectly well that personally I needed neither Brugmann nor Osthoff," and wrote his work "without anybody's help."
21. See the letter of L. Gautier to Streitberg (August 1919) and the latter's response in Amacker 1990.
22. "Apparently, under no circumstance did he want to appear as one *made in Germany*, and I realize now why he so often emphasized to us that he had come to Leipzig already all prepared" (Brugmann to Streitberg, December 1, 1914). In Villani 1990:31.
23. This attitude is particularly pronounced in Aarsleff 1981. The book summarily repudiates the "mysticism" of Romantic metaphysics, identifying virtually any positive development in the history of ideas with the "rationalism" of French tradition, from Condillac and *les philosophes* to Taine and Bréal. The few "German" authors to whom the book assumes a more benign attitude, such as Herder or Humboldt, earn this favor because of their perceived French connection.

24. E. Favre, who was present at the defense, claims in his gasping account that the young scholar, always extremely modest in his deportment, humbled his distinguished examiners by the thoroughness of his answers (cited in De Mauro 1967a:298).
25. See evaluations of Saussure's dissertation by Curtius and E. Windisch in Villani 1990:10–11.
26. "Due to the structural properties of the Indian phrase and to the loose style of the epos, it could be merely the loss of a hemistich that, in the blink of an eye, transformed an original subordinate genitive into the genitive absolute" (Saussure 1881:41).
27. A glowing picture of Saussure the teacher—*un vrai maître*—is given by Meillet in Saussure's obituary: "His poetic thinking often gave to the matter he exposed an imaginative form one could never forget. . . . He carefully prepared all he was going to say, but he gave his ideas a definitive aspect as he spoke . . . the listener was held in suspense in view of this thought in formation that evolved in front of him" (Meillet 1937 [1916], cited in Gadet 1987:9).
28. "I never attended Ferdinand de Saussure's course in general linguistics. But Ferdinand de Saussure fixed his thought on the subject very early. . . . The theories that he taught in that course in general linguistics were those that already inspired his class of comparative grammar two decades earlier at the L'Ecole des hautes études, which I took" (Meillet 1937 [1916]:33).
29. Koerner 1998/99 pointed out a curious paradox in Saussure literature: a highly popular phrase about the "system where everything is connected," which became a veritable mantra of structuralism, and was universally attributed to the *Course in General Linguistics*, was in fact nowhere to be seen in the book, nor was it present in Saussure's notes. Koerner traces the phrase to Meillet, who used it repeatedly in his works on Indo-European linguistics as early as 1893. According to Koerner's plausible construction, Meillet may have picked up the phrase from Saussure's lectures in Paris, in connection with his method of reconstruction; hence Meillet's use of it in his works on comparative grammar. Here is a possible clue to what stood behind Meillet's assertion that Saussure's theoretical ideas began to form "very early."
30. In a letter to Brugmann in December 1889, Streitberg speaks of hearing from one of Saussure's students that Saussure recently suffered from an "incurable psychological disorder" (*unheilbarer Geisteskrankheit verfallen sei*); the rumor was later denied by Saussure's brother-in-law, although "such a denial does not say much" (Villani 1990:15). Saussure's biographers avoid mentioning the reason for his leave. If Streitberg (whose extremely favorable predisposition

toward Saussure is undoubted) was correct, the episode repeated itself in 1906 when Saussure had to take a semester off from the University of Geneva because of extreme fatigue.

31. Apparently, as Benveniste noted (1965:22), Saussure failed to compile yearly reports in the last two years of his teaching at the École after his leave of absence.
32. In a letter of December 1891 to Gaston Paris, his former colleague at the École, Saussure speaks about a "small course" he teaches at Geneva to "three or four students who seem serious"; recalling the "preparedness" and "maturity" of his students in Paris, he nevertheless states that he has never regretted his decision, which, he predictably assures, was taken solely on personal grounds. See Décimo 1994/95:80.
33. Cited in De Mauro 1967a:312.
34. Ibid., 310–312.
35. *Mélanges de linguistique* 1908. Among the participants were Meillet, Grammond, Bally, Sechehaye, Wackernagel et al.
36. Letter to Meillet of March 20, 1911; Saussure 1964:121.
37. See the complete list of courses taught by Saussure at Geneva in Linda 1995/96:65–84.
38. In a letter to Streitberg on October 31, 1892, Saussure thanks him for inviting him to contribute to the Festschrift for August Leskien (one of his mentors at Leipzig), expressing his enthusiastic wish to participate; a year and a half later (June 24, 1894), he informs Streitberg that "various circumstances" have not allowed him to complete his article so far, but he is hoping to be able to send it soon (Villani 1990:15).
39. Cited in Starobinski 1979 [1971]:3.
40. "Severe to himself, disdainful of easy successes, content with pursuing [lit. 'walking along'] his uneasy reveries about the most delicate problems, yet showing utter repugnance to fixing his thought on a single answer, Ferdinand de Saussure has written little" (from the obituary by Noël Valois; in Saussure 1964:128). The words *promener sa rêverie inquiète* apparently alluded to Rousseau's late work, *Rêveries d'un promeneur solitaire*.
41. Saussure 1964:95.
42. Ibid.
43. Most of those who attended the courses are listed in De Mauro 1967a:320.
44. Linda (1998/99:223–224) even suggests that Saussure might have resisted teaching general linguistics; he did not do much preparation, judging by the scant preparatory notes he left.

## 2. The Writings

1. Cited in Rastier 2003:25.
2. Gautier 2005:69–70.
3. "Nothing would have given me more pleasure, and perhaps more benefit, than a collaboration of this kind—yet meantime I do see some practical difficulties for a project that, if realized, would have been ideal for me." Letter to Bally of December 15 (probably of 1911). Saussure 1994a:130–131.
4. Letter to Meillet of May 29, 1913. In Bally 1990:102–103.
5. "Your notes are of the highest interest; but what remorse do I have, thinking that I, too, could have kept a diary of my meetings with our *maître*; how much he told me, of which I should have kept notes." Bally to Gautier, March 5, 1913, cited in Linda 1998/99:226.
6. See Saussure 1964:124.
7. "Great was our deception: we found nothing or hardly anything that would correspond to the notebooks of his students; to a large extent F. de Saussure destroyed the rush drafts [*les brouillons hâtifs*] which he jotted down, day after day, as sketches of his presentation! His desk drawers yielded nothing but fairly old notes, which were certainly not without value, but impossible to use and to combine with the material of the three courses" (*CLG*, 7–8/xvii).
8. As later studies showed, Bally and Sechehaye did use some of Saussure's papers. Sechehaye made a somewhat abridged copy of a note by Saussure that contained important pronouncements on the general nature of language; the now famous note (identified by its beginning words, "unde exoriar?") was found and published later (Mejía 1997: 93–110). Also, a note on phonetics that closely corresponds to Sechehaye's preparatory notes was recently found in Saussure's papers at Harvard, evidence that those notes were taken from Saussure's own writing (Marchese 2003:333–339).
9. Cited in Godel 1957:30.
10. Ibid., 29–30.
11. Unpublished letter to L. Gautier in 1957, written in the wake of the appearance of Godel's book; cited in Bouquet 1998/99.
12. The most extensive notes were by Riedlinger, L. Caille, Gautier, Regard, G. Dégailler, F. Joseph, and Constantin. The editors eventually used two sets of notes from the first, three from the second, and five from the third course (Bouquet 1998/99:187–202).
13. See the same observation in Harris 2001:217.

14. Some additional pieces of Saussure's writing on the anagram appeared in Gandon 2003a.
15. "Les Burgondes et la langue burgonde en pays roman," delivered at the Société d'histoire et d'archéologie de Genève on December 15, 1904. The minutes of Saussure's talk were published (Saussure 1922b).
16. In these notes, Saussure mentions the "newborn century" (*siècle naissant*) and makes references to works of the "past century" (Saussure 1993a:179). According to Parret, Saussure's Vedic studies were inspired by the book of his friend and colleague Paul Oltramare, *L'histoire des idées philosophiques dans l'Inde* (1906). On Oltramare's influence on Saussure's Veda notes, see Parret 1995/96:86–87.
17. Bouquet (2003b:11) speaks of the "enigmatic" fate of Saussure's heritage: its enormous influence came before much of his writing was discovered.
18. Godel was the first to take note of these features of Saussure's sketch writing. He pointed out the obsessive recurrence of the same themes, in multiple variations; Godel observes that the impression is one of persistence and dissipation at the same time (1957:239).
19. "Nous nous demandons alors si la nature de cette chose, en tout cas double, de son essence, est plus forcièrement *historique*—ou plus forcièrement d'une nature abstraite, échappant aux forces historiques en vertu d'une donée fondamentale incoercible, qui est dans la jeu d'échecs la convention initiale reparaissant après chaque coup et dans la langue l'action totalement inéluctable des signes vis-à-vis de l'esprit qui s'établira de soi-méme aprés chaque événement, chaque coup" (*ELG*, 207/143–144); emphasis Saussure's; the passage begins in the middle, implying a main clause that is omitted.
20. "J'aurais dû dès lors vous prier de me décharger immédiatement du devoir de parler de l'oeuvre de Whitney en linguistique, alors même que cette occasion est de beaucoup" (*ELG*, 149/213–214).
21. Cited in Starobinski 1979 [1971]:3.
22. Saussure 1993a:197. Another characteristic sample of Saussure's writing can be seen in Engler's publication of a short fragment on the double nature of language that showed all the crossed-out alternatives. Engler interprets the proliferation of alternative versions in Saussure's writing as evidence of his search for the "most precise expression" (Engler 1997:201–202).
23. Analyzing one set of Saussure's letters (to his cousin, the Arabist Max van Brechem), Anouar (1974/75:17–18) notes that they are interrupted and resumed with different ink or on a sheet of paper of different format. The appearance of these letters recalls an example in the *Course* with which Saussure illustrated the irrelevance of the material substance of the representation of a sign:

"Whether I write letters on white or on black, etched or brought into relief, with a pen or a chisel, it has no consequence for their meaning" (*CLG*, 166/118).
24. Letter to Bally, August 7, 1906 (Saussure 1994a:114–115). See a discussion of Wagner's ideas about language from the perspective of structuralist "Saussurean linguistics": Ambrosini 1986.
25. Schlegel's *Philosophische Lehrjahre*, containing several thousand fragments, were published in full for the first time in the 1960s (Schlegel 1963).
26. *Athenaeum Fragmente*, no. 53 (Schlegel et al. 1798).
27. See, for example, Bouquet 1997; particularly strong statements to this effect can be found in works of Pétroff 1999:254, where "the other Saussure," emerging from the notes, is proclaimed to be "totally alien" to the structuralist tradition.
28. De Mauro (1967a), while using the term *vulgate* and refusing to accept the *Course* as anything more than a "summation" of Saussure's "doctrine" (as if there were an established doctrine of which one could make a summation), acknowledges nevertheless that our indebtedness to Bally and Sechehaye is "great and evident." Claude Hagège (2003) opposes the "exegetic" approach of those who see in the *Course* nothing more than Saussure's *vulgate* to a "historical" one, which upholds the book as an inexorable reality of twentieth-century linguistics.
29. Bouquet speaks about "two editorial paradigms" concerning Saussure's heritage: one considering the *Course in General Linguistics* to be Saussure's "oeuvre" in principle, while supplementing it with material drawn from the notes (as Godel did), the other taking Saussure's notes and "lectures" (that is, the students' notebooks) as his genuine "oeuvre" reflected only indirectly in the published book. Bouquet's preference for the latter approach extends to the point that he is willing to give priority quite uncritically to every source outside the book. For instance, he holds up Regard's notes as yet another piece of evidence against the book, despite the fact that they were expressly rejected by the editors as too free (1998/99:192–193).
30. The emphasis on "live speech," in contradistinction to fixed norms, was particularly vivid in Bally 1926 [1913]. The book, an earlier version of which appeared in 1913, soon after Saussure's death, can be read as a dialogue with, and presumably a complement to, the ideas of the *Course*, on whose preparation Bally was working at the same time.
31. In their preface to *ELG*, Bouquet and Engler (2002:11–13) concede that Saussure's newly recovered notes were "disparate and fragmentary," which made it necessary to group them thematically.
32. Commenting on "mixed notions" in the *Course* (for instance, treating *la langue* at different points as language in general, as the synchronic state of a language,

or as a generalization of different types of languages), Engler (2004) explains them as Saussure's "didactic intentions." Whether this was a result of intentional "simplifications" is problematic in view of similar discrepancies in Saussure's notes.

33. See this point made by Godel 1957:131.
34. As Hagège 2003:116 rightly points out, by comparing *CLG* with the newly discovered notes, one finds that much of the latter is already present in the *Course*. It was the "abruptness" of the formulations given in the *Course* that made them particularly influential, by virtue of leaving much to the reader's reflection.
35. Cf. Harris 2001.
36. See his commentary in Saussure 1967b:476–477.
37. Bouquet 2003:12. As a matter of fact, I could not find anything resembling the phrase in the *Course* in the book by Bopp. Perhaps Bouquet meant another work by that author.
38. As Engler (2004:58) justly noted, the meaning of the last sentence was "absolutely opposed to and incompatible with" the framework of the editors' own ideas and almost certainly a concession to Saussure's criticism of Sechehaye's book.
39. Lepschy (1979:31) does concede that the concluding sentence of the *Course* was probably a compression of Saussure's various pronouncements, which had probably been heard by several people.
40. De Mauro notes that the sentence in the *Course* "was not created ex nihilo," yet deems it unauthentic anyway (commentary to Saussure 1967b:452).
41. "Des incursions que nous venons de faire dans les domains limitrophes de notre science, il se dégage un enseignement tout négatif, mais d'autant plus intéressant qu'il concorde avec l'idée fondamentale de ce cours: *la linguistique a pour unique et véritable objet la langue envisagée en elle-même et pour elle-même*" (*CLG*, 317/230).

## 3. Antinomies of the Sign

1. This theme appears in the opening section of all three of Saussure's lecture courses. For instance, the first lecture of the first course begins with the words: "Starting from an internal principle, one could define linguistics as the science of language or of languages. But the question then immediately arises: what is language?" (Saussure 1996:1).
2. According to Godel, who was the first to appraise the note, it "represented perhaps the core of Saussure's reflections." It was one of the few notes of Saussure

to be used by the editors of the *Course* (Sechehaye made an incomplete copy of it). See Mejía 1997.
3. See in particular the most recent addition to Saussure's published notes on linguistics: Matsuzawa 2003.
4. In particular, Saussure rejected Sechehaye's suggestion that linguistics could be a branch of psychology (an opinion shared by many in the late nineteenth century) (*ELG*, 259/185).
5. "Le passé de la linguistique se compose d'un doute général sur son rôle, sur sa place, sur sa valeur, accompagné de colossals acquisitions sur les faits" (*ELG*, 116/79).
6. Derrida was apparently the first to trace the Husserlian approach in Saussure; cf. Strozier 1988:228. The idea did not find resonance in Saussurean studies, which generally tend to assume a defensive position when discussing Derrida's critique of Saussure. Komatsu 1993 attributes "significantly Husserlian" features in the *Course* to Bally and Sechehaye (whose familiarity with and interest in Husserl was known), citing the absence of "Husserlian" passages in students' lecture notes. Saussure's own notes, however (unconnected to his courses) give ample evidence of his preoccupation with questions of linguistic epistemology. Curiously enough, this time it is an excessive "philosophizing" in the *Course* that is attributed to the editors' bad influence; elsewhere, they have been accused of not understanding, and consequently having suppressed, philosophical aspects of Saussure's thought.
7. A curious feature of teleological concepts of language development is their rather naive connection with nationalist thinking. In the nineteenth century, German linguists often spoke of the richness and complexity of Indo-European morphology as a sign of the "organic" way of thinking of their speakers—in contradistinction to languages such as Chinese or Turkish with their more "mechanical" way of combining words, which ostensibly represented an earlier, more primitive stage of language development. From this perspective, French could be condemned as a "degenerate" language that had replaced many of the glorious Indo-European forms with "mechanical" analytical constructions. In the next century, however, the growing prestige of English, coupled with the erosion of the German linguistic monopoly, gave rise to a theory of "progress" in language, which took the simplification of forms in a language as a sign of a modern rationality and economy of thought replacing the feisty morphological idiosyncrasies of darker ages; see in particular Jespersen 1905. It should be to Saussure's credit that he never expressed the slightest sympathy with either side of this controversy.

8. Helmholtz 1996a [1895]:343.
9. Cf. Rickert's classification (1902) of all sciences as either "natural" or "historical"—an opposition that, according to Rickert, is grounded not in the substance of their objects of study but in the strategic approach they take.
10. Saussure was apparently not aware of Charles Peirce's "semiotics." Peirce's approach to the sign, however, was different from Saussure's.
11. In his third lecture course Saussure speaks about arbitrariness occupying "the place at the summit" in the hierarchy of the ideas discussed in the course (Saussure 1993b:76); if the sign were not arbitrary, one could not say that language consists of nothing but differences (76). See further comment in Bota 2002:141; Suenaga 1999:198. De Mauro (1967a:331) notes that Saussure's principle purpose in introducing the terms *signifier* and *signified*, late in the third course, was to establish the principle of arbitrariness "more rigorously."
12. Such has been the position of "conventionalists" against "naturalists" since Plato's *Cratylus* (Engler 1962:7).
13. Or, as Lacan expressed it, there is no reason why a giraffe could not be called an "elephant," and an elephant a "giraffe," in which case we would say that a giraffe has a trunk and an elephant has a long neck (Lacan 1973:290).
14. Jakobson 1978:111. Holdcroft 1991:55 points out that Saussure's explanation in this passage from the *Course* sounds "fairly casual"—a typical offhand remark given on the spur of the moment in a lecture. Other commentators have suggested "didactic intentions" that made Saussure simplify his notions, leading to their being misunderstood—an explanation to which he himself occasionally had recourse (Engler 1962:45).
15. The last point can be demonstrated by citing expressions in the two languages that involve the key word and are not directly translatable to each other—such as *Ça fait un effet boeuf* and *Er steht wie der Ochse am Berge* (Arrivé 2007:50). One can agree with Arrivé that by citing the words in isolation Saussure indeed made a "feeble demonstration" of his concept.
16. One of the sources of iconicity in language and other semiotic systems is synesthesia, a perceptual trait Saussure apparently possessed. In the 1890s, E. Claparède, a Genevan psychologist, distributed a questionnaire about the perception of sounds in colors. Among his respondents was "an eminent linguist" who gave an elaborate answer—in all probability, Saussure. Citing this episode, Mazzeo 2004 calls it "revanche de substance."
17. Jespersen 1933:109; cited in Engler 1962.
18. Cf., for example, Firth's "phonoaesthemes" (1930), i.e., clusters of etymologically nonrelated words whose partial phonic resemblance corresponds to an

overlap between their meanings: *flicker, flutter, flatter, fly, flow*. See also recent efforts to broaden the scope of lexical items that could be considered iconic: Lehmann 2006.

19. To rescue the concept, some scholars suggested that Saussure was in fact describing two qualitatively different phenomena of arbitrariness: "external," concerning the relations between signs, and "internal," concerning the link between a signifier and signified in a single sign, which is absolute. Engler 1962:52 was the first to express this idea; see also Suenaga 1999:199 and 2005:147; Arrivé 2007:48. Bouquet 1997:287–288 calls the two phenomena in question "systematic arbitrariness" and "the internal arbitrariness of the sign."

20. Cf. Finnish numerals *kahdeksan* "8" and *yhdeksän* "9," whose etymological forms refer, respectively, to *kaksi* "2" and *yksi* "1" (Gen. *kahden, yhden*)—implying their conceptualization as "ten without two" and "ten without one."

21. See in particular the definition of the sign in the *Encyclopédie ou Dictionnaire raisonné des sciences, des arts et des métiers*, vol. 15 (Paris, 1765): "Le signe est tout ce qui est destiné à représenter une chose. Le signe enferme deux idées, l'une de la chose qui représente, l'autre de la chose représentée." The 1897 edition (i.e., the one contemporary with Saussure's linguistic notes) of *La grande encyclopédie*, vol. 13, defines the phenomenon (which it calls *le symbole*) essentially the same way. As for the "sign," it is interpreted here more narrowly, as a symptom implying a certain meaning (smoke as a "sign" of fire), while defining it in the same "nomenclaturist" fashion": "Le signe est un phénomène apparent qui nous révèle l'existence d'un phénomène caché"; the existence of the "hidden phenomenon, independent of the one behind which it is "hidden," is never questioned.

22. Capt-Artaud 2003:234 claims that the oft-cited aphoristic formulation in the *Course*, "la langue est une forme et non une substance," is "apparently apocryphal." Even if it is, both the book and the notes abound in statements to a similar effect.

23. Normand 2000:128 makes a useful qualification when she points out that the direct application of Durkheim's concept to language was more typical of Meillet than Saussure. The former directly paraphrased Durkheim by proclaiming that "la langue est un fait social," while the latter preferred to speak about a "social product" or "social act" in connection with language.

24. An interesting antecedent to Saussure's thesis can be found in the critique of the idea of universal grammar by Destutt de Tracy. According to de Tracy, the impossibility of those "brilliant chimeras," universal grammars, can be attested by the fact that language usage is at the mercy of the infinite variety of intentions

that people apply to it at every moment: "If all the people on earth agreed today to speak the same language, immediately, with the first instance of its usage, they would alter and modify it in a thousand different ways in various lands, giving birth to distinct idioms that would distance one group of speakers from another. Language forms and composes itself bit by bit through usage, and without any general plan" (Destutt de Tracy 1817:368). Tracy's critique of the eighteenth-century rationalist approach to language finds a close parallel in Saussure's remarks about the futility of any attempt to create an artificial international language, a project that had gained great popularity in his time.

25. Culler 1986 [1976]. As Normand 2000:129 points out, a factor that had been overlooked for a long time was that arbitrariness intrudes into the social aspect of language, making it into a "socio-historical turbulence."
26. Maniglier 2006:46 argues that Saussure's "general linguistics" was never intended to be conceived of as a "sane edifice" for linguistic description but rather as the demonstration of its metaphysical impossibility. To this end, the author cites the famous passage from Saussure's 1894 letter to Meillet in which he acknowledges that one has to "stick" (*ténir*) to some doctrine "as if contrary to one's own conviction, and making the best, as it were, of exposing even one's doubts."
27. Maniglier (2006:462–463) perceptively compares this attitude in Saussure with Montaigne's approaches to the infinite diversity of human cultures and institutions.

## 4. Fragmentation and Progressivity

1. E. Favre, one of Saussure's Genevan companions in his Leipzig years, wrote effusively about the extraordinary abilities of his friend: "No subject, either poetry, literature, politics, fine arts, history, or natural science, was foreign to him. He wrote verses, he made drawings," etc. Cited in De Mauro 1967a:298.
2. Saussure's mother was an accomplished pianist (De Mauro 1967a:288).
3. The grammar's title, *Astadhyayi*, literally "eight chapters," reflects the division of its entries into eight major sections. A full German translation of *Astadhyayi* is available: Böhtlingk 1964.
4. Aarsleff's study (1981) goes to the extreme in identifying Saussure's views with the conventionalist approach to language of the philosophers of the French Enlightenment and Whitney. The author's principal thesis is Saussure's allegiance to eighteenth-century rationalism and, by the same token, his rejection of "Romantic" organicism. What Aarsleff's argument does not take into

account is the dramatic difference between the "eighteenth-century" Romanticism of the *Athenaeum* and the organicism of Schelling and Humboldt.
5. An exception to this trend, however limited, can be seen in some works by Engler, who pointed out parallels between Saussure and contemporary neo-Romantic schools in German philology headed by Carl Vossler and Leo Spitzer—both pointing back, in particular, to Schleiermacher (Engler 2001). Cf. also brief remarks by Starobinski and Rastier concerning the importance of Jena philosophy of language for Saussurean linguistic thought: Green et al. 2003.
6. *Cours de littérature dramatique de Schlegel*, trans. Albertine Adrienne Necker de Saussure (Paris, 1814).
7. For a detailed account of her life and major work, see Maurer 1938; Causse 1930; Bernardinis 1965. An interesting contextualization of Necker de Saussure's life, based on ample quotation from her diary and lifelong correspondence, can be found in Mestral Combremont 1946.
8. In Necker de Saussure's book one finds "some sensible remarks on language acquisition by infants" (Arivé 2007:20).
9. "Saissez donc le sens de l'évangile, mon fils, mais sans jamais le dépouiller de sa forme. Pénétrez-vous de l'esprit, mais en revenant sans cesse à sa lettre. Séparé de son enveloppe, l'esprit s'évapore ou s'altère."
10. As Maurer 1938:89 points out in this regard, the ideas of Schlegel, Novalis, Schleiermacher, and Jean Paul Richter concerning Romanticism were well-known to the author of *L'éducation progressive*.
11. All references to Necker de Saussure's book are taken from the 1836 edition.
12. Particularly powerful expressions of the idea can be found in Schlegel's essay "Über die Philosophie: An Dorothea" (1799c), in which he posits how a man and a woman can advance their understanding of philosophy by "teaching" it to each other.
13. In Schlegel's review of Kant's *Anthropologie in pragmatischer Hinsicht* (Schlegel 1799b:306).
14. "It is impossible to construct God without the Madonna" (*PhL*, 169, no. 540).
15. Maurer 1938:89–90 mentions Schlegel's *Lucinde* as a source for the concept of the woman/man dichotomy in Necker de Saussure's book.
16. Letter of December 1815. In Mestral Combremont 1946:139.
17. "Neither her faith not her cheerfulness were given her by nature. She struggled to attain them. In her fifties, she felt herself overcome with apathy and fatigue, almost numb" (Maurer 1938, 33).
18. Necker de Saussure's relationship with her elder son and elder daughter developed over the years into a state of almost complete mutual alienation; her

second son, more sanguine in his psychological disposition, died young. As for her younger daughter, she died, not long after her marriage, having to all appearances set herself on fire. In the last years of her life, Necker de Saussure found support in a strong mutual attachment with her granddaughter.

19. Cited in Mestral Combremont 1946:187.
20. Fichte 1988 [1794]:11 calls this thesis the "absolut-ersten, schlechthin unbedingten Grundsatz" (the absolutely primary, by necessity unconditional foundational proposition).
21. For a detailed argument to this effect concerning prosody, see Lepschy 1979:chapter 3. A counterargument suggested in Raggiunti 1982: 95—namely, that the evidence of prosody does not apply because it belongs to the *parole* while linearity is an attribute of the *langue*—looks rather lame. Cf. the school of functional linguistics (Halliday 1978), as well as some works of cognitive linguistics (Chafe 1994), which treat the "intonational unit" as a stationary unit of language.
22. Consequently, the idea that the anagram studies "offset" (Wunderli 1972:78–79) or "challenged" (Gadet 1987:113) the issue of linearity has gained considerable ground in poststructural Saussure literature.
23. Indeed, Joseph 2004:71 finds it difficult to explain why Saussure apparently gave such significance to the issue.
24. Arrivé 2007:62 remarks that by introducing the notion of linearity, Saussure "glided" from the domain of the sign to that of the signifier—an indeterminate fluidity of terminology that he finds typical of the *Course*. In this particular case, however, Saussure (or his editors) made the shift quite explicit by announcing it in the chapter's title: "Charactère linéaire du signifiant."
25. Quoted in Décimo 1994/95:79.
26. Cited in Parret 1995/96:117.
27. Cited in Mejía 1997:94.

## 5. Diachrony and History

1. The de facto appearance of *Mémoire sur le système primitif des voyelles dans les langues indo-européennes* (Saussure 1879) was in December 1878.
2. Thirty-five years later (and after Saussure's death), Brugmann still could not refrain from sarcasm when reminiscing about the way the young author of the *Mémoire* was celebrated in Switzerland "like a second [Franz] Bopp" (letter to W. Streitberg, November 11, 1914; cited in Villani 1990:30).

3. Brugmann and Delbrück 1886–1900.
4. "In the case of sound change we certainly must demand that it should make its appearance in the same way in every case in which the same phonetic conditions are present" (Paul 1889 [1880]:209).
5. Cf. Béguelin's remark that Saussure's adolescent "essay" contained, in a rudimentary form, his method employed in the *Mémoire*.
6. As a matter of fact, the term "laryngeals" belonged to the Danish comparatist, Saussure's contemporary Hermann Møller. Møller embraced Saussure's hypothesis in view of his own agenda, which was to prove that the Indo-European and Semitic language families originated from a common protolanguage. As early as 1879, Møller argued that Saussure's "coefficients" in Indo-European stems correspond to "laryngeal" consonants in a number of ostensibly related Semitic stems. Since Møller's idea of the protorelationship between the two families was not accepted in mainstream Indo-European studies, his argument in favor of Saussure's hypothesis had little impact. After the hypothesis was proven, however, Møller's term *laryngeals* became conventional. About all the vicissitudes of Saussure's hypothesis, see Gmür 1986.
7. At the time, Saussure's only fellow traveler in this paradigm shift was Baudouin de Courtenay—like Saussure, a prominent historical linguist who had come to appreciate the importance of approaching language as it is perceived by speakers. See Sljusareva 1971.
8. *Thèses* (1929), section 1C.
9. See the general discussion of this methodological principle in Martinet 1955.
10. See, for instance, Jakobson's radical redefinition of the history of the Slavic branch of Indo-European languages (Jakobson 1929). Regarding the extension of structural diachrony to earlier stages of Indo–European history, see Shevelov 1964.
11. This approach became the mainstream of comparative linguistics after Nicholas Trubetzkoy's seminal theoretical work (2001 [1939]) proclaimed the divergence of genetically related languages into separate branches and the convergence of unrelated languages into "linguistic unions" (*Sprachbünde*) as the two guiding principles simultaneously at work in the history of languages.
12. Bergson's central work, *L'évolution créatrice*, was published in 1907. A later work by Bergson (Bergson 2004 [1912]) dealt specifically with the question of the transmission of memory, which was central to Saussure's discussion of the history of legends.
13. Pétroff 1999:265 calls this "Heraclitus' perspective."

14. On the empirical level, it was at about that time that the traditional idea of dialects as compact formations gave way to the new understanding of the dialectal space as a continuum of overlapping features. The new approach resulted in the emergence of dialect atlases, consisting of a series of separate maps, each showing the distribution of a single distinct feature (the so-called isogloss). The earliest linguistic atlases appeared in Germany (1888) and France (1900s).
15. Wunderli 1990:45 argues that Saussure's insistence on the "blindness" of language development neglects to consider the norm, which could be envisioned as a relatively stable intermediary between language and speech. His suggestion does not take into account Saussure's strong antipathy to and profound skepticism about any deliberate activity of "language making." Indeed, any normalizing measure, for all its obvious immediate results, is always rife with unpredictable side effects, which makes its role in language development in the final analysis as unforeseeable as that of spontaneous speech.
16. Pétroff 1999:267–268 compares this attitude with Prigogine's theory of chaos (Prigogine and Stengers 1984), according to which the incessant course of transformation may "provoke the apparition of a new order."
17. See Arrivé 2007:187–188; Arsenjević 1998.
18. Starobinski (1979 [1971]:7) points to two principal types of modification according to Saussure: substitution of one name with another and change of a function assigned to a name.
19. Schlegel's letter to Christian Gottfried Körner, September 21–30, 1796 (Schlegel 1966:333).
20. "Der Historiker ist ein rückwärts gekehrter Prophet" (*AF*, no. 80).
21. "The most important scientific discoveries are *bons mots* of a kind. They are such due to the accidental suddenness of their origin, to the permutations of thoughts, and to the way their expression is thrown together in a Baroque fashion" (*AF*, no. 220).
22. Saussure's marginalization of writing earned him a rebuke from Derrida, who dubbed him a linguist of the "word." Saussure's perception of the disruptive forces at work in language was in fact not that far from Derrida's (Strozier 1988). Ironically, it was the perceived lack of those qualities in writing that made Saussure consider it a secondary phenomenon.
23. Cf. Altani-Voisin 2003.
24. "Ainsi il faut s'en tenir à une sorte de doctrine, comme malgré soi, et comme étant peut-être encore la meilleure maniere d'exposer les doutes eux-mêmes" (Saussure 2003a:377).

## 6. The Anagram

1. The book was preceded by a series of articles Starobinski published in the 1960s: Starobinski 1964, 1967, 1969.
2. See an annotated bibliography of early (1960–1979) studies of the anagram in Callus 2002.
3. Unlike other materials published in *L'Herne Saussure*, Saussure's writing on the anagram appeared tightly interwoven with the publisher's effusive celebrations of this "post-modern" Saussure (Gandon 2003a).
4. Letter of January 23, 1906 (Saussure 1964:106).
5. In his letter to Bally, which was apparently the first time he spoke publicly about the issue, Saussure used the word *Stichwort*. Callus (2002:175) cites the following terms which Saussure used as "more or less synonymous" on various occasions: *hypogram, leitwort, Stichwort, mot-thème, logogram, antigram, paragram, cryptogram, anagram*. To this Starobinski (1979 [1971]:14–15) adds "anaphony" and "hypogram" (29), both designating "imperfect" or "partial" versions of the phenomenon.
6. In the letter to Meillet of September 23, 1907—apparently following up an earlier mention of the subject—Saussure announces that he has decided to send Meillet his analysis of "Saturnian Latin" instead of the "Homeric anagram," first, because he found the issue "more fundamental" in Latin poetry than in Homer and, second, because these analyses turned out to be more compact, compared with the "15 to 20 notebooks" of his Homer studies (Saussure 1964:109).
7. Ibid., 113.
8. In this connection Saussure came to the conclusion that the assonance of Germanic epic verse was "total" rather than merely "initial" (i.e., confined to the lines' beginning) as was previously thought (ibid.).
9. In particular, Saussure analyzed Caesar's *Gallic Wars* and Cicero's letters (Gadet 1987:114).
10. "J'ai vainement essayé en ouvrant le volume à tous les endroits possibles de tomber sur un passage blanc." Cited in Gadet 1987:114.
11. See an extensive example of Saussure's analytical technique in Starobinski 1979 [1971]: 58–61.
12. Letter to Meillet of September 23, 1907 (Saussure 1964:113).
13. In the letter to Bally of August 7, 1906, Saussure calls his hypothesis about the omnipresence of anagrams in Homer "scary"; and yet, "in spite of myself, the proof that all Homeric texts are nothing but a continual cryptogram is

so compelling that nothing could deprive me of this conviction" (Saussure 1994a:114).
14. Cited in Saussure's letter of August 31 (ibid.).
15. Letter of January 8, 1908 (Saussure 1964:119).
16. Postcard of February 10, 1908. Published in Starobinski 1979 [1971]:127–128.
17. "When a first anagram appears, it seems like a flash of light. But when one sees that one can add to this a second, third, and even a fourth anagram, far from feeling relieved of doubt, one begins to lose confidence in the first discovery" (cited in Starobinski 1979 [1971]:101).
18. Starobinski 1964:259 called it the "strongest objection" to the concept of the anagram that one could construe any number of anagrams out of a few given lines of verse.
19. On some occasions Saussure even claimed that the borders of the relevant segment in the text within which an anagram appears are signaled by an identical sound combination at the beginning and the end of the passage. Saussure called such an enframed textual segment a "mannequin" (Starobinski 1979 [1971]:59–60).
20. With the anagram "one nails God to the text, so to speak" ("on rivait pour ansi dire le Dieu au texte"). Letter to Meillet, September 23, 1907 (Saussure 1964:116). Elsewhere Saussure spoke of the possibility that anagrams were relics of magic formulas, prayers, or funeral verses (Starobinski 1979 [1971]:41).
21. I disagree with Wunderli (1972:41) that in his treatment of the anagram Saussure "balanced" between the aesthetic and the mysterious. It seems, rather, that he tended to push the putative mystical origin into an unspecific primordial past in order to emphasize the self-contained (not outwardly motivated) nature of the subsequent tradition.
22. To this end, Saussure studied translations of Virgil by T. Johnson (c. 1800) in order to determine whether hypograms could be found there. His hypothesis was that the tradition stemmed from Latin classical poetry and extended through the Middle Ages and Renaissance to modern times (Bouquet 1986).
23. As Starobinski suggests elsewhere (1964:257), the process could go in either direction: from sound repetitions to the awareness of a name or from the idea of a name to echoing sound repetitions.
24. Cf. Bouquet's remark that Saussure's quest for anagrams is of interest only in relation to his theory of *la langue*; only in this opposition does it find its proper relevance (*valeur*): Green et al. 2003:302.
25. Letter to Meillet of December 15, 1907 (Saussure 1964:115).

## 7. Linguistics of Speech: An Unrealizable Promise

1. Bouquet, typically, accuses Bally of having "grievously distorted" Saussure's intentions concerning *la linguistique de la parole* (Green et al. 2003:294)—despite the fact that Bally specifically expressed his regret that Saussure was not more forthcoming on this matter. In fact, when Bouquet himself tries to present the case for a "pure" Saussure, his evidence does not go beyond vague general statements about Saussure's "two linguistics" (Bouquet 2000:135–136).
2. Bally and Bouquet find themselves in agreement in their attempt to explain this seemingly inexplicable omission: both suggested that Saussure chose not to include the linguistics of speech in his lecture course solely out of "didactic considerations" (Bouquet 2004).
3. This aspect of the structuralist reading of Saussure was upheld by Chomsky, who declared the opposition between "competence" and "performance" mainly for the purpose of excluding the latter from further consideration. His chief—and not unjustified—complaint against the *Course* was that its idea of inner linguistic knowledge dealt exclusively with single signs, making his *langue* an "inventory of elements" (Chomsky 1965:14). By including elaborate syntactic roles in the domain of linguistic competence, generative grammar made any notion of speech "performance," distinct from linguistic competence, superfluous or trivial (cf. in particular Chomsky 1993).
4. Sechehaye, in his contribution to the volume in honor of Saussure, pointed to this weakness in Bally's theory of style and discourse. He argued that to describe the expression that language receives in speech, one has to take into account subjective factors as well as objective ones (Sechehaye 1908a:168). Saussure, however, did not accept Sechehaye's argument.
5. Starobinski was the first to suggest that Saussure's anagrammatic studies meant at least a promise of a "linguistics of speech," on which the *Course* seemed to renege. The point has been reiterated in recent studies (Pétroff 1999:280; Green et al. 2003). Linda 1998/99:239–240 suggests that the introduction of the anagram potentially results in splitting the theory of the sign into three rather than two domains: "semiology" (general theory of different types of signs), "signology" (specifically addressing linguistic signs as they are constituted in *la langue*), and the study of signs in discourse, connected to the anagram.
6. Gandon (2003:202) ingeniously compares the anagram as a speech-enabler with the medieval symbolic construct of "The Mystical Mill," which "grinds" ancient reason, transforming it into "digestible flour" (*farine assimilable*).

7. See, for example, Holdcroft 1991:60; Gadet 1987:113–118 even asserts that the principle of linearity is "recused"—rescinded?—in the anagram, due to its "associative motivation," while Wunderli 1972:78–79 finds a parallel between the Saussurean anagram and Kristeva's idea of dissemination (1969a).
8. "Precise observation of the first moments of an emerging vélleité, which is the germ, as it were, would convince us that there, already, lies everything that will later merely evolve and explicate itself (*FDA*, no. 203).
9. "L'esprit de l'homme qui rêve se satisfait pleinement de ce qui lui arrive. L'angoissante question de la possibilité ne se pose pas" (Bréton 1973 [1924]:23).
10. Quoted from Renard 1987:114.
11. The importance of the Jena fragments for the beginning of modern theoretical linguistics in general, and for Saussure's thought in particular, was recently pointed out in a conversation between Starobinski, Rastier, Green, and Bouquet, published in *L'Herne Saussure* (Greene et al. 2003). Rastier emphasized the general importance of Schlegel's fragments, "qui n'ont rien perdu de leur actualité," while Starobinski traced Saussure's interest in Leo Spitzer's school of hermeneutics back to Schleiermacher.
12. For the early Romantics the particular epistemological value of the fragments lay in their ability to act as a "failed expression of the absolute" (Frank 1997:940), or, to put it somewhat differently, to make the non-accomplishment of cognition "endurable" (Heine 1974:51). This feature of the Jena fragments shows its kinship to the discursive mode of Wittgenstein's *Philosophical Investigations* (Balfour 2002).
13. Contemporaries compared the scope of change brought by Brown's theory and curative practices with the French Revolution (Gode 1941:159). On the impact of "Mesmerism" on the Romantics, see also Hammond 1994.
14. In particular, Mesmer's later perception of magnetism as "invisible fire" gained him the name of the modern Prometheus (Hammond 1994:55).
15. The transmutation of the concept, after it left the domain of science, into a powerful instigator of poetic images, social ideas, and popular beliefs is described in Darnton 1970 (see especially chapter 5, "From Mesmer to Hugo").
16. See Oppenheim 1985.
17. Flournoy's séances with Hélène Smith started in December 1894; Saussure joined them in 1897 and continued through a part of the next year (Fehr 1997:541–542).
18. Before Saussure, Flournoy consulted with some other experts in Sanskrit about Hélène's language. In particular, Léopold Favre, lieutenant colonel and a mem-

ber of the Asiatic Society in Paris, made transcriptions of early samples of Hélène's Sanskrit, which Saussure later analyzed (Décimo 1994:44).
19. See detailed description in Lepschy 1974.
20. Another pertinent feature of Hélène's "Sanskrit" was the total absence of the sound *f*. Victor Henry explained this by her subconscious identification of *f* with *Français* and a desire not to resemble French in any way.
21. In 1908 Flournoy published a review of Henri's book in *Archives de psychologie,* in which he expressed a skeptical, even mocking, attitude toward Henri's investigations, although discounting his own negative evaluation somewhat in view of the fact that he was not a linguist himself. About the whole episode, see Décimo 1994:45–47.
22. Cited in Lepschy 1974:191.
23. "Vous me prenez pour quelqu'un qui a completement deraillé du bon sens, et qui n'est pas loin del'idée fixe en matière d'hypograms." Cited in Bouquet 1986:8.
24. In 1907 Saussure wrote two letters to Gautier about the anagram; see Wunderli 1972.
25. Cited in Callus 2002:176.
26. Cf. Nava 1968.
27. Bouquet 1986 thinks, however, that Pascal's response would have presented a crucial test of Saussure's hypothesis: if no awareness of the anagram could be detected in the transmission of a tradition, he would have been prepared to acknowledge that the whole matter was "nebulous."
28. "—J'ai là des études commencées sur de nombreux sujets. Sur quelques-unes j'ai rédigé des centaines de pages. Je les abandonne. [Et pourquoi n'achèves-tu pas?]—Parce que plus on creuse, plus on rencontre d'obscurité et d'incertitude. . . . On ne percera jamais le mystère final du langage. Tout ce travail est vain." Cited from Mejía 2005:44.

## Conclusion

1. Cf. Maniglier's argument (2006:27) that, unlike Durkheim's notion of imperative "social facts," Saussure saw in the social character of language not an affirmation of the unity of the socium but, on the contrary, the uncontrollable variability of language in the hands of "speaking subjects."
2. Engler (2001:62–63) emphasizes the Neogrammarian roots of Saussure's non-idealist (dualist) approach to language, which separated him from such anti-positivist-minded contemporaries as Schuhardt and Vossler.

3. To draw from the title of the first chapter of Andrey Bely's memoirs (1995 [1921]) about the beginning of the century: "—And the dawns, dawns, dawns!"
4. "Es ist gleich tödlich für den Geist, ein System zu haben und keins zu haben" (*AF*, no. 53).
5. "A regiment of soldiers *en parade* is, according to the way of thinking of certain philosophers, a system" (*AF*, no. 46).
6. "Many thinkers lack it [progressivity]; they practice what they learn terminally and definitively, as a shoemaker practices his trade" (*BS*, no. 48).
7. "In his domain, he [Fichte] is, properly speaking, the Pope, possessing the infallible power to open and to close heaven and hell with his key" (Schlegel 1957:3, no. 2).

# Works Cited

Aarsleff, Hans. 1981. *From Locke to Saussure: Essays on the Study of Language and Intellectual History*. Minneapolis: University of Minnesota Press.

Altani-Voisin, Françoise. 2003. "Le don de l'Inde." In Simon Bouquet, ed., *L'Herne Saussure*, 79–93. Paris: l'Herne.

Amacker, René. 1990. "Correspondence Bally-Meillet (1906–1932)." CFS 43:124–126.

Ambrosini, Riccardo. 1986. "Speculazione linguistiche di Richard Wagner." In R. Ambrosini, ed., *Linguistica e musica da Richard Wagner a Ferdinand de Saussure*. Pisa: Giardini.

Anouar, Louca. 1974/75. "Lettres de Ferdinand de Saussure à Max van Brechem." CFS 29:13–36.

Arrivé, Michel. 2007. *À la recherche de Ferdinand de Saussure*. Paris: Presses universitaires de France.

Arsenjević, Milorad. 1998. "Manuscrit inédit de Ferdinand de Saussure à propos des noms de *Genthod, Écogia, Carouge* et *Jura*." CFS 51:275–288.

Badir, Sémir. 2001. *Saussure: La langue et sa représentations*. Paris: L'Harmattan.

Balfour, Ian. 2002. *Rhetoric of Romantic Prophecy*. Stanford: Stanford University Press.

Bally, Charles. 1926 [1913]. *Langage et la vie*. Paris: Payot.

—— 1932. *Linguistique générale et linguistique française*. Paris: E. Leroux.

——— 1990. "Correspondance Bally-Meillet." *CFS* 43:91–134.
Bally, Charles, and Albert Sechehaye. 1967 [1916]. "Préface de la première édition." In Ferdinand de Saussure, *Course de linguistique générale*, 7–11. Ed. Charles Bally and Albert Sechehaye, with Albert Riedlinger. Paris: Payot.
Barthes, Roland. 1957. *Mythologies*. Paris: Seuil.
——— 1987. *S/Z*. Paris: Seuil.
Baudrillard, Jean. 2001. *Impossible Exchange*. Trans. Chris Turner. London: Verso, 2001.
Béguelin, Marie-José. 2003. "Le méthode comparative et l'enseignement du *Mémoire*." In Simon Bouquet, ed., *L'Herne Saussure*, 150–164. Paris: l'Herne.
Behler, Ernst. 1992. *Frühromantik*. Berlin: Walter de Gruyter.
——— 1993. *Studien zur Romantik und zur idealistischen Philosophie*, 2. Paderborn: Schöningh.
——— 1993a. "Das Fragment der Frühromantik." In Ernst Behler, *Studien zur Romantik und zur idealistischen Philosophie*, 27–42. Paderborn: Schöningh.
Bely, Andrei. 1995 [1921]. *Vospominaniia ob A. A. Bloke*. Moscow: Respublika.
Benjamin, Walter. 1996 [1920]. *The Concept of Criticism in German Romanticism*. In Walter Benjamin, *Selected Writings*, 1:116–200. Cambridge: Belknap.
Bennington, Geoffrey. 2004. "Saussure and Derrida." In Carol Sanders, ed., *The Cambridge Companion to Saussure*, 186–204. Cambridge: Cambridge University Press.
Benveniste, Émile. 1965. *Ferdinand de Saussure à l'École des Hautes Études*. Paris: École Pratique des Hautes Études.
——— 1966a. "Nature du signe linguistique." In Émile Benveniste, *Problèmes de linguistique générale*, 49–55. Paris: Gallimard.
——— 1966b. "Saussure après un démi-siècle." In Émile Benveniste, *Problèmes de linguistique générale*, 32–45. Paris: Gallimard.
Bergson, Henri. 1907. *L'évolution créatrice*. Paris: H. Le Soudier.
——— 2004 [1912]. *Matter and Memory*. Mineola, NY: Dover.
Bernardinis, Anna Maria. 1965. *Il pensiero educativo di Albertine Necker de Saussure*. Firenze: Sansoni.
Bloomfield, Leonard. 1926. "A Set of Postulates for the Science of Language." *Language* 2:153–164.
Böhtlingk, Otto. 1964. *Panini's Grammatik*. Hildesheim: Georg Olms.
Bopp, Franz. 1816. *Über das Conjugationssystem der Sanskritsprache in Vergleichung mit jenem der griechischen, lateinischen, persischen und germanischen Sprache*. Frankfurt: n.p.
Bota, Cristian. 2002. "La question de l'ordre dans les cours et les écrits saussurienns de linguistique générale: Essai de refonte géometrique." *CFS* 55:139–167.

Bouquet, Simon. 1986. "Documents saussuriens retrouvés dans les archives d'Antoine Meillet au Collège de France." *CFS* 40:5–12.
—— 1997. *Introduction à la lecture de Saussure*. Paris: Payot and Rivages.
—— 1998/99. "Les deus paradigms éditoriaux de la linguistique générale de Ferdinand de Saussure." *CFS* 51:187–202.
—— 1999. "D'une théorie de la référence à une linguistique du texte: Saussure contre Saussure?" *CFS* 52:37–43.
—— 2000. "Sur la sémantique Saussurienne (Réponse à Gabriel Bergounioux)." *CFS* 53:135–39.
——, ed. 2003a. *L'Herne Saussure*. Paris: l'Herne.
—— 2003b. "Saussure après un siècle." In Simon Bouquet, ed., *L'Herne Saussure*, 11–15. Paris: l'Herne.
—— 2004. "Saussure's Unfinished Semantics." In Carol Sanders, ed., *The Cambridge Companion to Saussure*, 205–218. Cambridge: Cambridge University Press.
Bouquet, Simon, and Rudolf Engler. 2002. "Préface des éditeurs." 2002. *Écrits de linguistique générale*, 7–14. Ed. Simon Bouquet and Rudolf Engler. Paris: Gallimard.
Bréton, André. 1973 [1924]. *Manifestes du surréalisme*. Paris: Gallimard.
Brugmann, Karl, and Berthold Delbrück. 1886–1900. *Grundriss der vergleichenden Grammatik der indogermanischen Sprachen*, 1–5. Strassburg: Trübner.
Callus, Ivan. 2002. "*Jalonnante* and *Parathlipse*: Encountering New Terminology in Ferdinand de Saussure's Researches Into Anagrams." *CFS* 55:169–205.
Capt-Artaud, Marie-Claude. 2003. "La langue, mystérieux milieu intermédiaire." In Simon Bouquet, ed., *L'Herne Saussure*, 234–245. Paris: l'Herne.
Cardona, George. 1976. Panini: *A Survey of Research*. The Hague: Mouton.
Cassirer, Ernst. 1906–1907. *Das Erkenntnisproblem in der Philosophie und Wissenschaft der neueren Zeit*. Bd. 1–2. Berlin: Cassirer.
—— 1923–1929: *Philosophie der symbolischen Formen*. Bd. 1–3. Berlin: Cassirer.
Causse, Étienne. 1930. *Madame Necker de Saussure et l'éducation progressive*. Paris: Je sers.
Chafe, Wallace. 1994. *Discourse, Consciousness, and Time: The Flow and Displacement of Conscious Experience in Speaking and Writing*. Chicago: University of Chicago Press.
Chomsky, Noam. 1965. *Aspects of the Theory of Syntax*. Cambridge: MIT Press.
—— 1993: *Language and Thought*. Wakefield, RI: Bell.
Comte, Auguste. 1844. *Discourse sur l'esprit positif*. Paris: Carilian-Goeury and Dalmont.
Culler, Jonathan. 1986 [1976]. *Ferdinand de Saussure*. Rev. ed. Ithaca: Cornell University Press.

Darnton, Robert. 1970. *Mesmerism and the End of the Enlightenment in France.* New York: Schocken.
Décimo, Marc. 1994. "De quelques candidatures et affinités électives de 1904 à 1908, à travers d'un fragment de correspondance: Le fonds Michel Bréal." *CFS* 47:37–60.
—— 1994/1995. "Saussure à Paris." *CFS* 48:75–90.
De Mauro, Tullio. 1967a. "Notizie biografiche e critiche su Ferdinand de Saussure." In Ferdinand de Saussure, *Corso di linguistica generale*, 283–354. Ed. Tullio De Mauro. Bari: Laterza.
—— 1967b. "Introduzione." In Ferdinand de Saussure, *Corso di linguistica generale*, v–xix. Ed. Tullio De Mauro. Bari: Laterza.
—— 1991. "Ancora Saussure e la semantica." *CFS* 45:101–110.
De Mauro, Tullio, and Shigeaki Sugeta, eds. 1995. *Saussure and Linguistics Today.* Roma: Bulzoni.
Derrida, Jacques. 1976 [1967]. *Of Grammatology.* Baltimore: John Hopkins University Press.
Destutt de Tracy, Antoine-Louis-Claude. 1817. *Éléments d'idéologie*, part 2: *Grammaire.* Paris: Courcier.
Dyck, Martin. 1960. *Novalis and Mathematics: A Study of Friedrich von Hardenberg's Fragments on Mathematics and Its Relation to Magic, Music, Religion, Philosophy, Language, and Literature.* Chapel Hill: University of North Carolina Press.
Eco, Umberto. 1962. *Opera aperta: Forma e indeterminazione nelle poetiche contemporanee.* Milan: Bompiani.
—— 1994. *The Limits of Interpretation.* Bloomington: Indiana University Press.
—— 1999. *Kant and the Platypus: Essays on Language and Cognition.* San Diego: Harcourt.
Engler, Rudolf. 1962. "Théorie et critique d'un principe saussurien: L'arbitraire du sign." *CFS* 19:5–66.
—— 1987. "Charles Bally, Kritiker Saussure's?" *CFS* 41:55–64.
—— 1997: "Présentation" of Saussure's "De l'essence double du langage" *CFS* 50:201–202.
—— 2001: "Entre Bally, Spitzer, . . . Saussure." *CFS* 54:61–81.
—— 2003: "Polyphonie." In Simon Bouquet, ed., *L'Herne Saussure*, 16–19. Paris: l'Herne.
—— 2004: "The Making of the *Course de linguistique générale*." In Carol Sanders, ed., *The Cambridge Companion to Saussure*, 47–58. Cambridge: Cambridge University Press.
Fehr, Johann. 1992. "Die Theorie des Zeichens bei Saussure und Derrida oder Jacques Derridass Saussure-Lekture." *CFS* 46:35–55.

—— 1997. "Daten zu einer Biographie Ferdinand de Saussure." In J. Fehr, ed., *Linguistik und Semiologie. Notizen aus dem Nachlass. Texte, Briefe und Dokumente.* Frankfurt: Suhrkamp.

Fichte, Johann Gottlob. 1988 [1794]. *Grundlage der gesamten Wissenschaftslehre.* Hamburg, Felix Meiner.

Firth, John Rupert. 1930. *Speech.* London: Ernest Benn.

Flournoy, Théodore. 1900. *Des Indes à la planète Mars: Étude sur un cas de somnambulisme avec glossolalie.* Paris: F. Alcan.

Frank, Manfred. 1972. *Das Problem "Zeit" in der deutschen Romantik: Zeitbewußtsein und Bewußtsein von Zeitlichkeit in der frühromantische Philosophie und in Tieks Dichtung.* Padenborn: Winkler.

—— 1989. *Einführung in die frühromantische Ästhetik.* Frankfurt: Suhrkamp.

—— 1997. *"Unendliche Annäherung": Die Anfänge der philosophischen Frühromantik.* Frankfurt: Suhrkamp.

Frege, Gottlob. 1884. *Der Grundlagen der Arithmetik: Eine logisch-mathematische Untersuchung über den Begriff der Zahl.* Breslau: W. Koebner.

—— 1892. "Über Sinn und Bedeutung." *Zeitschrift über Philosophie und philosophische Kritik* 100:25–50.

Furton, Edward James. 1995. *A Medieval Semiotics: Reference and Representation in John St. Thomas's Theory of Signs.* New York: Peter Lang.

Gadet, Françoise. 1987. *Saussure: Une science de la langue.* Paris: Presses universitaires de France.

Gandon, Francis. 2003a. "Chaos des corps, chora des mots: Onze vers de Lucrèce sur l'illusion d'amoureuse." In Simon Bouquet, ed., *L'Herne Saussure,* 430–441. Paris: l'Herne.

—— 2003b. *De dangereux édifices: Saussure lecteur du Lucrece (Les cahiers d'anagrammes consacrés au De rerum natura).* Louvain: Peeters.

Gasparov, Boris. 1997. "Futurism and Phonology: Futurist Roots of Jakobson's Approach to Language." In Françoise Gadet and Patrick Sériot, eds., *Jakobson entre l'est et l'ouest (1915-1939): Un épisode de l'histoire de la culture européenne,* 109–130. Lausanne: Université de Lausanne.

Gautier, Léopold. 2005. "Entretien avec M. de Saussure, 6 Mai 1911." *CFS* 58:69–70.

Geertz, Clifford. 1973. *Interpretation of Cultures.* New York: Basic Books.

Gmür, Remo. 1986. *Das Schicksal von F. de Saussure's Mémoire: Eine Rezeptionsgeschichte.* Bern: Universität Bern, Institut für Sprachwissenschaft.

Gode, Alexander. 1941. *Natural Sciences in German Romanticism.* New York: Columbia University Press.

Godel, Robert. 1957. *Les sources manuscrites du Cours de linguistique générale de Ferdinand de Saussure.* Genève: E. Droz.

Green, André, François Rastier, and Jean Starobinski (in a dialogue with Simon Bouquet). 2003. "Interpréter: De la langue à la parole." In Simon Bouquet, ed., *L'Herne Saussure*, 293–306. Paris: l'Herne.

Hagège, Claude. 2003. "La vulgate et la lettre, ou Saussure par deux fois restitué: De l'arbitraire du signe et de la syntaxe dans le *Cours de linguistique générale*." *CFS* 56:111–124.

Halliday, M. A. K. 1978. *An Introduction to Functional Grammar*. London: E. Arnold.

Hammond, Saïd. 1994. *Mésmerisme et romantisme allemand (1766–1829)*. Paris: L'Harmattan.

Harris, Roy. 1987. *Reading Saussure: A Critial Commentary on the* Course de linguistique générale. London: Duckworth.

—— 2001. *Ferdinand de Saussure and His Interpreters*. Edinburgh: Edinburgh University Press.

Heine, Roland. 1974. *Transzendentalpoesie: Studien zu Friedrich Schlegel, Novalis und E. T. A. Hoffmann*. Bonn: Bouvier.

Helmholtz, Hermann von. 1996a [1895]. "On the Aim and Progress of Physical Science." In Hermann von Helmholtz, *Popular Lectures on Scientific Subjects*, 1:319–345. London: Routledge/Thoemmes.

—— 1996b [1895]. "The Recent Progress of the Theory of Vision." In Hermann von Helmholtz, *Popular Lectures on Scientific Subjects*, 1:175–276. London: Routledge/Thoemmes.

Henri, Victor. 1901. *Le langage martien*. Paris: Maisonneuve.

Hjelmslev, Louis. 1953. *Prolegomena to a Theory of Language*. Trans. F. Whitfield. Baltimore: Waverly.

Holdcroft, David. 1991. *Saussure: Signs, System, and Arbitrariness*. Cambridge: Cambridge University Press.

Humboldt, 30Wilhelm von. 1836. *Über die Kawi-sprache auf der Insel Java: Nebst einer Einleitung über die verschiedenheit des menschlichen Sprachbaues und ihren Einfluss auf die geistige Entwickelung des Menschengeschlechts*. Bd. 1. Berlin: Königliche Akademie der Wissenschaften.

Husserl, Edmund. 1901. *Logische Untersuchungen, Zweite Teil: Untersuchungen zur Phänomenologie und Theorie der Erkenntnis*. Halle: M. Niemeyer.

—— 1913. *Ideen zu einer reinen Phänomenologie und phänomenologischen Philosophie*. Halle: M. Niemeyer.

Jäger, Ludwig. 2003. "La pensée épistémologique de F. de Saussure." In Simon Bouquet, ed., *L'Herne Saussure*, 202–219. Paris: l'Herne.

Jakobson, Roman. 1929. *Remarques sur l'évolution phonologique du russe comparée à celle des autres langues slaves. Travaux du Cercle linguistique de Prague* 2.

―― 1960. "Closing Statement: Linguistics and Poetics." In Thomas A. Sebeok, ed., *Style in Language*, 350–77. New York: Wiley.
―― 1978. *Six Lectures on Sound and Meaning*. Hassocks: Harvester.
―― 1987. "Poetry of Grammar and Grammar of Poetry." In Roman Jakobson, *Language in Literature*, 121–144. Ed. K. Pomorska and S. Rudy. Cambridge: Harvard University Press.
Jakobson, Roman, and Iury Tynianov. 1985 [1928]. "Problems in the Study of Language and Literature." In Roman Jakobson, *Verbal Art, Verbal Sign, Verbal Time*, 25–27. Ed. K. Pomorska and S. Rudy. Minneapolis: University of Minnesota Press.
Jakobson, Roman, and Linda R. Waugh. 1987. *The Sound Shape of Language*. 2d ed. Berlin: Mouton de Gruyter.
Jespersen, Otto. 1905. *Growth and Structure of the English Language*. Leipzig: Teubner.
―― 1933. *Linguistica*. Copenhagen: Levin and Munksgaard.
Joseph, John E. 1988. "Saussure's Meeting with Whitney." *CFS* 42:205–214.
―― 2004. "The Linguistic Sign." In Carol Sanders, ed., *The Cambridge Companion to Saussure*, 59–75. Cambridge: Cambridge University Press.
Khlebnikov, Velimir. 1987 [1913]. "Our Fundamentals." In Velimir Khlebnikov, *Collected Works*, 1:376–391. Cambridge: Harvard University Press.
Kiparsky, Paul, and J. F. Staal. 1969. "Syntactic and Semantic Relations in Panini." *Foundations of Language* 5:83–117.
Koerner, E. F. K. 1998/99. "Noch Einmal on the History of the Concept of Language as a 'Système oú tout ce tient.'" *CFS* 51:203–221.
Komatsu, Eisuke. 1993. "Preface." In Saussure 1993.
Kristeva, Julia. 1969a. "L'engendrement de la formule." *Tel Quel* 37.
―― 1969b. *Semeiotiké: Recherches pour une sémanalyse*. Paris: Seuil.
―― 1980. "The Ethics in Linguistics." In Julia Kristeva, *Desire in Language: A Semiotic Approach to Literature and Art*. New York: Columbia University Press.
Lacan, Jacques. 1973. *Le Séminaire de Jacques Lacan*, vol. 11: *Les quatre concepts fondamentaux de la psychanalyse*. Paris: Seuil.
Lehmann, Christian. 2006. "Arbitraire du signe, iconicité et cercle onomatopoéique." In Friedrich Louis de Saussure, ed., *Nouveaux regards sur Saussure: Mélanges offerts à René Amacker*, 107–123. Genève: Droz.
Lepschy, Giulio. 1974. "Saussure e gli spiriti." In René Amacker, Tullio De Mauro, and Luis Prieto, eds., *Studi saussureani per Robert Godel*, 181–200. Milano: Società editrice.
―― 1979. *Intorno a Saussure*. Torino: Stampatori.
Lévi-Strauss, Claude. 1962. *La pensée sauvage*. Paris: Plon.

Linda, Markus. 1995/96. "Kommentiertes Verzeichnis der Vorlesungen F. de Saussures an der Universität Genf (1891–1913)." *CFS* 49:65–84.

—— 1998/1999. "Semiologie, signologie und 'sematologie' in den Notizen Ferdinand de Saussures." *CFS* 51:223–249.

Lotman, I. M. 1977 [1970]. *The Structure of the Artistic Text*. Ann Arbor: University of Michigan.

Maniglier, Patrice. 2006. *La vie énigmatique des signes: Saussure et la naissance du structuralisme*. Paris: Léo Scheer.

Marchese, Maria Pia. 2003. "Une source retrouvée du *Cours de linguistique générale* de Ferdinand de Saussure." *CFS* 56:333–339.

Martinet, André. 1955. *Économie des changements phonétiques: Traité de phonologie diachronique*. Berne: A. Francke.

Matsuzawa, Kazuhiro. 2003. "Notes pour un livre sur la linguistique générale." In Simon Bouquet, ed., *L'Herne Saussure*, 319–322. Paris: l'Herne.

Maurer, Paula. 1938. *Albertine Andrienne Necker de Saussure als pädadogische Schriftstellerin*. Bonn: Ludwig Leopold.

Mazzeo, Marco. 2004. "Les voyelles colorées: Saussure et la synesthésie." *CFS* 57:129–143.

Mazzone, Marco. 2004. "Proto-Concepts: On Non-Conceptual Content of Perception." *CFS* 57:145–160.

Meillet, Antoine. 1903. *Introduction a l'étude comparative des langues info-europeénnes*. Paris: Hachette.

—— 1937 [1916]: "Ferdinand de Saussure." In Antoine Meillet, *Linguistique historique et linguistique générale*, 2:174–184. Paris: Champion.

Mejía, Claudia. 1997. "Unde exoriar?" *CFS* 50:93–110.

—— 2005: "Sous le signe du doute: Présentation des textes de E. Constantin." *CFS* 58:43–67.

Mestral Combremont, Julie de. 1946. *Albertine Necker de Saussure*. Lausanne: Payot.

Michel, Willy. 1987. "Der 'innere Plural' in der Hermeneutik und Rollentheorie des Novalis." In Ernst Behler and Jochen Hörisch, eds., *Aktualität der Frühromantikk*, 33–50. Paderborn: F. Schöningh.

Misra, Vidya Niwas. 1964. "The Structural Framework of Panini's Linguistic Analysis." In Horace G. Lunt, ed., *Proceedings of the Ninth International Congress of Linguists*, 743–747. The Hague: Mouton.

Müller, Friedrich Max. 1881. *Vorlesungen über den Ursprung und die Entwickelung der Religion, mit besonderer Rücksicht auf die Religionen des alten Indiens*. Strassburg: Trübner.

Myers, Frederic W. H. 1903. *Human Personality and Its Survival of Bodily Death*. Vol. 1. New York: Longmans, Green.

Natorp, Paul. 1910. *Die logischen Grundlagen der exakten Wissenschaften*. Leipzig: Teubner.

Nava, Giuseppe. 1968. "Lettres de Ferdinand de Saussure à Giovanni Pascal." *CFS* 24:73–81.

Necker de Saussure, Adrienne Albertine. 1820. *Notice sur la vie et les écrits de Mme de Staël*. Paris.

—— 1829–32. *L'éducation progressive, ou étude du cours de la vie*. Vols. 1–2. Paris: Librairie-éditeur.

—— 1837. *L'éducation progressive*, vol. 3: *Étude de la vie des femmes*. Paris: Librairie-éditeur.

Normand, Claudine. 2000. *Saussure*. Paris: Les belles lettres.

—— 2004. "System, Arbitrariness, Value." In Carol Sanders, ed., *The Cambridge Companion to Saussure*, 88–106. Cambridge: Cambridge University Press.

Novalis 1901. *Novalis Schriften*. Vol. 2. Ed. Ernst Heilborn. Berlin: Georg Reimer.

—— 1981. *Novalis Schriften. Die Werke Friedrich von Hardenberg*, Bd. 2: *Das philosophische Werk*. Ed. Richard Samuel. Stuttgart: Kohlhammer.

—— 1983. *Novalis Schriften: Die Werke Friedrich von Hardenberg*, Bd. 3: *Das philosophische Werk II*, Ed. Richard Samuel. Stuttgart: Kohlhammer.

Ogden, C. K., and I. A. Richards. 1923. *The Meaning of Meaning: A Study of the Influence of Language Upon Thought and of the Science of Symbolism*. London: K. Paul, Trench, Trubner.

Oltramare, Paul. 1906. *L'histoire des idées philosophiques dans l'Inde*. Paris: Ernest Leroux.

Oppenheim, Janet. 1985. *The Other World: Spiritualism and Psychical Research in England, 1850–1914*. New York: Cambridge University Press.

Parret, Hermann. 1995/96. "Réflexions Saussuriennes sur le Temps et le Moi." *CFS* 49:85–122.

—— 2003. "Métaphysique saussurienne de la voix et de l'oreille dans les manuscrits de Genève at de Harvard." In Simon Bouquet, ed., *L'Herne Saussure*, 62–78. Paris: l'Herne.

Paul, Hermann. 1889 [1880]. *Principles of the History of Language*. London: Swan Sonnenschein.

Pétroff, André-Jean. 1999. "La langue, l'ordre et le désordre: Les analyses de Ferdinand de *Saussure*." *CFS* 52:253–281.

Piaget, Jean. 1968. *Le strucuralisme*. Paris: Presses universitaires de France.

Pictet, Adolphe. 1856. *De beau dans la nature, l'art et la poésie*. Paris: J. Cherbuliez.

——— 1859–63. *Origines indo-européennes: Essai de paléontologie linguistique.* Vols. 1–2. Paris: J. Cherbuliez.

Prigogine, Ilya, and Isabelle Stengers. 1984. *Order Out of Chaos: Man's New Dialogue with Nature.* Toronto: Bantam.

Raggiunti, Renzo. 1982. *Problemi filosofici nelle teorie linguistiche di Ferdinand de Saussure.* Roma: Armando.

Rastier, François. 2001. "Du signe aux plans du langage." *CFS* 54:177–200.

——— 2003. "Le silence de Saussure ou l'ontologie refusée." In Simon Bouquet, ed., *L'Herne Saussure,* 23–51. Paris: l'Herne.

Renard, Jean-Claude. 1987. *L'"expérience intérieure" de Georges Bataiile ou la négation du Mystère.* Paris: Seuil, 1987.

Rickert, Heinrich. 1902. *Die Grenzen der naturwissencheflichen Begriffsbildung: Eine logische Einleitung in die historischen Wissenschaften.* Tübingen: Mohr.

Roggenbuck, Simone. 1998. *Saussure und Derrida: Linguistik und Philosophie.* Tübingen: Francke.

Russell, Bertrand. 1897. *An Essay on the Foundation of the Geometry.* Cambridge: At the University Press.

Sanders, Carol, ed. 2004. *The Cambridge Companion to Saussure.* Cambridge: Cambridge University Press.

Saussure, Ferdinand de. 1879. *Mémoire sur le système primitif des voyelles dans les langues indo-européennes.* Leipzig: Teubner.

——— 1881. *De l'emploi du génitif absolu en Sanscrit.* Genève: J.-G. Fick.

——— 1922a [1894]. "À propos de l'accentuation lituanienne. (Intonation et accent proprement dit.)" In Ferdinand de Saussure, *Recueil des publications scientifiques de Ferdinand de Saussure,* 490–512. Heidelberg: C. Winter.

——— 1922b. "Les Burgondes et la langue burgonde en pays roman." In Ferdinand de Saussure, *Recueil des publications scientifiques de Ferdinand de Saussure,* 606–607. Heidelberg: C. Winter.

——— 1922c. *Recueil des publications scientifiques de Ferdinand de Saussure.* Heidelberg: C. Winter.

——— 1960 [1903]. ["Souvenirs d'enfance et d'études"]. *CFS* 17:15–25.

——— 1964. "Lettres de Ferdinand de Saussure à Antoine Meillet publiées par Emile Benveniste." *CFS* 21:93–134.

——— 1967a [1916]. *Cours de linguistique générale.* Ed. Charles Bally and Albert Sechehaye, with Albert Riedlinger. Paris: Payot.

——— 1967b. *Corso di linguistica generale.* Ed. Tullio De Mauro. Bari: Laterza.

——— 1968–74. *Cours de linguistique générale.* Ed. Rudolf Engler. Vols. 1 and 2 (*Appendice*). Wiesbaden: Harrassowitz.

—— 1978. "Essai pour réduire les mots du grec, du latin et de l'allemand à un petit nombre de racines." Published by Boyd Davis. CFS 32:73–101.
—— 1986. *Course in General Linguistics*. Ed. and trans. Roy Harris. Chicago: Open Court.
—— 1993a. "Les manuscrits saussuriens de Harvard." Published by Hermann Parret. CFS 47:179–234.
—— 1993b. *Troisiéme cours de linguistique générale (1910–1011) d'après les cahiers d'Émile Constantine*. Ed. Eisuke Komatsu. Trans. Roy Harris. Oxford: Pergamon.
—— 1994a. "Correspondance Bally-Saussure." CFS 48:91–134.
—— 1994b. *Manuscritti di Harvard, a cura di Herman Parret*. Roma: Laterza.
—— 1996. *Premier cours de linguistique générale (1907) d'après les cahiers d'Albert Riedlinger*. Ed. Eisuke Komatsu. Trans. George Wolf. Oxford: Pergamon.
—— 1997. *Dexième cours de linguistique générale (1908–1909) d'après les cahiers d'Albert Riedlinger et Charles Parois*. Ed. Eisuke Komatsu. Oxford: Pergamon.
—— 2002. *Écrits de linguistique générale*. Ed. Simon Bouquet and Rudolf Engler. Paris: Gallimard.
—— 2003a. "La légende de Sigfrid et l'histoire Burgonde." Presented by Béatrice Turpin. In Simon Bouquet, ed., *L'Herne Saussure*, 360–429. Paris: l'Herne.
—— 2003b. "Notes sur l'accentuation lituanienne." Presented by Ludwig Jäger, Mareike Buss, and Lorella Ghiotti. In Simon Bouquet, ed., *L'Herne Saussure*, 328–350. Paris: l'Herne.
—— 2006. *Writings in General Linguistics*. Oxford: Oxford University Press.
Saussure, Friedrich Louis de, ed. 2006. *Nouveaux regards sur Saussure: Mélanges offerts à René Amacker*. Genève: Droz.
Saussure, Léopold de. 1899. *Psychologie de la colonisation français dans les rapports avec les sociétés indigènes*. Paris: F. Alcan.
Saussure, René de. 1911. *Principes logiques de la construction des mots en esperanto*. Geneva: Kündig.
Schlegel, Friedrich. 1799a. *Lucinde*. Berlin: H. Frölich.
—— 1799b. "Notizen." In *Athenaeum* 2/2:301–306. Berlin.
—— 1799c. "Über die Philosophie: An Dorothea." *Athenaeum* 2:2. Berlin.
—— 1800. "Ideen." *Athenaeum* 3:1. Berlin.
—— 1808. *Über die Sprache und die Weisheit der Indien*. Heidelberg: Mohr and Zimmer.
—— 1957. *Literary Notebooks, 1797–1801*. Ed. Hans Eichner. Toronto: University of Toronto Press.
—— 1963. *Philosophische Lehrjahre*, part 1. In Ernst Behler, ed., *Kritische Friedrich-Schlege-Ausgabe*. Vol. 18. Munich: F. Schöningh.

——— 1966. *Briefe von und an Friedrich und Dorothea Schlegel.* In Ernst Behler, ed., *Kritische Friedrich-Schlegel-Ausgabe.* Vol. 23. Munich: F. Schöningh.
Schlegel, Friedrich, August Wilhelm Schlegel, Friedrich von Hardenberg (Novalis), and Friedrich Schleiermacher. 1798. "Athenaeum Fragmente." *Athenaeum* 1:2. Berlin.
Schleicher, August. 1866. *Compendium der vergleichende Grammatik der indogermanischen Sprachen.* Weimar: Böhlau.
Schuchardt, Hugo. 1885. *Über die Lautgesetze: Gegen die Junggrammatiker.* Berlin: Oppenheim.
Sechehaye, Albert. 1908a. "La stylistique et la linguistique théorique." In *Mélanges de linguistique offerts à M. Ferdinand de Saussure,* 153–187. Paris: Champion.
——— 1908b. *Programme et méthodes de la linguistique théorique.* Paris: Champion.
Sériot, Patrick, ed. 2005. *Un paradigme perdu: La linguistique marriste.* Cahiers de ILSL 20. Lausanne: Université de Lausanne.
Seyhan, Azade 1992: *Representation and Its Discontents: The Critical Legacy of German Romanticism.* Berkeley: University of California Press.
Shevelov, Iurii. 1964: *A Prehistory of Slavic: The Historical Phonology of Common Slavic.* Heidelberg: C. Winter.
Sievers, Eduard. 1901. *Grundzüge der Phonetik, zur Einführung in das Studium der Lautlehre der indogermanischen Sprachen.* Leipzig: Breitkoph and Härtel.
Simone, Raffaele. 2006. "Saussure après un siècle." In *Nouveaux regards sur Saussure: Mélanges offerts à René Amacker,* 35–54. Ed. Louis Saussure. Geneva: Droz.
Sliusareva [sic], Natalja. 2004. *Teoriia F. de Sossiura v svete sovremennoi lingvistiki.* Moscow: Éditorial USSR.
Sljusareva, Natalja. 1971. "Deux lettres de Ferdinand de Saussure à Baudouin de Courtenay." *CFS* 27:7–17.
Spencer, Herbert. 1862–1897. *The System of Synthetic Philosophy.* 10 vols. New York: Appleton.
Stancati, Claudia. 2004. "Saussure à l'ombre des philosophes: Quelle philosophie pour la linguistique générale?" *CFS* 57:185–207.
Starobinski, Jean. 1964. "Les anagrammes de Ferdinand de Saussure, textes inédites." *Mercure de France* 350:243–262.
——— 1967. "Les mots sous les mots: Textes inédites des cahiers d'anagrammes de Ferdinand de Saussure." In *To Honor Roman Jakobson,* 3:1906–1917. The Hague: Mouton.
——— 1969. "Le texte dans le texte: Extraits inédits des cahiers d'anagrammes de Ferdinand de Saussure." *Tel Quel* 37:3–33.
——— 1979 [1971]. *Words for Words: The Anagrams of Ferdinand de Saussure.* New Haven: Yale University Press.

Strozier, Robert. 1988. *Saussure, Derrida, and the Metaphysics of Subjectivity*. Berlin: Mouton de Gruyter.

Suenaga, Akatane. 1999. "De deux arbitraires, absolut et rélatif, à une arbitraire primaire: Le fait linguistique et le devenir du signe chez Saussure."*CFS* 52:189–200.

—— 2005. *Saussure, un système de paradoxes: Langue, parole, arbitraire et inconscient*. Limoges: Lambert-Lucas, 2005.

Tesnière, Lucien. 1959. *Eléments de syntaxe structurale*. Paris: Klincksieck.

*Thèses*. 1929. *Travaux du Cercle linguistique de Prague* 1.

Todorov, Tzvetan. 1967. *Littérature et signification*. Paris: Larousse.

Trubetzkoy, N. S. 1939. *Grundzüge der Phonologie: Travaux du Cercle linguistique de Prague* 7.

—— 2001 [1939]. "Thoughts on Indo-European Problem." In *Studies in General Linguistics and Language Structure*, 87–98. Ed. Anatoly Liberman. Durham: Duke University Press.

Turpin, Béatrice. 2003. "Légendes et récits d"Europe du Nord: de Sigfrid à Tristan." In Simon Bouquet, ed., *L'Herne Saussure*, 351–359. Paris: l'Herne.

Utaker, Arild. 1990. *Pour une ontologie du langage: Wittgenstein et Saussure*. Bergen: Ariadne.

Veselovskii, A. N. 1896. *Skazaniia o Vavilone, skinii i sv. Grale*. St. Petersburg: Akademiia nauk.

Vilela, Isabel. 1998/99. "Saussure pró: A unidade Saussuriana presente no *Curso*, nos *Anagaramas* e na análise de Lacan." *CFS* 51:251–272.

Villani, Paola. 1990. "Documenti saussureani conservati a Lipsia e a Berlino." *CFS* 44:3–36.

Voloshinov, V. N. 1973 [1928]. *Marxism and the Philosophy of Language*. New York: Seminar.

Whitney, William Dwight. 1876. *The Life and Growth of Language: An Outline of Linguistic Science*. New York: Appleton.

Wittgenstein, Ludwig. 1998 [1921]. *Logisch-philosophische Abhandlung, Tractatus logico-philosophicus*. Frankfurt: Suhrkamp.

—— 2001 [1953]. *Philosophical Investigations—Philosophische Untersuchingen*. Oxford: Blackwell.

Wunderli, Peter. 1972. *Ferdinand de Saussure und die Anagramme: Linguistik und Literatur*. Tübingen: Max Niemeyer.

—— 1990. *Principes de diachronie: Contribution a l'exégèse du Cours de linguistique générale de Ferdinand de Saussure*. Frankfurt: Peter Lang.

—— 2004. "Saussure's Anagrams." In Carol Sanders, ed., *The Cambridge Companion to Saussure*, 174–185. Cambridge: Cambridge University Press.

# Index

Aarsleff, H., 186, 196
Actualization, 151, 153, 155
Aeschylus, 167
Altani-Voisin, F., 200
Amacker, R., 6, 187
Anagram, 5, 43–45, 51, 105, 139–49, 154, 155, 160, 161, 167, 168, 184, 190, 198, 201–5; ad hoc rules, 141, 143, 144, 146, 148, 149, 202 integration in, 154–59; and linguistics of speech, 141, 147–49, 154, 154, 160, 203; the meaning of, 145–48, 202, 203; and the oneiric, 5, 161–63, 184, 202; theme word (*Stichwort*), 142, 143, 145; *see also* arbitrariness
Anouar, L., 190
arbitrariness 10, 17, 42, 59, 64, 65, 68, 70–76, 78–82, 85, 85, 89, 97, 104, 105, 118, 143, 144, 147–52, 154–56, 158, 160, 163, 171, 181, 182, 194–96; in the anagram, 143, 144, 147–49, 155, 160; critique of the concept, 42, 71–73, 80, 86; and the duality of the sign 70, 74–76,
82, 97, 105, 154; and motivation, 72, 73, 75, 76, 85, 86; relative, 57, 73, 195; as the principle of freedom, 17, 59, 64, 68, 79, 82, 86, 89, 97, 118, 147, 148, 155, 181, 196
Aristotle, 67, 76
Arrivé, M., 29, 34, 168, 184, 194, 195, 198, 200
Arsenjević, M., 200
Avenarius, R., 176

Bach, J. S., 88, 146
Bakhtin, M. M., 3, 42, 81, 174, 180
Balfour, I., 204
Bally, Ch., 2, 4, 28, 30, 35, 37, 39, 40, 42, 45, 53–55, 58, 140, 144–47, 151–53, 162, 163, 183, 185, 188, 189, 191, 193, 201, 203
Barthes, R., 3, 55
Bataille, G., 158
Baudelaire, Ch., 145
Baudouin de Courtenay, J., 2, 29, 186, 199
Baudrillard, J., 158
Béguelin, M.-J., 113, 199

Bely, A., 206
Benjamin, W., 18, 92, 180
Bennington, G. 184
Benveniste, É., 2, 15, 28, 29, 42, 73, 140, 188
Bergson, H., 64, 88, 119, 199
Bernardinis, A. M., 185
*Bestimmende* vs. *Bestimmte, see* Novalis
Bloomfield, L., 2, 58, 171, 183
Böhtlingk, O., 196
Bopp, F., 22, 23, 58, 112, 192, 198
Bota, Ch., 34, 194
Bouquet, S., 34, 38, 184, 189–92, 195, 202, 203–5
Bréal, M., 22, 29, 30, 186
Brechem, M. von, 190
Brémond, C., 3
Bréton, A., 158, 204
Brown, J., 161, 162, 204
Brugmann, K., 23–26, 111, 174, 185–87, 198, 199

Caesar, 201
Caille, L., 189
Calderon de la Barca, P., 159
Callus, I., 144, 201, 205
Capt-Artaud, M.-C., 195
Cassirer, E., 3, 174, 175, 179
Causse, É., 197
Chafe, W., 198
Chamfort, N., 51
Chateaubriand, F.-R., 18, 145
chess game and language, 49, 118, 119, 121, 130, 151, 153
Chomsky, N., 3, 203
Cicero, 83, 201
Claparède, E., 194
Comte, A., 170, 171
Condillac, É., 66, 90, 186
Constant, B., 18, 92
Constantin, É. 189
conventionality of language, 6, 25, 26, 48, 49, 66, 68, 70–73, 75, 76, 80–82, 86, 89, 97, 118, 171, 190, 194, 196; Saussure and French *philosophes*, 25, 26, 66, 71, 89, 90, 97, 186, 196

Crue, B., 185
Culler, J., 74, 82, 196
Curtius, G., 16, 24, 187

Darnton, R., 204
Darwin, Ch., 170
David, J.-E., 168, 169
Décimo, M., 188, 198, 205
Dégailler, G., 198
Delbrück, B., 111, 199
De Mauro, T., 22, 29, 34, 58, 123, 183, 186–88, 191, 192, 194, 196
Derrida, J., 3, 43, 184, 193, 200
Descartes, R., 45
Destutt de Tracy, A., 195, 196
Diachrony, 41, 117, 119, 123, 130, 131–33, 151, 173, 179, 199; and history 117, 119, 123, 130, 131, 132, 173; "structural diachrony," 119, 120, 199
differential value, *see* sign
diversity of languages, 3, 35, 52, 59, 60, 70, 86, 125, 133, 175, 193, 195, 196
duality of the sign, *see* sign
duration, *see* language evolution
Durkheim, É., 80, 195, 205

Eco, U., 184
Einstein, A., 114, 177
Engler, R., 43, 55, 183, 184, 190–92, 194, 195, 197, 205

Favre, E., 29, 187, 196
Favre, F., 43
Favre, L., 204
Fehr, J., 44, 204
Fichte, J. G., 101, 102, 128, 177, 178, 198, 206
Firth, J. R., 183, 194
Flournoy, Th., 163–68, 204, 205
form vs. substance, *see langue*
fragment, *see* Romanticism
Frank, M., 204
Frege, G., 2, 3, 90, 174, 175, 179
French *philosophes*, *see* conventionality
Freud, S., 3, 114, 158, 162, 163, 167, 177
Furton, E. J., 73

Gadet, F., 74, 184, 185, 187, 198, 201, 204
Gandon, F., 184, 201, 203
Gasparov, B., 185
Gautier, L., 34, 35, 37, 38, 40, 43, 168, 185, 186, 189, 205
Geertz, C., 3
genitive/genitive absolute, 26–28, 84, 89, 187
Gmür, R., 26, 199
Gode, A., 204
Godel, R., 5, 6, 28, 41, 43, 57, 140, 185, 189–92
Goethe, J. W., 18
Grammond, M., 28, 188
Green, A., 197, 202–4
Grimm, J., 19

Hagège, C., 184, 191, 192
Halliday, M. A. K., 198
Hamann, J. G., 90
Hammond, S., 204
Harris, R., 104, 106, 107, 183, 189, 192
Hegel, G. F., 18, 45
Heine, R., 204
Hélène Smith (É.-C.Müller), 163–67, 204, 205; Hélène's "Martian Language," 164, 166, 167, Hélène's "Sanskrit," 165–67, 204, 205
Helmholtz, H. von, 64, 65, 68, 194
Henri, V., 166, 167, 205
Herder, J. G., 90, 186
Herodotus, 21
Hjelmslev, L., 2, 177
Holdcroft, D., 105, 194, 204
Homer, 19, 135, 141, 143, 145, 147, 162, 201
Horace, 145
Hrozny, B., 115
Hugo, V., 162, 204
Humboldt, W. von, 72, 78, 89, 186, 197
Husserl, E., 10, 65, 176, 179, 193

immutability vs. mutability, 41, 59, 60, 81–83, 96, 97, 107, 117, 118, 120, 133, 150, 152, 153–55
Indo-European proto-language

(*Ursprache*), 20, 23, 19, 112, 113, 116, 118; reconstruction of, 20, 112, 113–15
integration: as opposed to differentiation, 124, 134, 135, 154–59; in history ("rhymed" development), 135–36; *see also* anagram; Novalis

Jakobson, R., 3, 9, 16, 21, 42–44, 53, 71–73, 104, 105, 177, 184, 185, 194, 199
James, W., 163
Jean Paul (Richter), 18, 197
Jena, *see* Romanticism
Jespersen, O., 193, 194
Johnson, T., 202
Joseph, F., 189
Joseph, J., 26, 73, 198
*Junggrammatiker, see* Leipzig school

Kant, E., 9, 11, 18, 25, 45, 52, 64, 86, 90, 98–101, 109, 131, 161, 173, 175, 177, 178, 180, 197
Karcevsky, S., 2, 37
Khlebnikov, V., 21, 72, 177
Kierkegaard, S., 51
Kiparsky, P., 88
Koerner, E. F. K., 187
Komatsu, E., 193
Körner, Ch. G., 200
Kristeva, J., 184, 204
Kruszewski, M., 29
Kuryłowicz, J., 115

Lacan, J., 3, 194
La Fontaine, J., de 21
language as the object of linguistics: postulated (not empirical), 9, 10, 29, 41, 45, 52, 63, 64–66, 132–134, 175, 181; linguistics and the foundations of science, 9, 64, 65, 88, 91, 134, 170, 175; uniqueness of linguistics, 17, 58, 60, 65, 66–69, 132, 134; plurality of approaches ("Unde exoriar?"), 10, 45, 63–65, 70, 108, 109, 131, 173, 194
language evolution/change, 25, 35, 36, 41, 44, 47, 59, 60, 68, 79, 80–83, 88, 94,

language evolution/change (*continued*) 103, 107, 112, 117–19, 121, 122, 126, 127, 129–31, 134, 148, 150–52, 171, 174, 199; accidental/haphazard, 59, 60, 82 103, 121, 122, 126, 127, 129, 131, 134, 148, 200; evolution as duration, 35, 36, 47, 80–82, 88, 107, 119, 121, 131, 134, 150, 199; initial (proto-) state, 49, 79, 112, 116, 125, 126, 128, 202; unconscious character of, 79, 82, 83, 131

language laws/rules, 29, 31, 60, 80, 84, 88, 112, 118, s120–23, 133, 141, 144, 148, 153, 171, 174; rules as conventions of scholarship, 27, 28, 80, 84, 121–23, 135

*langue*, 1–4, 7, 9, 10, 50, 53, 54, 60, 65, 77, 78, 80, 82, 83, 85, 86, 88, 100, 107, 120, 149–51, 153, 154, 157, 160, 167, 173, 191, 192, 195, 196, 202, 203; immanent, 50, 58, 60, 83, 85, 107, 192; as postulated phenomenon, 60, 65, 85, 86, 120, 122, 123, 130, 131, 153, 154, 173; relative/oppositive (as a pure form), 50, 77, 78, 150, 151, 153, 154, 157, 195; volatile, 10, 60, 80, 82, 88, 107, 122, 123, 130, 131, 151

laringeals, *see* Saussure: *Mémoire* . . .

linguistic racism/nationalism, *see* structural types of languages

La Rochefoucauld, F., 51

Lehmann, Ch., 195

Leipzig school in linguistics (Neogrammarians, *Junggrammatiker*), 9, 17, 22–26, 29, 31, 60, 65, 70, 88, 90, 121, 111, 112, 114, 121, 171, 173–76; Saussure's critique of, 9, 17, 26, 60, 70, 88, 90, 105, 121

Lepschy, G., 58, 167, 184, 192, 198, 205

Leskien, A., 188

Lévi-Strauss, C., 3, 184

Linda, M., 40, 188, 189, 203

linearity, 104–7, 155, 198, 204

Lotman, Iu. M., 3

Lucretius, 143, 145

Malevich, K., 114, 177

Maniglier, P., 184, 196, 205

Marchese, M. P., 189

"Martian language," *see* Hélène Smith

Martinet, A., 199

Marx, K., 3

Matsuzawa, K., 34, 193

Maurer, P., 93, 185, 197

Mazzeo, M., 194

Mazzone, M., 79

Meillet, A., 28, 30, 33, 38–40, 42, 43, 45, 114, 120, 140, 145, 146, 168, 187–89, 195, 196, 201, 202

Mejía, C., 144, 189, 193, 198, 205

Mendeleev, D. I., 65

Mesmer, F. A., 161, 162, 204

Mestral Combremont, J. de, 95, 197, 198

Misra, V. N., 88

Møller, H., 186, 199

Montaigne, M. de, 196

Mukařovský, J., 3

Müller, É.-C., *see* Hélène Smith

Müller, M., 125

Mutability, *see* immutability

Myers, F. W. H., 167

Mystery, *see* anagram

Natorp, P., 175

Nava, G., 205

Necker de Saussure, A. A., 18, 58, 92–101, 110, 197, 198; child development as differentiation, 93–96; double nature of child's consciousness, 95–97; immanence of child's consciousness, 58, 95, 96; *L'éducation progressive*, 18, 19, 58, 93, 97, 100, 197; progressive education, the principle of, 18, 92, 96, 97; progressive education as a Romantic concept, 97, 98–100; progressive education and women, 99, 100

Neogrammarians, *see* Leipzig school

neo-Kantian epistemology, 9, 11, 25, 52, 90, 131, 161, 180

Nietzsche, F., 3, 36, 51, 158

Nomenclaturism, *see* sign

Normand, C., 2, 3, 184, 195, 196

Novalis (Friedrich von Hardenberg), 11, 18, 51, 90, 91, 100–104, 106, 107, 110, 128, 148, 152, 156–63, 167, 168, 178, 180–82, 197; asymmetry, 106, 107; differentiation vs. integration, 156–59; duality of the sign (*das Bestimmende* vs. *das Bestimmte*), 91, 102, 103, 106; immanence of language, 103, 104; representational character of cognition, 101, 102; symbiosis, 102, 103; *see also* sign

Ogden, C. K., 2, 73
Oltramare, P., 190
Oneiric, *see* anagram
Oppenheim, J., 204
organism as language metaphor, 48, 60, 89, 122, 133, 160, 172–73, 176, 181, 193, 196, 197
Osthoff, H., 23, 24, 26, 185, 186
Ostwald, W., 65, 175

Panini grammar (*Astadhyayi*), 88, 89, 196
Paris, G., 106, 188
Parret, H., 44, 45, 190, 198
Pascal, G., 168, 205
Paul, H., 199
Peirce, Ch., S., 3, 194
Pétroff, A.-J., 191, 199, 200, 203
Phenomenology, 9, 10, 25, 45, 64, 65
Picasso, P., 180
Piaget, J., 3, 177
Pictet, A., 11, 18, 19–21, 24, 93, 112, 135, 172, 185
Plato, 194
Positivism, 9, 29, 45, 53, 64, 65, 90, 114, 129, 170, 171, 174, 175, 205; Saussure's critique of, 9, 29, 64, 90, 114, 129, 174
Prigogine, I., 200
Progressivity, *see* Necker de Saussure; Romanticism

Raggiunti, R., 198
Rastier, F., 47, 189, 197, 204
Regard, P.-F., 39, 42, 189, 191

Renard, J.-C., 204
"rhymed" development, *see* integration in history
Richards, I. A., 2, 73
Rickert, H., 131, 175, 194
Riedlinger, A., 34, 37, 41, 42, 183, 189
Rig Veda, 19, 44, 108, 134, 135, 141, 158, 162, 190
Romanticism: the *Athenaeum,* 51, 55, 91, 92, 108, 129, 160, 177, 178, 180–82, 191, 197; accidents and coincidences, 94, 98, 128–30, 200; dynamic character of consciousness (progressivity) 52, 97–99, 108, 128, 134, 159, 177, 178, 181, 182; early (Jena) as distinct from high Romanticism, 11, 18, 19, 51, 52, 90–93, 98, 99, 100–2, 109, 110, 128, 130, 133, 134, 156, 160–62, 172–74, 178–81, 197, 204; fragment/fragmentariness, 11, 51, 52, 55, 99–101, 106–8, 128, 156, 158, 159, 177–79, 181, 182, 191, 204; potentialization 128, 159–61, 178; "Romantic poetry," 156, 159, 177, 178
"Romantic linguistics": its poor empirical base, 11, 19, 20, 24; Saussure's critique of, 11, 20, 112, 172
Rousseau, J.-J., 18, 66, 90, 185, 188
Russell, B., 175

St. Augustine, 66
Saussure, H. de, 17
Saussure, H. B. de, 17, 18
Saussure, L. de, 35
Saussure, Madam de, 39, 40
Saussure, N.-Th. de, 17
Saussure, R. (Saussure's son), 44
Saussure, R. de, 17, 18
Saussure, family background, 16–18, 21, 30, 32, 35, 43, 44, 87, 88, 92, 93, 100, 124, 185; Lotharingy/Burgundy, symbolic significance, 16, 24, 25, 44, 90, 124–26
Saussure, personal traits, 8, 9, 15, 21–23, 29–34, 37, 38, 48, 52, 56, 69, 77, 85, 89, 91, 122, 129, 132–34, 136, 140, 145, 154,

Saussure, personal traits (*continued*)
160, 163, 168, 179, 180, 182, 196, 202, 202; Germany and "Germans" 16, 17, 22–25, 31, 48, 72, 89, 90, 111, 172, 186; "graphophobia," 31, 32, 45; Saussurean "Christology," 5, 7, 15, 33, 34, 46, 81, 177, 191

Saussure, as teacher, 28, 30, 34, 37, 39, 40, 45, 88–90, 140, 154, 170, 174, 187, 188

Saussure, works: dissertation (*De l'emploi du genitif absolu . . .*), 16, 26–28, 47, 84, 89, 171, 187; lecture at the Historical and Archeological Society, 32, 124, 190; notes on the anagram, 5, 6, 43, 44, 140–44, 146, 147, 154, 168; notes on ancient legends, 6, 44, 124–28, 133, 135, 136, 184, 200; notes on Hindu philosophy ("Harvard papers"), 6, 44, 108, 109, 135, 162, 190; notes on Lithuanian (Balto-Slavic) accentuation, 29, 33, 120, 125, 132, 133, 175, 176; "Souvenirs d'enfance et d'études," 16, 19, 22, 24, 31, 34, 45, 185, 186

—*Course in General Linguistics,* its influence, 1–3, 42; poststructuralist interpretation/critique, 3–5, 10, 43, 53, 80, 158, 184, 191, 196; structuralist interpretation, 1–6, 8, 52, 55, 57–59, 80, 84, 88, 92, 109, 118, 119, 140, 177, 179, 191, 199, 203

—*Course in General Linguistics*, text and sources: as compiled by Bally and Sechehaye 4, 5, 28, 39–42, 53, 54, 56; critique of Bally and Sechehaye's edition, 6–8, 33, 38, 53–55, 57, 58, 81, 109, 194, 203; lecture courses in general linguistics, 1, 4, 22, 34, 35, 37–46, 56, 58, 63, 88, 117, 123, 130, 133, 140, 154, 160, 168, 188, 189, 192, 194; notes for the courses, 4, 40, 42, 45, 189; rhetorical features, 15, 35, 52, 56–60, 82, 85, 104, 150; students' notes, 5, 35, 39, 40, 130, 189, 193

—"Essay on reducing words of Greek, Latin, and German . . . ," 20, 21, 185, 199

—*Mémoire sur la système promitif,* 19, 22, 24, 25, 26, 28, 31, 32, 39, 111, 114, 116, 117, 119, 120, 123, 133, 173, 198, 199; laryngeals, 114, 115, 186, 189; method, 113, 114–17; reception, 26, 31, 111, 114, 115, 119, 123; syllabic sonants, priority in discovering, 22–24, 31, 114

—notes on linguistics: discovery, 5, 29, 38, 43, 52, 53, 64; fragmentariness, 7, 46–52; polemical emphasis, 8, 9, 21, 23, 48, 49, 65, 78, 88, 89, 91, 118, 132, 172; relation to the *Course,* 7, 52, 53, 56

"Saussurism," 6, 8, 9, 52

"Saussurology," 6–8, 25, 26, 81

Schelling, F. W. J., 19, 162, 172, 197

Schiller, F., 19

Schlegel, A. W., 18, 92, 93, 100, 197

Schlegel, F., 11, 18, 19, 51, 52, 91, 99, 100, 122, 128, 129, 134, 159, 160, 177, 178, 180–82, 191, 197, 200, 204, 204

Schleicher, A., 48, 49, 60, 89, 112, 122

Schleiermacher, F., 18, 92, 197, 204

Schoenberg, A., 114, 177

Schuhardt, H., 29, 121, 205

Sechehaye, A., 2, 5, 30, 37, 40, 42, 54, 55, 183, 188, 189, 191–93, 203

semiology/semiotics, 3, 52, 70, 80, 99, 102, 130, 132, 134, 139, 154, 157, 160, 177–79, 194, 203

Shakespeare, W., 71

Shevelov, Iu., 199

Sievers, E., 49, 50

sign, 1, 3, 4, 26, 28, 41, 42, 47–50, 57, 60, 64, 65–80, 81, 82–86, 88, 89, 94–97, 99, 101–8, 118, 121, 123, 127, 129, 132, 133, 134, 139, 142, 146, 148, 149, 151–57, 161, 164, 173, 178, 190, 194–96, 203; critique of nomenclaturism, 67, 71, 72, 104, 123, 164, 195; differential value (*valeur*) 41, 57, 75, 77–79, 94, 107, 108, 134, 148, 154, 157; dual nature of, 48, 66–70, 74, 76, 81, 85, 88, 89, 95, 97, 101–3, 132, 195; signifier and signified, 42, 67, 70–77, 80, 81, 83, 94, 96, 102–7, 118, 129, 142,

146, 148, 149, 152, 154, 155, 164, 194–96; *see also* arbitratiness; integration; linearity; Novalis
Sljusareva, N., 186, 199
Smith, *see* Hélène Smith
speech (*la parole*), linguistics of, 1–3, 6, 7, 10, 50, 54, 57, 83, 85, 89, 131, 141, 142, 147–56, 169, 160, 173, 177, 179, 191, 198, 200, 203; incompatibility with linguistics of language, 85, 150–54, 156; *see also* anagram; integration
Spencer, H., 170, 171
Spitzer, L., 197, 204
Staal, J. F., 88
Staël, G. de, 18, 92, 93, 100
Stancati C., 18, 87
Starobinski, J. 5, 43, 44, 140, 141, 143, 144, 146, 147, 155, 184, 188, 190, 197, 200–4
status vs. motus, 130–32
Stengers, I., 200
Streitberg, W., 24, 31, 185–88, 198
Strozier, R., 193, 200
structural types of languages: immanence, 60, 75, 154, 172; linguistic nationalism/racism, refutation of, 35, 57, 172, 193; unlimited variety of 59, 71, 133, 155, 157
Suenaga, A. 194, 195
syllabic sonants, *see* Saussure: *Mémoire . . .*
synchrony, 1, 6, 27, 40, 41, 47, 55, 117–20, 123, 130–33, 150, 151, 173, 179, 191

Taine, H., 186
Tesnière, L., 105
Todorov, T., 3
Trubetzkoy, N., 2, 183, 199
Tynianov, Iu. N., 184

*Ursprache, see* Indo-European

*valeur, see* sign
Valois, N., 185, 188
Verner, C., 31
Veselovsky, A. N., 125
Vilela, I., 144
Villani, P., 31, 185–88, 198
Villon, F., 141
Virgil, 141, 145, 202
Voloshinov, V. N., 3, 42
Vossler, C., 197, 205

Wackernagel, J., 31, 89, 188
Wagner, R., 51, 87, 126, 146, 191
Waugh, L., 43, 72, 104
Wertheimer, J., 22, 33, 38
Whitney, W. D., 26, 48, 49, 66, 89, 97, 171, 190, 196
Windisch, E., 187
Wittgenstein, L., 2, 3, 52, 78, 174, 204
Wunderli, P., 184, 198, 200, 202, 204, 205

Zarnke, F., 26